CLINICAL INTERVENTIONS IN CRIMINAL JUSTICE SETTINGS

CLINICAL INTERVENTIONS IN CRIMINAL JUSTICE SETTINGS

Evidence-Based Practice

GEORGE T. PATTERSON

WARREN K. GRAHAM

Silberman School of Social Work
Hunter College, City University of New York
NY, United States

ELSEVIER

ACADEMIC PRESS
An imprint of Elsevier

Academic Press is an imprint of Elsevier
125 London Wall, London EC2Y 5AS, United Kingdom
525 B Street, Suite 1800, San Diego, CA 92101-4495, United States
50 Hampshire Street, 5th Floor, Cambridge, MA 02139, United States
The Boulevard, Langford Lane, Kidlington, Oxford OX5 1GB, United Kingdom

Library of Congress Cataloging-in-Publication Data
A catalog record for this book is available from the Library of Congress

British Library Cataloguing-in-Publication Data
A catalogue record for this book is available from the British Library

ISBN: 978-0-12-811381-3

For information on all Academic Press publications visit our website at https://www.elsevier.com/books-and-journals

Publisher: Nikki Levy
Acquisitions Editor: Emily Ekle
Editorial Project Manager: Barbara Makinster
Production Project Manager: Poulouse Joseph
Cover Designer: Matthew Limbert

Typeset by TNQ Books and Journals

CONTENTS

PREFACE

Evidence-based practice emerged in the medical field as an approach that relied on research findings to improve patient care. Since its origins, evidence-based practices have been implemented in counseling, nursing, psychology, and social work, among other fields. More recently, the criminal justice system has implemented evidence-based practices to improve inmate classification, diversion procedures, reduce recidivism, and enhance mental health, substance abuse, and individual and family treatment outcomes. Implementation of evidence-based practices and principles in the criminal justice system have the potential to improve public safety and public health, reduce the costs associated with incarceration, and reduce recidivism thereby reforming the criminal justice system.

Often when clinicians consider clinical interventions that are evidence-based, they may think of manualized, replicable therapies, such as Functional Family Therapy or Aggression Replacement Training. In the criminal justice system, crime prevention programs that are grounded in evidence-based *principles* are also widely used. Evidence-based principles may incorporate components of clinical evidence-based interventions such as an intervention provided for more than 90 days in duration. However, such an intervention is not a specific manualized, replicable intervention. Moreover, a crime prevention program such as the use of police patrol is not a clinical intervention. Therefore, in addition to focusing on evidence-based clinical interventions, we also briefly examine the implementation of evidence-based *principles* in the criminal justice system. However, evidence-based clinical interventions for criminal justice populations are the primary focus of the book.

It is important to recognize that the criminal justice system is comprised of four components: legislation, law enforcement, courts, and corrections, each of which is further divided into subcomponents. For example, the corrections system includes institutional facilities, such as jails and prisons, as well as community-based supervision settings such as probation and parole. These criminal justice components and subcomponents place unique needs and challenges on offenders and former offenders due to the mandates associated with them. For example, a former offender placed on parole while living in the community may be mandated to comply with parole conditions or face violations which could result in a variety of sanctions including re-incarceration. Or, the parolee could be released from prison with no parole conditions.

In addition to the aforementioned considerations, criminal justice populations are characterized by distinctive subpopulations. These subpopulations are racially and ethnically diverse, representing large numbers of people of color, and increasingly more women. These subpopulations also include low-level offenders, chronic repeat offenders, violent offenders, sex offenders, offenders incarcerated short-term in jails and long-term in prisons, recently released offenders, and mandated and voluntary populations, among others.

Furthermore, criminal justice populations experience multiple social problems often concurrently. These social problems include poverty, low levels of education and employment skills, unemployment, inadequate housing, and lack of healthcare, to mention a few. Additional social problems include alcohol and substance use and abuse, mental illness, co-occurring disorders, and criminal offending behavior.

We refer to individuals who are involved with the criminal justice system (legislation, law enforcement, courts, and/or corrections) as criminal justice populations. Criminal justice populations include both youth and adults. Each of these subpopulations requires clinical interventions that focus on their unique needs. It is our hope that this book contributes to a better understanding of these unique clinical needs.

The idea for this book emerged from our shared commitment to providing clinical interventions to criminal justice populations, and our shared experiences teaching clinical interventions for criminal justice populations to our students. These experiences have convinced us that a book is needed that can be used a teaching resources for students, as well as a resource for practitioners in the field to gain a deeper understanding of clinical evidence-based practices for criminal justice populations.

This book is intended for clinical students, clinical practitioners including counselors, nurses, psychologists, and social workers; as well as nonclinical criminal justice practitioners including lawyers, judges, and probation and parole officers who seek to increase their understanding of clinical interventions provided to criminal justice populations. The book will be useful for those directly employed in criminal justice organizations, as well as those employed in noncriminal justice organizations.

We present in lay terms the need for clinical interventions, how they are rated and become classified as evidence-based, and distinguish between evidence-based practices and evidence-based *principles* used in the criminal justice system. Consequently, the goals of the book are: (1) to provide a summary of evidence-based practices and principles that have been demonstrated to be effective for criminal justice populations; (2) to examine the major clinical issues that are relevant for implementing evidence-based practices and principles with criminal justice populations or within the criminal justice settings; (3) to simplify an understanding of the need for evidence-based practices and principles in the criminal justice system supporting the present direction of its use; and (4) to provide clinical and non-clinical readers with easy to understand tools to evaluate and implement evidence-based practices and principles.

We recognize the influence and intersectionality of social problems on criminal behavior and criminal justice system involvement. We also recognize the need for high-quality, effective clinical interventions for this population. Thus, the latter is the focus of this book with attention given to the view that social problems, criminal behavior, and criminal justice system involvement can be ameliorated using effective clinical interventions. It is our hope that clinical interventions based on evidence-based practices and principles will transform the criminal justice system by reducing the criminal justice population, reducing recidivism and offending behavior, enhance public safety and public health, and increase individuals' ability to lead productive lives.

ACKNOWLEDGMENTS

Numerous publications are available that focus on the topics of evidence-based practice, the criminal justice system, and clinical practice, both separately and combined. This represents a substantial body of knowledge. First and foremost, we acknowledge this body of work and the dedicated professionals who created it. We acknowledge the work we included in this book as well as the work we did not include. It was not possible to include all of the publications, resources, and creative as well as innovative criminal justice initiatives that support effective interventions with criminal justice populations.

We are grateful to several individuals for making our ideas for this book a reality. We are thankful and appreciative of the encouragement we received from Emily Ekle, Senior Acquisitions Editor, Psychology at Elsevier Academic Press. Your support for our vision, obtaining reviews in response to our initial proposal, and assistance with the contract are much appreciated. We also thank Barbara Makinster, Senior Editorial Project Manager at Elsevier Academic Press for your assistance with the manuscript, patience and answers to our many questions. Also, we acknowledge the assistance of Poulouse Joseph, Production Project Manager at Elsevier Academic Press for managing the manuscript corrections. Thank you Jacob Gutter for formatting the figures.

Additionally, I acknowledge the law enforcement officers who serve at the front end of the criminal justice system. These officers enforce legislation that results in criminal justice system involvement, but also provide service function interventions that result in diversion and attend to the 24 h a day, 7 days a week service needs of communities. A special thank you to those law enforcement organizations that hire police social workers to assist with these service functions. I also acknowledge the funding awarded by the New York Community Trust to support *A Pilot Study to Examine the Relationship between Substance Use, Mental Illness, and HIV Risk and/or Progression among Recently Incarcerated Women Returning to the East Harlem Neighborhood.* The funding was instrumental for examining the utility of the Level of Service Inventory-Revised among these women in addition to the Risk-Need-Responsivity model.

To the many criminal justice practitioners who embrace the idea that research informs practice and practice informs research, and use this as a foundation to provide clinical interventions to criminal justice populations.

Finally, to my family and friends thank you for your support and encouragement throughout the writing of this book.

George T. Patterson

There are many people who, over the years, helped shape this book, from idea to conceptual reality. Thanks to Rosalie Fitzgerald, Lynn Pinto, Nancy Matles, and all of my NYS Office of Court Administration family; Gregg Roth and Arianne Reyer, Nassau County Deputy County Attorney's Office; and LaQueta Robbins-Kennedy of the Nassau County Juvenile Detention Center.

Special thanks to all of the Judges and Justices I've partnered with and learned from; Honorable Associate Justice Ruth C. Balkin, Hon. Hope Zimmerman, Judge John G. Marks, Judge Robin Kent, Judge Conrad Singer, and Justice Michele M. Woodard.

To Dr. Charlene Lane, Dr. Patricia Dempsey, and Rev. Dr. Craig Wright whose mentorship has allowed me to dream big, faithfully, incredibly, and whose wisdom keeps me within due bounds.

Finally, to my family for always believing in me, and never allowing me to give up.

Warren K. Graham

CHAPTER 1

Introduction to Evidence-Based Practices and Principles in the Criminal Justice System

George T. Patterson

GOALS OF THE BOOK

The goals of the book are: (1) to provide a summary of evidence-based practices and principles that have been demonstrated to be effective for criminal justice populations; (2) to examine the major clinical issues that are relevant for adopting evidence-based practices and principles with criminal justice populations or within criminal justice settings; (3) to simplify an understanding of the need for evidence-based practices and principles in the criminal justice system, and support the present direction of its use; and (4) to provide clinical and nonclinical readers with easy to understand tools to evaluate and implement evidence-based practices and principles.

THE CRIMINAL JUSTICE SYSTEM

The Adult Criminal Justice System

The adult criminal justice system is comprised of four components; legislation, law enforcement, courts, and corrections. Each of these four components is comprised of subcomponents. Furthermore, each component and subcomponent has a specific function. Typically, individuals who are involved in the criminal justice system move from one component to the next. Individuals are processed by each component, of the criminal justice system, if applicable, which has a unique function. Each of these criminal justice components and subcomponents contributes to unique circumstances among offenders and former offenders due to the role of each component. These circumstances may affect the types of interventions criminal justice populations receive, as well as intervention outcomes.

Clinical Interventions in Criminal Justice Settings
ISBN 978-0-12-811381-3
http://dx.doi.org/10.1016/B978-0-12-811381-3.00001-9

In general, the legislative component is responsible for enacting laws that define offending behavior, as well as supporting interventions and a host of other societal laws. For instance, since the mid-1990s, the Washington State legislature has enacted and supported legislation that promotes the use evidence-based interventions in the adult criminal justice system and juvenile justice system (Aos, Mayfield, Miller, & Yen, 2006).

The law enforcement component enforces laws and provides a variety of service functions, many of which are in response to non-crime situations. In law enforcement settings, evidence-based practice takes the form of using data and empirical evidence to improve policing outcomes. Examples include reducing crime incidents or diverting individuals to appropriate resources.

The court component is comprised of numerous court structures such as civil courts, adult criminal courts, and specialty courts such as drug courts, mental health courts, and domestic violence courts, among others. These courts hear specific types of cases. Courts provide justice in response to a range of criminal, non-criminal, and social matters. Justice options can include punishment, treatment focused on rehabilitation, or a combination of these two options.

The corrections component includes institutional facilities, such as city or county jails, and State, Federal and private prisons, as well as community-based supervision settings including probation and parole. A former offender released from prison may be placed on parole supervision while living in the community. The former offender may be mandated to comply with parole conditions or face violations, which could result in a variety of sanctions including re-incarceration. These conditions may be drug testing or participating in a treatment program, for example. Conversely, a parolee may be released from prison without conditions.

Undeniably, the criminal justice system is comprised of complex organizations. These organizations operate on many levels including local, state, federal, and tribal levels. These organizations share many common features although differences are found due to legislative and regional differences. Among these differences are the types of interventions provided to offenders and former offenders. Criminal justice systems vary in the level of interventions offered, some of which are legislated whereas others are not. For example, some police departments hire police social workers to assist them with their services functions. This is not mandated among all law enforcement agencies. On the other hand, physical and mental health services are mandated among correctional facilities.

Evidence-based practices can be implemented in each of the four components of the criminal justice system and integrated with processing procedures. Several recommendations have been developed. Chandler, Fletcher, and Volkow (2009) identified the criminal justice stages of entry, prosecution, adjudication, sentencing, corrections, and reentry. These stages trace offenders' movement through the criminal justice components from arrest, through court, to incarceration or community-supervision. Interventions include screening and referrals, or community-based services, drug courts, and drug treatment throughout the components of the criminal justice system. The authors identified law enforcement officers, judges, prosecutors, juries, probation officers, correctional officers, and community-based service providers, among others as criminal justice practitioners capable of implementing effective interventions.

Another model suggests that the criminal justice settings of law enforcement, courts, jails, prisons, and probation and parole can separately provide interventions ranging from screening and integrated services to mental health and substance abuse treatment, including drug courts. When individuals with mental illness receive empirically supported interventions in each component of the criminal justice system, it will reduce processing in subsequent components of the criminal justice system (Kennedy-Hendricks, Huskamp, Rutkow, & Barry, 2016). This model is also applicable for individuals without mental illness, since diversion approaches can result in clinical interventions and less criminal justice system involvement.

The Juvenile Justice System

The juvenile justice system mirrors the adult criminal justice system in terms of the four components previously identified. Commonly referred to as the juvenile justice system, the distinguishing features of the four components and subcomponents are based on the age of the youth, which varies according to jurisdiction. Another distinguishing feature is the legislative component, which mandates different processing procedures for youth and defines juvenile delinquency. The juvenile justice system is comprised of separate sentencing guidelines, court structures, juvenile secure and non-secure detention facilities, juvenile probation officers, and statutes that define delinquency and status offenses, which are age-related offenses.

PUBLIC SAFETY AND PUBLIC HEALTH

Perhaps the distinguishing feature of clinical interventions provided in criminal justice settings is the focus on public safety and public health issues. In clinical settings, public health concerns may be the only clinical focus, where criminal justice settings emphasize both public safety and public health concerns. Consequently, clinicians require an understanding of public safety issues. Some clinicians may be uncomfortable with the emphasis on public safety found in criminal justice settings. However, both public safety and public health affect criminal justice populations and the two issues must be addressed.

Public safety refers to protecting the public from victimization and preventing future crimes. Perhaps the most well known method for achieving public safety is incapacitation, which is the incarceration of offenders. However, public safety can also be achieved by providing evidence-based practices (Carter, Gibel, Giguere, & Stroker, 2007).

Public health and public safety risks are often increased due to the lack of evidence-based interventions, health care, and other needed services for offenders and former offenders (Patterson, 2013). Given the sizeable involvement of criminal justice populations in substance use and abuse, public health and public safety can be enhanced through providing interventions focused on substance use in the criminal justice system (Chandler et al., 2009).

Moreover, public health practitioners should recognize that public safety is a fundamental issue in the criminal justice system. Practitioners should engage in efforts to develop and implement additional public health initiatives in criminal justice settings. However, practitioners are sometimes reluctant to provide interventions to criminal justice populations because of public safety concerns (Belenko & Wexler, 2007).

Criminal justice populations often have multiple needs in addition to experiencing public safety and public health risks. This combination of factors has resulted in extensive research focused on addressing these issues. This research has focused on improving public safety and public health, and has been conducted in both the adult criminal justice system and juvenile justice systems (Henderson, Taxman, & Young, 2008).

Public Health

Criminal justice populations are disproportionately represented within low-income communities of color. These populations experience inadequate health care services and consequently poor physical and mental health. When combined with criminal justice system involvement, particularly incarceration where these physical and mental health care needs are not met, returning to low-income urban communities increases public health risks (Binswanger, Redmond, Steiner, & Hicks, 2011; Dumont, Brockman, Dickman, Alexander, & Rich, 2012).

SIZE AND SCOPE OF CRIMINAL JUSTICE POPULATIONS

Prisons and Jails

As of 2015, the U.S. prison population incarcerated in State and Federal prisons was 1,526,800 prisoners (Kaeble & Glaze, 2016). Although the number of inmates admitted to city and county jails decreased over a seven-year period from 2008 to 2015, 721,300 jail inmates comprised the average daily population in jails in 2015. The prison and jail population represented 33.4% of the total correctional population (Minton & Zeng, 2016).

Probation and Parole

In 2015, 3,789,800 adults were under probation supervision. This figure represents 56.2% of the U.S. correctional population. Also during 2015, 870,000 adults were under parole supervision, representing 12.9% of the correctional population. Combined, adults under probation and parole supervision comprised 69.1% of the total correctional population in 2015 (Kaeble & Glaze, 2016).

Reentry

Estimates suggest that each year approximately 650,000 individuals are released from State and Federal prisons and reenter local communities (U.S. Department of Justice, Office of Justice Programs, n.d.). The most recent reentry statistics suggest that during 2011, 688,384 inmates and prisoners were released from jails and Federal prisons. These 688,384 releases were more than the 668,800 inmates and prisoners that were admitted in 2011 (Carson & Sabol, 2011).

Low-Level Offenders

A decrease of 28,600 prisoners from 2011 to 2012 coincided with the enactment of California's Public Safety Realignment Policy, which diverted low-level offenders from State prisons to jails and community supervision (Carson, 2015). In November 2015, the Federal government released approximately 6000 low-level prisoners from Federal prisons. These offenders were primarily nonviolent drug offenders. Approximately 40,000 more offenders are eligible for release in the future (Grimson, 2015). The release of these low-level drug offenders was intended to ease overcrowding in Federal prisons and the punitive sentences given to drug offenders (Horwitz, 2015). However, it is uncertain whether these trends will continue in the future, and how many low-level offenders will actually be released.

Recidivism

In perhaps the most comprehensive study investigating recidivism rates among prisoners released in 30 states in 2005, 67.0% were rearrested by 2008 (three years after release), and 76.6% were rearrested by 2010 (five years after release). This study also tracked the types of crimes that resulted in rearrests:

- 82.1% were property offenses
- 76.9% were drug offenses
- 73.6% were public order offenses
- 71.3% were violent crime offenses (Durose, Cooper, & Snyder, 2014)

Mental Illness

The most recent comprehensive report assessing mental illness rates among inmates and prisoners found that mid-year 2005, 56% of State prisoners reported experiencing a mental health problem. Similarly, 45% of Federal prisoners and 64% of jail inmates reported mental health problems (James & Glaze, 2006). These figures show that nearly half of all Federal prisoners, and more than half of all State prisoners and jail inmates reported experiencing a mental health problem. More jail inmates experienced mental health problems than other incarcerated groups.

Substance Abuse

James and Glaze (2006) also reported that 56% of State and Federal prisoners, and 53% of jail inmates experienced substance dependence or substance abuse. Comparable to the rates of mental illness, more than half of prisoners and inmates experience substance abuse. Moreover, 49% of State prisoners and 42% of jail inmates reported using drugs during the month of their arrest.

Co-Occurring Disorders

Also at mid-year 2005, 74% of State prisoners who experienced mental health problems also experienced substance dependence or substance abuse. Among jail inmates, 76% who experienced mental health problems also experienced substance dependence or substance abuse. These figures clearly show that more prisoners and inmates experience co-occurring disorders than either mental health problems or substance use alone.

Juveniles

In 2013, approximately 1.1 million juvenile delinquency cases were processed in juvenile courts, although the number of juvenile court cases has decreased 44% from 1997 to 2013. More than 4000 of these juvenile cases were waived, or transferred to the adult criminal justice system. More than 25% of juvenile delinquency court cases were female youth (Furdella & Puzzanchera, 2015).

EVIDENCE-BASED PRACTICE

Evidence-based practice originated in the medical field. An early definition of evidence-based medicine states, "evidence based medicine is the process of systematically finding, appraising, and using contemporaneous research findings as the basis for clinical decisions" (Rosenberg & Donald, 1995, p. 1122).

Sackett, Rosenberg, Gray, Haynes, and Richardson (1996) traced the origins of evidence-based medicine to mid-19th century Paris, France. Sackett et al. stated, "evidence-based medicine is the conscientious, explicit, and judicious use of current best evidence in making decisions about the care of individual patients" (p. 71). Furthermore, the authors articulated "the practice of evidence-based medicine means integrating individual clinical expertise with the best available external clinical evidence from systematic research" (p. 71). More recently, Straus, Richardson, Glasziou, and Haynes (2005) provided a definition of evidence-based medicine suggesting that "evidence-based medicine (EBM) requires the integration of the best research evidence with our clinical expertise and our patient's unique values and circumstances" (p. 1).

The above definition, although it defines EBM, appears to be a widely cited definition of evidence-based practice. Indeed, the very definition of evidence-based practice originated with the definition of EBM. Throughout the book we embrace this latter definition.

Straus et al. (2005) also defined the four major concepts associated with evidence-based medicine. Best research evidence is valid clinical research that informs practice. Such research is provisional as more recent research evidence supplants outdated evidence. Clinical expertise refers to the practitioner's clinical skills and clinical judgment. Patient values are "the unique preferences, concerns and experiences" (p. 1) that individuals maintain when they engage in clinical interventions. Finally, patient circumstances refers to the individual's clinical needs as well as the setting in which the intervention is provided.

Fig. 1.1 illustrates Straus et al.'s (2005) conceptualization of EBM. In our view, the definition and concepts are applicable to criminal justice settings

Figure 1.1 Overview of evidence-based practice.

and criminal justice populations, and consistent with contemporary definitions of evidence-based practice.

General Implementation Benefits

Straus et al. (2005) suggest that when implemented properly, evidence-based practices can improve client outcomes in several ways that are beneficial to both clinicians and clients. Clinicians benefit from the ability to provide better interventions, to interpret clinical findings, and to choose effective interventions. Clients benefit from receiving effective assessment, prevention, and intervention.

General Implementation Challenges

Straus et al. (2005) also acknowledge the many challenges and criticisms associated with evidence-based practices. In general, the challenges result from lack of knowledge and understanding of the definition of evidence-based practice, acquiring the necessary skills to locate, retrieve, and assess the validity of an evidence-based practice, acquiring resources needed for intervention implementation, participating in the most appropriate approaches for teaching and learning the skills, integrating new interventions into practice, and being mindful of the time needed to practice new skills.

EVIDENCE-BASED PRACTICE IN THE CRIMINAL JUSTICE SYSTEM

Since its origins in the medical field, evidence-based practices have been implemented in nursing, social work, psychology, and counseling, among

Figure 1.2 Overview of evidence-based practice in the criminal justice system.

other disciplines. In Fig. 1.2, we illustrate the application of Straus et al.'s (2005) conceptualization of EBM in criminal justice settings. As the figure shows, the same concepts that are applicable in EBM are applicable in criminal justice settings. However, several additional considerations are needed.

Numerous resources are available for locating and retrieving best evidence relevant for criminal justice populations. Some of the resources are described in the appendix. Behavioral outcomes among criminal justice populations are much more varied than in typical clinical settings and include reductions in crime, delinquency, recidivism, and arrests, which are associated with public safety, as well as public health outcomes. Consequently, best evidence should include these outcomes and be relevant for the criminal justice settings and a specific criminal justice population.

Clinical expertise requires prior clinical experience with criminal justice populations as well as knowledge about relevant intervention outcomes. As subsequent chapters examine further, the use of actuarial risk assessment instruments have been demonstrated to be more effective than clinical judgment alone. Clinical expertise in criminal justice settings should also include the use of actuarial risk assessment instruments. Thus, clinical judgment when used in criminal justice settings should be supported with the use of actuarial risk assessment instruments.

Patient values such as cultural beliefs about mental illness and mental health treatment should not be ignored. Certainly, demographic characteristics are an important consideration when implementing evidence-based practices. The intervention should be relevant to the client's demographic characteristics, but also the client's presenting problems. Other important considerations include values associated offending behavior, biopsychosocial well-being, age, race/ethnicity, and preferred clinical outcomes.

Patient circumstances such as views toward the criminal justice system and prior experiences in the criminal justice system may also impact intervention efficacy. These experiences need to be acknowledged. We understand patient circumstances to include criminal justice mandates since criminal justice settings may impose mandates on behavior. Furthermore, the criminal justice and juvenile justice systems are comprised of numerous complex organizations.

The "What Works" Literature

Asserting that little empirical evidence supports the effectiveness of interventions for offenders in institutional and community-based settings, Martinson (1974) published a summary of a previously unpublished report. The original unpublished report contained a study wherein Martinson and colleagues reviewed 231 studies that were published between 1945 and 1967. These were evaluation studies utilizing comparison groups and reporting data focused on a range of outcomes such as recidivism, education, and employment. Martinson concluded that none of the interventions resulted in positive outcomes on recidivism, education, and/or employment.

Five years later, Martinson (1979) reported that based on the results of a second study, he did not maintain his previous assertions that no interventions were effective. Martinson further argued, "I protested at the slogan used by the media to sum up what I said "nothing works"" (p. 254). Martinson suggested a new framework to describe interventions for offenders, which categorized interventions in three categories; beneficial, neutral, and or detrimental. Noting that Martinson's (1974) initial conclusions were based on a study with several limitations, nonetheless the conclusions did have an adverse impact on correctional policy (Sarre, 2001).

As studies investigating the efficacy of interventions for offenders and former offenders continued to be conducted and reviewed, this literature was recognized as "the 'what works' literature" (Latessa & Lowenkamp, 2005, p. 521–535). As the "what works" literature further developed it transformed community-based supervision of former offenders (Bourgon, Gutierrez, & Ashton, 2011), and provided empirical evidence that rehabilitation interventions were effective (Cullen, Smith, Lowenkamp, & Latessa, 2009).

Sherman et al. (1998) describe the events that resulted in the development of listings identifying what works, what doesn't, what's promising, and what's unknown. In 1996, legislation was passed mandating the U.S. Attorney General to present to Congress with a report describing the effectiveness of State and local crime interventions that were funded by the U.S. Department of Justice. Later, in 1997, the report was presented to Congress describing the results of a systematic review that examined over 500 program evaluation studies investigating crime prevention interventions. The systematic review defined a crime prevention intervention or program as any intervention resulting in fewer crime outcomes. Primary outcomes included crime and risk factors for criminal behavior.

As part of the systematic review, Sherman and colleagues developed the Maryland Scale of Scientific Methods (described in greater detail in Chapter 2) to assess the level of internal validity reported in each study. These activities produced four categories of interventions (what works, what doesn't, what's promising, and what's unknown). These categories are also described in greater detail in Chapter 2.

We observed that many of the crime prevention interventions can be grouped in several of the criminal justice system components described earlier. The following examples point out these observations:

What Works

Law Enforcement

Examples of what works in law enforcement include "extra police patrols in high crime hot spots" and "arresting domestic abusers" (p. 8).

Corrections

Examples in corrections settings include "incarceration of offenders who will continue to commit crimes" and "drug treatment in prison" (p. 8).

What's Promising

Law Enforcement

What's promising in law enforcement settings include "gang offender monitoring by community workers and probation and police officers" (p. 9) and "proactive drunk driving arrests with breath testing" (p. 10).

Corrections

In corrections settings, such interventions include "gang offender monitoring by community workers and probation and police officers" (p. 9) and "prison-based vocational education" (p. 11).

What Doesn't Work

Law Enforcement

Examples of what doesn't work in law enforcement settings include "neighborhood watch programs organized with police" and "storefront police officers" (p. 9).

Courts

An example of what doesn't work in the court component of the criminal justice system is "diversion from court to job training" (p. 9).

Corrections

What doesn't work in corrections settings include "rehabilitation programs using counseling" and "intensive supervision on parole or probation (ISP)" (p. 9).

The Use of Evidence-Based *Principles* in the Criminal Justice System

On December 6–7, 2006, a conference was held in Philadelphia, PA. The goals of the conference were to identify the unique challenges encountered when implementing, sustaining, and disseminating evidence-based drug treatments in criminal justice settings. In May 2007, the Center for Evidence-based Interventions for Crime and Addiction published *Implementing Evidence-based Drug Treatment in Criminal Justice Settings: Final Conference Report* (Belenko & Wexler, 2007). The report summarized numerous issues and recommendations identified during the conference. Perhaps a major conclusion that came out of the conference was "...placing more emphasis on evidence-based principles rather than practices. Such principles (e.g., use of behavioral and cognitive behavioral methods, targeting criminogenic risks and needs, monitoring and accountability, continuity of care) may be easier to implement than new interventions and have a substantial scientific base" (p. 27).

Much of the "What Works" literature describes empirically-based interventions that are *principles*. Others are evidence-based clinical interventions. This distinction is important to recognize since one type of intervention may be more appropriate than the other for a specific criminal justice setting or population.

In fact, eight principles for effective offender and former offender interventions have been recommended based on empirical evidence demonstrating the efficacy of these principles. This evidence also suggests that these principles should be implemented in chronological order as follows:

1. Use actuarial risk assessment instruments to assess criminogenic needs.
2. Use motivation techniques to increase offender and former offenders' motivation to change behavior that results in criminal justice system involvement.
3. Target interventions based on the risk-need-responsivity model, provide interventions to high risk offenders and former offenders that last 3–9 months in duration and involve 40%–70% of their time.
4. Provide staff training and skill development in evidence-based practices that employ cognitive–behavioral approaches.
5. Use positive reinforcements to change behaviors.
6. Assist offenders and former offenders with developing and maintaining community-based, pro-social activities that support behavioral change.
7. Use reliable and valid outcomes measures to evaluate intervention implementation.
8. Use outcome measures to enhance the accountability and integrity of the intervention (National Institute of Corrections, n.d.).

THE AUTHORS' PERSPECTIVE

At the end of this chapter, we repeat our perspective on the use of evidence-based practices and evidence-based principles in criminal justice settings. Terms such as practices, principles, programs, and evidence-based practices are often used to describe the interventions given to criminal justice populations. Later in the book, we will discuss the differences between these terms. As clinicians, we use the term evidence-based practices to refer to clinical interventions intended to improve psychosocial and behavioral outcomes. These clinical interventions are grounded in empirical evidence demonstrating the efficacy of the intervention. Furthermore, when implemented individuals are engaged in the intervention over a period of time lasting from several weeks to several months. Clearly, the organizational setting must have the capacity to provide ongoing treatment.

Functional family therapy, for example, is an empirically supported, evidence-based practice. This clinical intervention consists of three phases. The first phase is engagement and motivation. As we shall see many principles are suggested for criminal justice populations. One widely recommended principle suggests that motivation should be increased among offenders and former offenders. In our view, increasing motivation alone is a *component* of a (clinical) evidence-based practice not a clinical intervention. However, possessing clinical skills can be an asset for enhancing offender and former offenders' motivation and certainly when providing functional family therapy.

In many criminal justice settings, named clinical interventions that are evidence-based (such as functional family) may not be realistic. For example, probation and parole officers may not provide the intervention, but refer individuals to organizations that provide interventions to criminal justice populations. Indeed, for-profit and nonprofit organizations also provide interventions to criminal justice populations.

Our view is that most interventions implemented in criminal justice settings are based on evidence-based *principles*. This occurs for a variety of reasons given the complexity of the criminal justice system and multiple needs of criminal justice populations. Acquiring clinical skills is essential for understanding criminal justice outcomes.

SUMMARY

In this chapter, we briefly introduced the four components of the adult criminal justice system and juvenile justice system, described the characteristics of criminal justice populations, and traced the emergence of evidence-based practice in criminal justice settings. In Chapter 2, we will provide a basic overview of research concepts necessary for understanding evidence-based practice.

REFERENCES

Aos, S., Mayfield, J., Miller, M., & Yen, W. (2006). *Evidence-based treatment of alcohol, drug, and mental health disorders: Potential benefits, costs, and fiscal impacts for Washington State*. Olympia: Washington State Institute for Public Policy.

Belenko, S., & Wexler, H. K. (2007). *Implementing evidence-based drug treatment in criminal justice settings: Final conference report*. Retrieved from www.tresearch.org/law_ethics/CEICAFinalReport2006.pdf.

Binswanger, I. A., Redmond, N., Steiner, J. F., & Hicks, L. R. (2011). Health disparities and the criminal justice system: An agenda for further research and action. *Journal of Urban Health*, *89*(1), 98–107.

Bourgon, G., Gutierrez, L., & Ashton, J. (2011). From case management to change agent: The evolution of what works' community supervision. *Irish Probation Journal*, *8*, 28–48.

Carson, E.A. (2015). *Prisoners in 2014*. U.S. Department of Justice, Office of Justice Programs, Bureau of Justice Statistics.

Carson, E. A., & Sabol, W. J. (2011). *Prisoners in 2011*. U.S. Department of Justice, Office of Justice Programs, Bureau of Justice Statistics.

Carter, M. M., Gibel, S., Giguere, R., & Stroker, R. (2007). *Increasing public safety through successful offender reentry: Evidence-based and emerging practices in corrections*. Silver Spring, MD: Center for Effective Public Policy.

Chandler, R. K., Fletcher, B. W., & Volkow, N. D. (2009). Treating drug abuse and addiction in the criminal justice system: Improving public health and safety. *JAMA, 301*(2), 183–190.

Cullen, F. T., Smith, P., Lowenkamp, C. T., & Latessa, E. J. (2009). Nothing works revisited: Deconstructing Farabee's rethinking rehabilitation. *Victims and Offenders, 4*, 101–123.

Dumont, D. M., Brockman, B., Dickman, S., Alexander, N., & Rich, J. D. (2012). Public health and the epidemic of incarceration. *Annual Review of Public Health, 33*, 325–339.

Durose, M. R., Cooper, A. D., & Snyder, H. N. (2014). *Recidivism of prisoners released in 30 states in 2005: Patterns from 2005 to 2010*. Washington, DC: U.S. Department of Justice, Office of Justice Programs, Bureau of Justice Statistics.

Furdella, J., & Puzzanchera, C. (2015). *Delinquency cases in juvenile court*. U.S. Department of Justice, Office of Justice Programs, Office of Juvenile Justice and Delinquency Prevention.

Grimson, M. (2015). *6,000 federal prisoners to be granted early release*. NBC News. Retrieved from http://www.nbcnews.com/news/us-news/6-000-federal-prisoners-be-granted-early-release-report-n439491.

Henderson, C. E., Taxman, F. S., & Young, D. W. (2008). A Rasch model analysis of evidence-based treatment practices in the criminal justice system. *Drug and Alcohol Dependence, 93*, 163–175.

Horwitz, S. (2015). *Justice department set to free 6,000 prisoners, largest one-time release*. Retrieved from https://www.washingtonpost.com/world/national-security/justice-department-about-to-free-6000-prisoners-largest-one-time-release/2015/10/06/961f4c9a-6ba2-11e5-aa5b-f78a98956699_story.html?utm_term=.763b02ad3b96.

James, D. J., & Glaze, L. E. (2006). *Mental health problems of prison and jail inmates*. U.S. Department of Justice, Office of Justice Programs, Bureau of Justice Statistics.

Kaeble, D., & Glaze, L. (2016). *Correctional populations in the United States, 2015*. U.S. Department of Justice, Office of Justice Programs, Bureau of Justice Statistics.

Kennedy-Hendricks, A., Huskamp, H. A., Rutkow, L., & Barry, C. L. (2016). Improving access to care and reducing involvement in the criminal justice for people with mental illness. *Health Affairs, 35*(6), 1076–1083.

Latessa, E. J., & Lowenkamp, C. (2005). *What works in reducing recidivism?* (Vol. 3). University of St. Thomas Law Journal.

Martinson, R. (1974). What works? - Questions and answers about prison reform. *The Public Interest, 35*, 22–54.

Martinson, R. (1979). New findings, new views: A note of caution regarding sentencing reform. *Hofstra Law Review*, 7, 243–258.

Minton, T. D., & Zeng, Z. (2016). *Jail inmates in 2015*. U.S. Department of Justice, Office of Justice Programs, Bureau of Justice Statistics.

National Institute of Corrections. (n.d.). *The principles of effective interventions*. Retrieved from https://nicic.gov/theprinciplesofeffectiveinterventions.

Patterson, G. T. (2013). Prisoner reentry: A public health or public safety issue for social work practice? *Social Work in Public Health, 28*, 129–141.

Rosenberg, W., & Donald, A. (1995). Evidence based medicine: An approach to clinical problem-solving. *British Medical Journal, 310*(6987), 1122–1126.

Sackett, D. L., Rosenberg, W. M., Gray, J. A., Haynes, R. B., & Richardson, W. S. (1996). Evidenced based medicine: What it is and what it isn't. *British Medical Journal, 312*, 71–72.

Sarre, R. (2001). Beyond 'what works?' A 25-year jubilee retrospective of Robert Martinson's famous article. *Australian & New Zealand Journal of Criminology, 34*(1), 38–46.

Sherman, L. W., Gottfredson, D. C., MacKenzie, D. L., Eck, J., Reuter, P., & Bushway, S. D. (1998). *Preventing crime: What works, what doesn't, what's promising*. Washington, DC: U.S.Department of Justice, Department of Justice, Office of Justice Programs, National Institute of Justice.

Straus, S. E., Richardson, W. S., Glasziou, P., & Haynes, R. B. (2005). *Evidence-based medicine: How to practice and teach EBM* (3rd ed.). Edinburgh: Elsevier.

U.S. Department of Justice, Office of Justice Programs. (n.d.). *Reentry*. Retrieved from http://www.reentry.gov.

FURTHER READING

Aos, S., Miller, M., & Drake, E. (2006). *Evidence-based adult corrections programs: What works and what does not work*. Olympia: Washington State Institute for Public Policy.

Friedman, P. D., Taxman, F. S., & Henderson, C. E. (2007). Evidence-based treatment practices for drug-involved adults in the criminal justice. *Journal of Substance Abuse Treatment, 32*, 267–277.

Kim, K., Becker-Cohen, M., & Serakos, M. (2015). *The processing and treatment of mentally ill persons in the criminal justice system*. Washington, DC: Urban Institute.

Prendergast, M. L. (2011). Issues in defining and applying evidence-based practices criteria for treatment of criminal-justice involved clients. *Journal of Psychoactive Drugs, 43*(S1), 10–18.

CHAPTER 2

Using Evidence to Inform Clinical Practice

George T. Patterson

THE ROLE OF THEORY IN RESEARCH AND CLINICAL PRACTICE

A theory is defined as "a set of interrelated, abstract propositions or statements that offers an explanation of some phenomenon" (Skidmore, as cited in Monette, Sullivan, DeJong, & Hilton, 2014, pp. 26–27). Theoretical frameworks are used to guide both research and clinical practice. In research, abstract theoretical concepts are measured and tested. Some theories are more difficult to measure and test than others because the abstract theoretical concepts must be defined and measured, a process known as operationalization.

Freud's psychoanalytic theory, for example, is comprised of three major abstract theoretical concepts; the id, ego, and superego. These concepts are difficult to concretely measure and quantify, and this is particularly true when relying on reliable and valid standardized instruments, given that no instruments measure these three abstract concepts.

Complicating the process of measuring abstract theoretical concepts is the fact that concepts can be measured in different ways among studies. Furthermore, definitions and measurement approaches should be based on theoretical frameworks. For example, crime or offending behavior, and recidivism are two abstract theoretical concepts that are often investigated in criminal justice studies. However, researchers often define and measure crime and recidivism in different ways using different data sources. This results in different measurement approaches across studies.

The following two studies illustrate how differently recidivism can be defined and measured. Durose, Cooper, and Snyder (2014) defined and measured recidivism as: (1) an arrest occurring within 5 years after release from prison, (2) an arrest occurring within 5 years after release from prison that involved court adjudication or disposition, (3) an arrest occurring within 5 years after release from prison that involved a court conviction, (4)

Clinical Interventions in Criminal Justice Settings
ISBN 978-0-12-811381-3
http://dx.doi.org/10.1016/B978-0-12-811381-3.00002-0

an arrest occurring within 5 years after release from prison that involved a jail or prison sentence, and (5) an arrest or technical violation of conditional release occurring within 5 years after release from prison. Clearly, studies investigating intervention efficacy will use a period much less than 5 years. In contrast, Pérez (2009) defined and measured recidivism as the number of new arrests, new incarcerations, and new convictions that occurred 18 months after probationers completed substance abuse treatment.

Common among these definitions of recidivism are events and situations that identify recidivism, and a timeframe in which these events must occur. Between these two examples, the timeframe ranged from 18 months to 5 years.

The measurement of recidivism is important to understand, given that the correctional intervention literature describes the importance of evidence-based practices and principles for reducing recidivism (Aos, Miller, & Drake, 2006; Casey, Warren, & Elek, 2011; Gendreau, Little, & Goggin, 1996).

In clinical practice, theory informs clinicians and clients about what to anticipate over the course of an intervention and how the intervention produces clinical and behavioral changes. Theory aids in understanding the central components of an intervention and explains how and why the intervention produces the desired outcomes. Applying a theoretical framework also informs practitioners about techniques to use in intervention, and if an interventions consists of several phases, which techniques to use during a specific phase and why they should be used in sequential order. Theory also influences implementation fidelity (Miller & Miller, 2015).

Actuarial risk assessment instruments are also grounded in theory and measurement methods. In the same way that research studies and clinical interventions are guided by different theoretical frameworks, actuarial risk assessment instruments, which are the focus of Chapter 6, are also guided by theoretical frameworks. In fact, these instruments have been developed based on different theoretical frameworks and different measurement methods (Casey et al., 2014).

Bonta and Andrews (2017) emphasize the relevance of theory for understanding offending behavior. They suggest that theories identify causes for offending behavior and once causation is known interventions can be developed that address these causes. Thus, theoretical frameworks, causes of offending behaviors, and clinical interventions are all linked. Importantly, Bonta and Andrews recognized that criminological theories such as strain theory, subcultural theory, labeling theory, and Marxist or conflict theory posit that social class background is the cause of offending behavior. These are assumptions that are not supported by empirical evidence. Other criminological theories, such as control theory and differential association theory, posit that some communities are unable to promote appropriate norms. In response to these theoretical limitations, Bonta and Andrews proposed the General Personality and Cognitive Social Learning (GPCSL) theory based on social learning theory.

SOCIAL LEARNING THEORY

Social learning theory is a theoretical framework that guides several evidence-based practices and approaches to assessment for criminal justice populations. Social learning theory is based on several theoretical assumptions. Individuals learn behaviors, attitudes, and behavioral consequences from other individuals in their social environment (Bandura, 1977). It stands to reason that if individuals learn certain behaviors, attitudes, and behavioral consequences from others, these can be unlearned or changed through observing, imitating, or modeling others. Bandura's research conducted in the 1960s and 1970s focused on the role of observational learning of behaviors and attitudes, as well as opportunities for intervention that emphasize observational learning, modeling, and self-efficacy (Grusec, 1992).

Several evidence-based interventions relevant for criminal justice populations are grounded in social learning theory. Multidimensional treatment foster care for youth (Chamberlain, 2003) and functional family therapy (Sexton & Alexander, 2003) for at-risk youth and their families are evidence-based interventions presented in subsequent chapters that are based on social learning theory.

General Personality and Cognitive Social Learning Theory

The Risk-Need-Responsivity model (Bonta & Andrews, 2007, 2017), examined in greater detail in Chapter 6, was developed based on the GPCSL theory. Empirical evidence supports the GPCSL theory, which posits that behaviors, including offending behavior, are learned.

INTERVENTION OUTCOMES ARE PROVISIONAL

As a result of theory testing and research findings that replicate intervention efficacy, lists that identify evidence-based practices are provisional. As studies are replicated, improved measurement approaches are developed and utilized, and more rigorous research designs utilized, this newer evidence will provide empirical support for an evidence-based intervention. This particularly applies to advances made in medicine, but other fields as well. Consequently, lists of evidence-based practices for criminal justice populations change as new evidence emerges that result from research findings. Noting the importance of theory testing and emerging research findings, Sherman et al. (1998) reported that their listings of what works, what doesn't, and what's promising, is provisional.

PRETEST AND POSTTEST MEASUREMENT

The importance of defining and measuring abstract theoretical concepts makes this a good starting point for discussing basic research methodology. The measurement process involves determining which intervention outcomes, including clinical outcomes, are relevant for a particular criminal justice population and subsequently how these outcomes will be measured. Throughout the book, particularly in Chapter 4, clinical and behavioral intervention outcomes relevant for criminal justice populations are discussed.

As we saw, outcome measures must be theoretically linked to the intervention. To assess behavioral or other changes that occur as a result of participating in an evidence-based intervention, it is important to measure pretest and posttest outcomes. Theoretically, if an evidence-based practice or principle does not target anger, for example, with specific effective anger management techniques to reduce angry emotions or behavior, it is unlikely that the behavior will change. The intervention should be comprised of components that target a specific social problem.

A pretest is a measurement of an attitude, perception, or behavior conducted prior to an offender or former offender participating in an intervention. It serves as a baseline that can be used for comparison after an intervention has been completed.

Pretest measurement is a fundamental step in a research study to assess intervention effectiveness. Conducting a pretest is also important in clinical practice. For instance, actuarial risk assessment instruments should be administered prior to delivering an intervention to assess levels of risk and need. The purpose of subsequent administration is to assess whether risks and needs have been reduced.

Actuarial instruments can be re-administered after offenders or former offenders complete an intervention to assess whether risk levels have been reduced after participating in an intervention. This is known as a posttest. A posttest is a measurement of the same behavior that was measured in the pretest using the same measurement approach or instrument. For instance, if a standardized instrument was used at pretest to assess criminal thinking, the same instrument should be administered at posttest. In this way, comparisons can be made to assess changes in criminal thinking after participating in an intervention.

MEASUREMENT APPROACHES

The measurement of intervention outcomes generally takes two forms: subjective measurement and objective measurement. These approaches vary in rigor.

Subjective Measurement

Subjective measurement refers to a measurement approach based on what individuals report about their attitudes, perceptions, or behaviors. This is also known as self-report and is the most common type of measurement approach. When an offender or former offender completes a standardized instrument, they are providing self-report responses. Similarly, when offenders or former offenders are administered and complete an actuarial risk assessment instrument, they are providing self-report responses since they themselves identify their responses to questions.

Most evidence-based clinical practices utilize self-report measures. Individuals complete a standardized instrument prior to participating in an intervention (pretest), and again after completing an intervention (posttest). The standardized instrument can be administered several times prior to participating in an intervention as well as several times after completing the intervention.

Objective Measurement

Whereas the measurement of attitudes and perceptions rely on self-report, some behaviors are documented. To increase the trustworthiness of self-report responses, objective measurement approaches may be used alone or in combination with subjective measurement approaches. Objective measurement approaches are considered to be a better approach than subjective approaches. Examples of objective measurement approaches include obtaining information from official documents such as arrest records, school, and/or employment records.

Reliability

Reliability refers to the ability of a standardized instrument to produce similar results each time the instrument is administered among the same individuals, or different individuals. Cronbach's alpha is a commonly used approach to describe the reliability of an instrument. Cronbach's alpha ranges from 0.00 to 1.00. The closer that alpha is to 1.00, the more acceptable the reliability of the instrument. For example, 0.90 demonstrates that the instrument is a reliable instrument, whereas an alpha of 0.67 is less acceptable.

Test–Retest Reliability

Because standardized instruments are often administered more than once to the same individuals, it is important that the instrument continue to produce similar results each time. This is known as test–retest reliability. In other words, an individual's familiarity with the instrument should not influence the results during subsequent administration. Standardized instruments should demonstrate and report acceptable reliability including test–retest reliability.

Validity

Validity refers to the ability of a standardized instrument to accurately measure the attitude, perception, or behavior it purports to measure. For instance, if an instrument purports to measure criminal thinking, it should measure that concept and not some other concept such as anger. Whereas reliability is reported numerically, validity is not. The methods for establishing the various types of reliability and validity are beyond the scope of this book. Standardized instruments should also demonstrate and report acceptable validity.

SAMPLING

In addition to the type of study design and type of data that are used to assess clinical intervention effectiveness, several other issues require consideration such as sample size, sampling technique, response rate, and attrition or drop-outs. Research participants volunteer to participate in research studies and make an informed decision about whether to participate based on the information they are provided about the study. Ethical boards, such as an Institutional Review Board (IRB), review all procedures in advance and require signed informed consent.

The techniques employed to obtain a sample of research participants has implications for assessing clinical intervention effectiveness since sampling procedures vary ranging from weak to robust. Two types of sampling techniques are probability and nonprobability samples. With probability sampling, every individual in the population has an equal chance of being selected to participate in the study. On the other hand, with nonprobability sampling, all individuals in the population do not have an equal chance to be included in the study sample. A convenience sample is a form of nonprobability sampling, and as the name implies, it is a sample of convenience. Therefore, the potential for bias exists.

While a full discussion of statistical power is beyond the scope of this book, the sample size must be large enough to allow confidence in the results. Likewise, it is important to understand and examine the responses rate; the number of research study participants who complete and return questionnaires. The attrition or dropout rate is also important to examine because the characteristics of study participants who drop out of the study may affect the study results.

RESEARCH DESIGNS

Three types of research designs are employed to assess intervention outcomes: pre-experimental, quasi-experimental, and experimental designs. The type of research design used to investigate clinical intervention effectiveness is important because the strongest designs control for threats to internal validity. The primary goal of the research design is to reduce extraneous variability, or other factors, that might affect intervention outcomes thereby increasing confidence that the intervention itself resulted in positive outcomes. Research designs range in rigor from simple to complex designs, and range in strength from a weak or strong ability to control for threats to internal validity.

The types of research studies that provide the strongest evidence also employ quantitative data. Such studies employ statistics and statistical significance to rule out the possibility that positive intervention outcomes could have occurred by chance.

Internal Validity

The three research designs vary in their ability to reduce threats to internal validity. Internal validity refers to the ability to understand and reduce factors other than the intervention that can influence intervention outcomes.

The following example employs frequently used scientific notation, where (X) represents the independent variable, or the intervention which is considered the cause and occurs first; and (O) represents the dependent variable, the effect or intervention outcome, and it occurs second in sequential order. To further illustrate, if the independent variable (X) is the evidence-based practice and the dependent variable (O) is recidivism, internal validity helps to understand that the evidence-based practice, and not sanctions, resulted in less recidivism.

Campbell and Stanley (1963) identified seven threats to internal validity:

1. History refers to events that occur in communities, for example. If during the course of a study, a community makes major changes between pretest and posttest regarding how low-level offenders are managed in the criminal justice system, this may impact the study outcomes.
2. Maturation refers to changes that occur solely based on the passage of time. In other words, an intervention may not produce positive outcomes if these outcomes occurred merely with the passage of time between pretest and posttest.
3. Testing refers to the administration of a standardized instrument more than one time. When study participants are administered certain instruments more than once, their scores tend to be higher upon subsequent administration. Thus, an outcome could be the result of testing rather than resulting from an intervention.
4. Instrumentation is related to testing, and refers to changes made in the administration of a standardized instrument. For instance, if the posttest is administered by a different individual, that individual may change or use different the instructions, thereby possibly affecting outcomes.
5. Statistical regression refers to recruiting samples of offenders or former offenders at either high risk or low risk for recidivating. When assessing risk levels by administering an instrument a second time, these individuals may have different scores which could be lower or higher. This is known as regression toward the mean, and may incorrectly suggest higher or lower risk. This will occur even in the absence of an intervention.
6. Selection occurs when study participants are assigned to control and experimental groups without using random assignment. For instance, it could be that high-risk offenders are placed in the control group, and low-risk offender placed in the experimental group. Clearly, this will affect outcomes. Risk levels should be similar between the two groups, which can be achieved using random assignment.
7. Experimental attrition refers to study participants dropping out of the study, either from the control or experimental group. The characteristics of study participants who drop out could affect intervention outcomes.

Causation

Causation is more difficult to determine in social science research. This occurs because numerous social, psychological, biological, neurological, and behavioral factors contribute to offending behavior and criminal justice system involvement. For these reasons, we cannot be completely certain that any one or combination of these factors caused offending behavior. However, based on replication of research studies that employ the most rigorous research designs and empirical evidence, we increase our confidence in which of these factors contributes to offending behavior and criminal justice system involvement.

External Validity

External validity refers to the degree to which an evidence-based practice, which was tested in a research study among a sample of study participants, is generalized to real world settings and other populations.

Pre-Experimental Designs

Numerous variations of pre-experimental designs exist. For example, a pre-experimental design could use only a posttest measuring a clinical outcome after an intervention has been given. Obviously, this approach is very limited because pre-intervention measurements were not conducted, thus no comparisons can be made between pretest and posttest intervention outcomes. Conversely, only a pretest could be administered. Therefore, only a basic design will be discussed as an illustration.

A Basic Example

In this basic example, scientific notation is used to illustrate the design. Pretest and posttest measurements are denoted by (O). The intervention is (X). Thus, only one group of study participants are administered a pretest prior to participating in the intervention, and administered a posttest which is the same measurement instrument, upon completing the intervention.

Group 1 O X O

Pre-experimental designs are the weakest types of research designs for minimizing threats to internal validity. Such designs do not employ random assignment to control or experimental groups, and consequently lack control or experimental groups. Due to these limitations, pre-experimental designs are not acceptable for categorizing an intervention as an evidence-based intervention. Although pre-experimental designs are weak regarding internal validity, such designs can provide useful information.

Case Example

Pre-experimental designs are weak research designs for minimizing threats to internal validity. Consequently, such designs cannot be employed to assess intervention effectiveness. However, pre-experimental designs can be useful for other purposes when implementing evidence-based practices and principles in criminal justice settings or with criminal justice populations. This case example describes the use of a one-group pretest–posttest pre-experimental design.

Most research describing the utility of the Level of Service Inventory-Revised (LSI-R) (Andrews & Bonta, 1995) for female offenders has examined its utility compared to men, or its ability to predict recidivism among female offenders. The purpose of this pilot study was to examine the feasibility of implementing the LSI-R among a sample of women of color in a large urban environment. Another purpose of this study was to conduct a basic cost analysis to determine the cost of implementing the LSI-R, training needs among staff to administer the LSI-R and interpret scores, and the feasibility of administering in a social service agency to female offenders with criminal justice system involvement.

The following procedures were used to recruit participants: (1) agency staff distributed flyers at intake to all clients who received services from the outpatient, aftercare, and residential programs, and (2) signed consent was obtained and study participants were given a copy of the consent form. Twenty women were recruited within 30 days after discharge from the agency who were in the aftercare program, an additional 20 women participating in the agency's residential program, and 20 participating in the agency's outpatient services program were recruited using these procedures. Thus, a total of 60 female participants were included in the pilot study so that they were evenly divided among the three programs, and completed the pretest LSI-R. At posttest, 36 participants completed the LSI-R. Each participant was given a $20 gift card for her participation in the pretest interview, and again for the posttest interview. Study participants were re-consented according to IRB requirements at the end of 12 months during the two-year pilot study. Participants varied in their level of former offending, history of prior offenses, and number of current offenses, as well as probation and parole supervision.

Study results associated with scoring and interpreting the LSI-R demonstrated the ease of administering and scoring the instrument. Only the residential program results are discussed here. At intake, the mean LSI-R score among residential program participants was 25.35 (SD = 5.76). Six months later at posttest, the mean LSI-R score was 16.80.

The user's manual accompanying the LSI-R states that scores of 20 or more indicate halfway house placement for females is not appropriate unless intensive supervision and interventions are provided (Andrews & Bonta, 1995).

Study results examining the costs of administering the LSI-R to all pilot study participants showed that at the time the pilot study was conducted, the costs of the LSI-R questionnaire including the Manual, Interview Guides, and QuickScore forms, including shipping and handling, were approximately $1000. These costs were funded by a foundation grant awarded to support the pilot study aims. No costs were incurred for training. It is important to examine the purchase costs, utility, and administration efforts of the LSI-R (Morash, 2009). Such information was useful for contributing to decision-making about its use in a gender-responsive social service agency.

Quasi-Experimental Designs

Quasi-experimental designs are an improvement upon pre-experimental designs because group comparisons can be made. However, the groups lack random assignment, which means that these designs do not minimize threats to internal validity. These designs are also are not acceptable when used for categorizing interventions as evidence-based practices, although the Coalition for Evidence-Based Policy (2014) suggests that quasi-experimental designs can provide valid evidence about intervention if numerous conditions are met.

A Basic Example

The basic example shows two groups of study participants. Group 1 received the intervention, whereas Group 2 did not. Both groups completed a pretest and posttest with Group 1 completing these before and after participating in an intervention. Because Group 2 did not participate in an intervention, these measurements were taken after a period of time, preferably the same period of time as Group 1. However, participants are not randomly assigned to groups, therefore this design does not minimize threats to internal validity.

Group 1 O X O

Group 2 O O

Experimental Designs

Experimental designs are the most robust research designs and the strongest in internal validity because they employ pretest and posttest measures, and random assignment to control and experimental groups. The experimental group receives the intervention and the control does not. These designs also emphasize quantitative research methods, which focus on statistics and statistical significance.

The principles underlying random assignment suggest that participates with a high number of prior arrests, for example, are likely to be equally assigned to the control and experimental groups. Thus, those participants with more arrests are unlikely to be overrepresented in the control or experimental group. If this were to occur, an intervention could be shown to be an effective due to this high-risk population being overrepresented (or underrepresented) in one of the groups.

A Basic Example

Group 1 R O X O

Group 2 O O

This basic example also shows two groups of study participants. Group 1 received the intervention, whereas Group 2 did not. Both groups completed a pretest and posttest, with Group 1 completing these before and after participating in an intervention. Similar to a quasi-experimental design, Group 2 did not participate in an intervention. Study participants were randomly assigned to groups therefore this design does minimize threats to internal validity.

Randomized Controlled Trials

A randomized controlled trial (RCT) is synonymous with the type of research design just described. These designs are the most robust research designs. As such, these designs include rigorous pretest and posttest measures, often involving subjective and objective measures, and random assignment to a control group and experimental group to minimize threats to internal validity. RCTs are the gold standard for investigating intervention effectiveness, and subsequently categorizing an intervention as an evidence-based practice.

Sackett, Rosenberg, Gray, Haynes, and Richardson (1996) noted that "evidence-based medicine is not restricted to randomized trials and meta-analyses" (p. 72). The authors suggested that while RCTs are considered the gold standard for investigating intervention efficacy, cross-sectional studies or other less robust designs can be used when RCTS have not been conducted or are not feasible.

The Use of Randomized Controlled Trials in Criminal Justice Settings

Many challenges arise that limit the use of RCTs in real world criminal justice settings. These include: public safety risks, decisions about jail and prison overcrowding, agencies responding to court orders to provide treatment, civil rights and due process concerns, and possible criminal justice sanctions for offenders and former offenders who unsuccessfully participate in an RCT (Belenko & Wexler, 2007).

Prendergast (2011) also noted several challenges associated with implementing RCTS in criminal justice settings. Study participants often cannot be randomly assigned to control and experimental groups due to ethical or practical reasons particularly in corrections settings, and because interventions are comprised of numerous components but often developed and tested as a single intervention disentangling necessary and unnecessary intervention components is difficult.

RANKING EMPIRICAL EVIDENCE

Fig. 2.1 illustrates a basic overview of the strength of empirical evidence and the types of research methods used to obtain the empirical evidence. The figure shows the strongest empirical evidence is located vertically at the top of the figure. Followed by promising and weakest evidence, in descending order. Horizontally, the figure shows the research methods that are used to collect data. The methods range from case studies, the weakest methods for obtaining empirical evidence to RCTs representing the strongest research method for obtaining evidence.

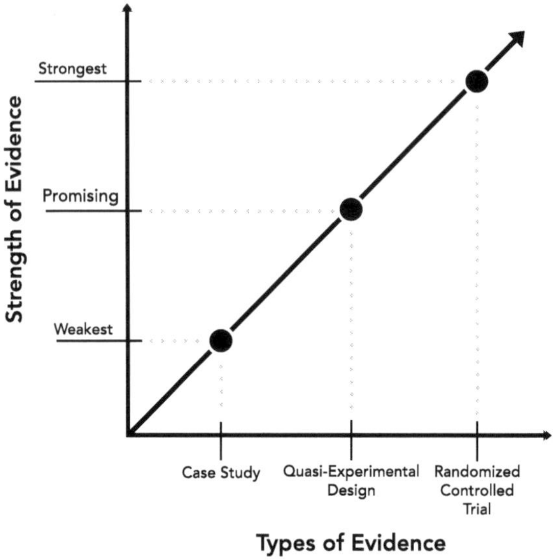

Figure 2.1 Overview of research evidence and the strength of evidence.

RESEARCH METHODS NOT USED TO ASSESS CLINICAL INTERVENTIONS

The National Institute of Justice (Crimesolutions.org, 2011) indicates that as a part of their evidence-based rating and classification process, research studies that employ non-experimental methods, and qualitative methods such as ethnographic and case studies are not acceptable for consideration or review. While mixed methodology designs are acceptable for assessing clinical intervention effectiveness, only the quantitative data of the methodology are used to assess intervention effectiveness.

Qualitative studies use words and narratives, and lack statistics and statistical significance, which is important to rule out that a clinical outcome was obtained by chance. As we saw, intervention efficacy should be obtained based on the efficacy of the intervention alone, and not based on chance or extraneous factors.

Qualitative studies (studies that rely on words and narratives) such as case studies do not provide evidence about clinical effectiveness but may add contextual information about offenders or former offenders' experiences. Mixed methodology research designs, which include both quantitative and qualitative data, have been recommended for examining program fidelity in criminal settings (Miller & Miller, 2015).

Case Example

Qualitative data can inform the implementation of evidence-based practice in criminal justice settings (Miller & Miller, 2015). However, this informs about implementation quality and not intervention effectiveness. This case example shows how qualitative data can inform about the implementation of the LSI-R.

Assessing the feasibly of implementing the LSI-R to assess risks and needs also included examining how the female population, primarily women of color, responded to the LSI-R as well as their perspectives regarding the utility of its use. To achieve these aims, two focus groups were conducted with a sample of women who completed the LSI-R at pretest and posttest. The qualitative data was used to provide contextual information about women's experiences completing the LS-R.

Sample focus group questions included: (1) what are your thoughts about the LSI-R, (2) is it too long, (3) is it relevant to female offending behavior, and (4) what were your thoughts while you were answering the questions. Sample responses from focus group participants included:

> *I didn't want to put my name on it because I have legal issues. I felt the information might be used against me, thought it was a trick question, I was just coming back from prison. I gave 10 minutes of grief before I answered and signed the consent form. No problem with the LSI-R. Because I was mandated I was concerned about answering the questions. Yes, the questions were relevant for women. This LSI-R may benefit other women in the program I think it was good, I was open, I tell everything. Don't remember all of the questions, but I feel it did apply to women. It is appropriate for women.*

Based on the results of the focus groups, the findings suggest that the sample of former female offenders responded well to completing the LSI-R. While study participants did initially express some hesitancy regarding answering the LSI-R questionnaire and signing the informed consent, due to concerns about how the information would be used, these concerns were minimized through explaining its purpose and addressing their concerns.

A Case in Point: The Maryland Scale of Scientific Methods

The development and implementation of the Maryland Scale of Scientific Methods (Sherman et al., 1998) was described in Chapter 1. The Maryland Scale of Scientific Methods was developed to rate evaluation studies of crime prevention programs based on internal validity. Studies are rated on five levels that range from Level 1, the weakest studies in terms of internal validity, to Level 5, representing the strongest studies in terms of internal validity. Evaluation studies were then categorized into four areas: (1) what works, (2) what doesn't, (3) what's promising, and (4) what's unknown.

Table 2.1 illustrates the Maryland Scale of Scientific Methods. It illustrates many of the concepts that were discussed in this chapter. First, it is important to note that in this table, X refers to the concept being present, whereas O refers to the absence of a concept. This represents a different use of these symbols from the scientific notation previously presented. In Table 2.1, research designs appear first (A). Horizontally, the table shows four major research design components. Level 5, representing the highest methods score, contains all of the four components: pretest and posttest measurement (before-after), use of a comparison group (control), comparisons of more than one program in the evaluation (multiple units), and use of random assignment to an experimental and control group. The relevance of each of these components was examined earlier in this chapter.

Table 2.1 The Maryland scale of scientific methods

A. Research designs

	Before-after	Control	Multiple units	Randomization
Methods score				
Level 1	O	O	X	O
Level 2	X	O	O[a]	O
Level 3	X	X	O	O
Level 4	X	X	X	O
Level 5	X	X	X	X

B. Threats to internal validity

	Causal direction	History	Chance factors	Selection bias
Methods score				
Level 1	X	X	X	X
Level 2	O	X	X	X
Level 3	O	O	X	X
Level 4	O	O	O	X
Level 5	O	O	O	O

Key: *O*, absent; *X*, present.
[a]Except where a comparison unit is employed without demonstrated comparability.
Originally published by the National Institute of Justice, U.S. Department of Justice.

Vertically, the five methods scores are displayed. Level 1 represents the lowest methods score. This score is given when an evaluation study lacks pretest and posttest measurement, a comparison group, and random assignment. However, multiple crime prevention programs may be included in the study.

Table 2.1 also shows various threats to internal validity (B), and how these threats are associated with methods scores. As the table shows, Level 5, representing the highest level, is not influenced by internal validity factors such as causal direction, history, chance factors, or selection bias.

Sherman et al. (1998) described the differences among the five levels in the following summary:

Level 1. Correlation between a crime prevention program and a measure of crime or crime risk factors at a single point in time.

Level 2. Temporal sequence between the program and the crime or risk outcome clearly observed, or the presence of a comparison group without demonstrated comparability to the treatment group.

Level 3. A comparison between two or more comparable units of analysis, one with and one without the program.

Level 4. Comparison between multiple units with and without the program, controlling for other factors, or using comparison units that evidence only minor differences.

Level 5. Random assignment and analysis of comparable units to program and comparison groups. (Originally published by the National Institute of Justice, U.S. Department of Justice.)

SUMMARY

This chapter provided a basic overview of research methodology used to rate and classify clinical interventions as evidence-based practices. Knowledge of research methodology is essential to understand what constitutes best available evidence. The concepts presented in this chapter are discussed in Chapter 5, which focuses on how organizations rate and classify interventions as evidence-based, and again in Chapter 6, which focuses on actuarial risk assessment instruments.

REFERENCES

Andrews, D. A., & Bonta, J. (1995). *The level of service inventory - Revised*. Toronto: Multi-Health Systems.

Aos, S., Miller, M., & Drake, E. (2006). *Evidence-based adult corrections programs: What works and what does not*. Olympia: Washington State Institute for Public Policy.

Bandura, A. (1977). *Social learning theory*. Englewood Cliffs, NJ: Prentice-Hall.

Belenko, S., & Wexler, H. K. (2007). *Implementing evidence-based drug treatment in criminal justice settings: Final conference report*. Retrieved from www.tresearch.org/law_ethics/CEICAFinalReport2006.pdf.

Bonta, J., & Andrews, D. A. (2007). Risk-need-responsivity model for offender assessment and rehabilitation. *Rehabilitation, 6*(1), 1–22.

Bonta, J., & Andrews, D. A. (2017). *The psychology of criminal conduct* (6th ed.). New York: Routledge.

Campbell, D. T., & Stanley, J. C. (1963). *Experimental and quasi-experimental designs for research*. Chicago, IL: Rand McNally.

Casey, P. M., Elek, J. K., Warren, R. K., Cheesman, F., Kleiman, M., & Ostrom, B. (2014). *Offender risk & needs assessment instruments: A primer for courts*. Williamsburg, VA: National Center for State Courts.

Casey, P. M., Warren, R. K., & Elek, J. K. (2011). *Using offender risk and needs assessment information at sentencing: Guidance for courts from a national working group*. Williamsburg, VA: National Center for State Courts.

Chamberlain, P. (2003). The Oregon multidimensional treatment foster care model: Features, outcomes, and progress in dissemination. *Cognitive and Behavioral Practice, 10*(4), 303–312.

Coalition for Evidence-Based Policy. (2014). *Which study designs are capable of producing valid evidence about a program's effectiveness?: A brief overview*. Retrieved from http://coalition-4evidence.org/wp-content/uploads/2014/10/Which-Study-Designs-are-Capable-of-Producing-Valid-Evidence-of-Effectiveness.pdf.

Durose, M. R., Cooper, A. D., & Snyder, H. N. (2014). *Recidivism of prisoners released in 30 states in 2005: Patterns from 2005 to 2010*. Washington, DC: U.S. Department of Justice, Office of Justice Programs, Bureau of Justice Statistics.

Gendreau, P., Little, T., & Goggin, C. (1996). A meta-analysis of adult offender recidivism: What works!. *Criminology, 34*(4), 575–607.

Grusec, J. E. (1992). Social learning theory and developmental psychology: The legacies of Robert Sears and Albert Bandura. *Developmental Psychology, 28*(5), 776–786.

Miller, J. M., & Miller, H. V. (2015). Rethinking program fidelity for criminal justice. *Criminology & Public Policy, 14*(2), 339–349.

Monette, D. R., Sullivan, T. J., DeJong, C. R., & Hilton, T. P. (2014). *Applied social research: A tool for the human services* (9th ed.). Belmont, CA: Brooks/Cole/Thomson Learning.

Morash, M. (2009). A great debate over using the level of service inventory – Revised (LSI-R) with women offenders. *Criminology & Public Policy, 8*(1), 173–181.

National Institute of Justice. (2011). *About crimesolutions.gov: Program review and rating from start to finish - Crimesolutions.gov*. Retrieved from https://www.crimesolutions.gov/about_starttofinish.aspx.

Pérez, D. M. (2009). Applying evidence-based practices to community corrections supervision: An evaluation of residential substance abuse treatment for high-risk probationers. *Journal of Contemporary Criminal Justice, 25*(4), 442–458.

Prendergast, M. L. (2011). Issues defining and applying evidence-based practices criteria for treatment of criminal-justice involved clients. *Journal of Psychoactive Drugs*, 7, 10–18.

Sackett, D. L., Rosenberg, W. M. C., Gray, J. A. M., Haynes, R. B., & Richardson, W. S. (1996). Evidence based medicine: What it is and what it isn't. *British Medical Journal, 312*(7023), 71–72.

Sexton, T. L., & Alexander, J. F. (2003). Functional family therapy: A mature clinical model for working with at-risk adolescents and their families. In T. L. Sexton, G. R. Weeks, & M. S. Robbins (Eds.), *Handbook of family therapy: The science and practice of working with families and couples* (pp. 323–348). New York: Brunner-Routledge.

Sherman, L. W., Gottfredson, D. C., MacKenzie, D. L., Eck, J., Reuter, P., & Bushway, S. D. (1998). *Preventing crime: What works, what doesn't, what's promising*. Washington, DC: U.S. Department of Justice, Office of Justice Programs, National Institute of Justice.

Skidmore, W. (1979). *Theoretical thinking in sociology*. New York: Cambridge University Press.

FURTHER READING

Timmons-Mitchell, J., Bender, M. B., Kishna, M. A., & Michelle, C. C. (2006). An independent effectiveness trial of multisystemic therapy with juvenile justice youth. *Journal of Clinical Child and Adolescent Psychology*, *35*(2), 227–236.

Weisburd, D., Lum, C. M., & Petrosino, A. (2001). Does research design affect study outcomes in criminal justice? *The Annals of the American Academy of Political and Social Science*, *578*(1), 50–70.

CHAPTER 3

An Overview of Implementation Fidelity

George T. Patterson

FIDELITY DEFINED

Tracing the history of treatment fidelity and identifying how the concept has changed over time, Bellg et al. (2004) suggest that the concept first appeared in the behavioral intervention literature published in the late 1970s and early 1980s. However, the first article to define treatment fidelity and introduce guidelines for improving treatment fidelity published by Moncher and Prinz in 1991. "Fidelity is the extent to which delivery of an intervention, modality, or treatment adheres to program design (i.e., theory and delivery protocol)" (Miller & Miller, 2015, p. 340). Fidelity is an essential component for the implementation of evidence-based practices and principles (Blandford & Osher, 2012; Przybylski & Orchowsky, 2015; Welsh, Sullivan, & Olds, 2010), and it is also relevant for the implementation of standardized instruments such as actuarial risk assessment instruments (Casey et al., 2014). Treatment fidelity is defined as "...the methodological strategies used to monitor and enhance the reliability and validity of behavioral interventions. It also refers to the methodological practices used to ensure that a research study reliably and validly tests a clinical intervention" (Bellg et al., 2004, p. 443).

IMPLEMENTATION FIDELITY

Concepts similar in scope to fidelity and treatment fidelity include implementation and implementation fidelity. Implementation fidelity is defined as "the degree to which a program's implementation in any real-world setting matches what was stated in the original program model" (Przybylski & Orchowsky, 2015, p. 3). Fixsen, Naoom, Blase, Friedman, and Wallace (2005) provided the following definition of implementation: "a specified set of activities designed to put into practice an activity or program of known dimensions" (p. 5).

Clinical Interventions in Criminal Justice Settings
ISBN 978-0-12-811381-3
http://dx.doi.org/10.1016/B978-0-12-811381-3.00003-2

A common theme among these varied concepts is the need to implement an intervention in real world settings in the same manner the intervention was developed and tested in research studies.

Accordingly, evidence-based practices must be implemented with fidelity to benefit criminal justice populations (Belenko & Wexler, 2007). Indeed, the primary cause of evidence-based practices having poor outcomes is a "lack of fidelity" (Welsch et al., p. 18). For these reasons, the National Institute of Justice (CrimeSolutions.gov) includes fidelity as part of the eight-step evidence-based rating process. Program fidelity is rated based on how well the intervention is implemented consistent with its original development, and is assessed on the basis of documentation and adherence (CrimeSolutions.gov, n.d.).

IMPLEMENTATION FIDELITY BARRIERS AND CHALLENGES

Evidence-based practices that demonstrate effectiveness in research studies may not demonstrate the same level of effectiveness in real world criminal justice settings or with criminal justice populations. In order to achieve the anticipated positive results of the evidence-based practices on the behavior of criminal justice populations, an evidence-based practice must be implemented and sustained with fidelity (Przybylski & Orchowsky, 2015). Implementing evidence-based practices in real world settings is certainly a challenging endeavor (Aarons, Hurlburt, & Horwitz, 2011; Gearing et al., 2011).

Whereas evidence-based practices are most effective when implemented with fidelity, attaining and maintaining fidelity among different practitioners can be a challenge. Organizational factors such as the agency's mission, administrative oversight, and culture are key factors that contribute to poor outcomes when evidence-based practices are implemented (Belenko & Wexler, 2007). Certainly, a host of factors contribute to poor outcomes. In a similar way, Welsh et al. (2010) suggested that the implementation of evidence-based practices can be negatively affected by the diversity found among the client population and practitioners in real world settings, which differ from the research study environment. The authors also argue that during implementation in real world settings, the evidence-based practice may be delivered to a population with lower risk levels than those who participated in the research study, lack of organizational resources for training and other needs, the diversity found among the clinical skill level of intervention providers, and the fact that the intervention developer is no longer overseeing implementation of the intervention and training intervention providers. Finally, interventions often need to be tailored to meet individual's needs, and therefore should have some degree of flexibility, a factor also recognized by Blanford and Osher (2012). All of these factors contribute to decrease the efficacy of evidence-based practices in real world settings.

Scanning the table of contents and reference lists of some volumes devoted to the implementation of evidence-based practices will show that fidelity, integrity, or implementation fidelity in criminal justice settings are given scant attention. The journal *Implementation Science* acknowledges the lack of implementation research in many health and behavioral health settings and is devoted to disseminating a wide range of topics related to theory, intervention development, and implementation evaluation. This resource can be invaluable for conducting implementation efforts in criminal justice settings and with criminal justice populations.

The results of a process evaluation conducted among 42 sites that implemented eight of the Blueprints for Violence Prevention evidence-based practices found several challenges associated with implementing these intervention in real world settings. Bivariate analyses revealed that the skills possessed by intervention providers, the quality and quantity of training and technical assistance, and community and organizational characteristics are all factors associated with implementation efficacy (Mihalic & Irwin, 2003).

IMPROVING TREATMENT FIDELITY IN RESEARCH AND CLINICAL PRACTICE

Gearing et al. (2011) provide suggestions for researchers and clinicians implementing evidence-based practices in real world criminal justice and social service settings that can be used to improve intervention implementation and fidelity. The authors recommend that clinicians first assess whether the agency has sufficient resources to assess implementation fidelity. It is our view that oftentimes in real world settings, such tasks are beyond the expertise of administrators and staff. Employing the expertise of a professional requires financial resources, which may be limited in some social service agencies. Second, Gearing et al. recommend that organizational characteristics be considered since some evidence-based practices may be more congruent with the agency mission than others. Once again, it is our view that the characteristics of the criminal justice are important, given that some evidence-based practices are more appropriate for some settings and not others. Third, the authors recommend that the standardized instruments used to assess fidelity should also be congruent with the agency mission, culture, and needs. Administering and analyzing data collected from such instruments is also often beyond the expertise of administrators and staff. Finally, the authors recommend that assessment of implementation fidelity be established as an ongoing process conducted at the beginning and throughout the course of intervention delivery. Given agency lack of expertise in this area, achieving this goal can also present challenges.

The Treatment Fidelity Workgroup of the National Institute of Health Behavior Change Consortium (BBC) has focused on identifying treatment fidelity concepts and strategies in health behavior intervention research. The BBC recognized five factors to consider for improving treatment fidelity in research studies: (1) study design, (2) provider training, (3) intervention delivery, (4) participants involvement in the intervention, and (5) participants use of intervention skills (Bellg et al., 2004). Although the BBC provided these recommendations for researchers, it is our view that several of these recommendations are applicable for improving treatment fidelity in criminal justice and social service settings implementing evidence-based practices. Perhaps two factors are most relevant for improving the implementation of evidence-based practices in these settings; provider training and treatment delivery. Therefore, these two factors are reviewed in detail since they can also be useful in the implementation and delivery of evidence-based clinical practices beyond the research environment. While not exhaustive, the following examples illustrate their recommendations:

Monitoring and Improving Provider Training

- Training should be standardized among all intervention providers. This should be accomplished by employing standardized training materials and manuals, case scenarios, and role-playing.
- Skill development should be enhanced among all intervention providers. This should be accomplished by developing and employing transparent performance standards, observing provider intervention implementation employing standardized case scenarios and role plays, use checklist, provide pre-and post-training, and give providers certification prior to implementing the intervention as well as during the process of intervention delivery.

- Providers should maintain the same skills and skill set they acquired during training throughout intervention delivery and "drift" should be reduced. Drift refers to diminished intervention skills or providing an intervention inconsistent with protocols. This can be accomplished by offering ongoing supervision and/or booster sessions, or audio or videotaping intervention sessions.
- Recognize differences in provider orientations, profession, and skill sets, and provide training that acknowledges these differences. This can be accomplished by providing all providers intensive training, or developing and providing training based on prior clinical expertise or profession.

Monitoring and Improving Intervention Delivery

Three of four recommendations are useful for improving implementation fidelity in criminal justice and social service settings. The fourth recommendation concerns randomization, and experimental and control groups which is applicable for research and not clinical practice:

- Intervention delivery can be improved by examining complaints received from intervention participants and attitudes toward the intervention provider.
- Intervention delivery should be delivered in the same manner among all providers. This should be assessed employing intervention protocols and manuals, and supervisor ratings of audio and videotapes.
- Intervention delivery should offer all components and dosage associated with the model as developed. This should be also be assessed by employing supervisor ratings of audio and videotapes. Intervention providers could also complete a checklist after each intervention sessions to identify the intervention components that were delivered.

The most effective intervention provider training "protocols combine theory and discussion, demonstration, practice and feedback, and coaching" (Belenko & Wexler, 2007, p. 29). This view supports the need to utilize manualized protocols.

Other guidelines that were derived from research have been proposed to improve the fidelity of evidence-based practices (Przyblski & Orchowski, 2015). In their review of approaches to improve implementation fidelity, Przyblski and Orchowski suggest that fidelity should be measured and monitored throughout the implementation process, and these are critical tasks when implementing evidence-based interventions. Their suggestions for improving implementation fidelity include:

1. develop rigorous fidelity criteria and conduct fidelity assessments.
2. develop and use implementation checklists.
3. measure and monitor implementation fidelity.

MEASURING IMPLEMENTATION FIDELITY

As mentioned, some of the recommendations for improving implementation fidelity are gleaned from improving fidelity during the research process. However, these recommendations can also serve as guidelines for implementation in real world criminal justice settings. No uniform method for defining, assessing and improving implantation fidelity has been developed (Gearing et al., 2011). Indeed, no single approach to defining and measuring implementation employing reliable and valid standardized instruments exists. Moreover, as we saw in Chapter 2, the quality of the sources of information collected during the measurement process may vary.

Measuring implementation fidelity requires a unique skill set. As previously mentioned, this skill set is often beyond the scope and expertise of agency administrators and staff. As Schoenwald et al. (2011) pointed out, the measurement of implementation fidelity involves numbers, scoring instruments, and data analysis performed based on the common levels of measurement. Skilled researchers spend a great deal of time, effort, and financial resources seeking Institutional Review Board (IRB) approvals and informed consent, planning and implementing research methods and measurement approaches, and collecting and analyzing data. It stands to reason that the majority of clinically trained administrative and agency staff, or criminal justice practitioners, will be ineffective at performing these tasks.

Employing incorrect measurement or methods to obtain information about implementation fidelity can perhaps be as harmful as having no information. This occurs because clinical decisions will be based on the measurement outcomes, and if these outcomes are not correctly attributed to the intervention, then subsequent clinical decisions that will be made about the intervention or intervention outcomes will also be incorrect.

In addition, as Carroll et al. (2007) assert, clinicians and researchers will only be informed concerning whether an intervention is effective by measuring implementation fidelity. Examining research studies published between 2000 and 2007, the authors found that assessing implementation fidelity involves measuring five factors: (1) how closely the implemented intervention adheres to the developed model, (2) the dosage of intervention that individuals receive, (3) the quality of intervention delivery, (4) how individuals participating in the intervention respond to the intervention, and (5) identifying the intervention components that are most likely to produce the intended outcomes.

The measurement of these five factors supports the previous point regarding the need for specialized skills to measure implementation fidelity. Moreover, the five factors also demonstrate that information should to be collected from multiple stakeholders. Without doubt implementation outcomes are very different from clinical outcomes (Proctor et al., 2011). This further supports the need to possess a unique skill set supporting abilities to collect and analyze data from multiple stakeholders that are associated with the implementation process and not clinical outcomes.

Missett and Foster (2015) examined whether published studies describing the implementation of evidence-based curricular interventions measured and reported implementation fidelity. The authors included studies published between 2004 and 2013, and found that while many of these studies acknowledged the importance of implementation fidelity, the measurement approaches were often not reported. Few studies measured implementation fidelity. Studies also did not report implementation fidelity information such as the measurement approach that was used. In other words, the use of reliable and valid standardized instruments was not mentioned among the studies.

Interestingly, this example is not unique to the field of education and can also be found in criminal justice settings. Emshoff et al. (1987) evaluated four educational and three criminal justice programs to assess implementation fidelity among the programs. These programs did not utilize reliable and valid standardized instruments to measure implementation fidelity. The authors developed their own methods for measuring fidelity. The reliability and validity (psychometric properties) of their instrument were not reported. This is perhaps also the case with implementation fidelity concerning evidence-based practice interventions in real world criminal justice settings. It is unlikely that such settings have established and implemented elaborate methods for measuring implementation fidelity.

Beidas et al. (2016) describe a plan to conduct a future study involving a randomized controlled trial. Their plan describes the Fidelity, Accuracy: Comparing Three Strategies (Project FACTS). The main goal of Project FACTS was to compare three methods for measuring implementation fidelity to determine which measurement approach yields valid information and is most cost-effective. Because the report described a planned future study, no results were reported. While the report did not present study results, their review of the most commonly used approaches for measuring implementation fidelity and the strengths and limitations associated with these approaches is useful. The three approaches reviewed included: (1) self-report, (2) chart simulated recall, and (3) behavioral rehearsal. The evidence-based intervention was cognitive behavioral therapy (CBT).

Self-report measurement approaches are the least accurate approach to measuring implementation fidelity because intervention providers could misinterpret questionnaire items, forget what occurred during the intervention session thereby resulting in accurate information, or be influenced by social desirability. Chart simulated recall is a measurement approach used most often in medical research and is rarely used in mental health research to assess implementation fidelity among evidence-based practices. It involves having the intervention provider review the chart or records of an individual who received the intervention. In this way, the chart review helps the intervention provider to remember details of what occurred during the intervention session thereby reducing self-report bias based totally on recall.

Behavioral rehearsal is a role-play approach to measurement, in which the intervention provider and a trained person acting as the intervention recipient role-play the enactment of CBT.

The authors hypothesized that this measurement approach would be more effective than the other two approaches because it affords intervention providers with opportunities to ponder and discuss the actions and interventions they provided while implementing an intervention. Furthermore, the authors suggested that this approach would be the most valid approach because a trained person or supervisor directly observes the intervention provider role-playing CBT, thereby providing an opportunity to assess demonstrated skills and competencies. Finally, the authors report that direct observation as an approach for measuring implementation fidelity is considered the gold standard. However, this approach is very costly and requires additional resources that limit its use.

Beidas et al. (2016) proposed to examine the cost-effectiveness of various approaches to measuring implementation fidelity although their proposal did not provide cost results. Proctor et al. (2011) found that among the eight factors to consider for implementation outcomes cost-benefits and cost-effectiveness associated with both intervention implementation and sustainability are also common factors to assess.

IMPLEMENTATION FIDELITY IN CRIMINAL JUSTICE SETTINGS

Among the many factors to consider and assess for implementation fidelity such as organizational factors and organizational change, implementing evidence-based practices in criminal justice settings also requires that consideration be given to public safety and public health issues (Taxman, Henderson, & Belenko, 2009). These factors have been discussed elsewhere in the book. These factors also present additional challenges when evidence-based practices are implemented in criminal justice settings.

Implementation fidelity in criminal justice settings is characterized by poor conceptualization, and the sole use of quantitative research designs and quantitative data, which do not fully measure important information about implementation fidelity (Miller & Miller, 2015). Remarking on the lack of available reliable and valid standardized instruments to measure implementation fidelity in criminal justice settings, the authors describe the Justice Program Fidelity Scale. The scale is purported to provide "robust and systematic measurement of implementation intensity and modality adherence demonstrated by criminal justice programs" (p. 340), and measures five domains: (1) adherence, (2) exposure, (3) intervention delivery, (4) participant engagement, and (5) program differentiation. Reliability and validity are not reported.

In addition to the numerous factors that need to be considered to measure implementation fidelity, Bond, Drake, Rapp, McHugo, and Xie (2009) suggest that client level factors, such as developing and implementing an individualized treatment for intervention recipients, and quality improvement factors, such as providing training and supervision are neglected areas of measurement. Describing some of the work of the National Implementing Evidence-Based Practices Project, the authors describe the development of the five-item Individualization Scale, and the five-item Quality Improvement Scale. These scales demonstrate good reliability and validity and for measuring these two areas. Although not specific to criminal justice settings, these scales were pilot tests in 49 mental health center sites.

Case Example

A case example described in greater detail in Chapter 10, shows that in real world settings, criminal justice populations rarely benefit from the measurement and analysis of implementation fidelity. The concepts presented in this chapter, including treatment fidelity, implementation fidelity, and implementation, are typically given little attention in real world criminal justice settings, or social service agencies providing interventions for criminal justice populations.

An external evaluation was conducted that examined intervention outcomes following the implementation of an evidence-based practice relevant for women involved in the criminal justice system. The newly implemented intervention had not been previously provided by the social service agency.

The goals of this newly implemented gender-responsive intervention were to increase access to: (1) HIV prevention and intervention, (2) substance abuse treatment, (3) HIV testing, (4) treatment for co-occurring disorders, and (5) risk reduction for HIV. The primary goals of the evaluation were to assess changes that occurred in these behavioral health outcomes.

Most often when program evaluations are conducted in criminal justice settings, such evaluations tend to focus on outcome designs and intervention outcomes with less emphasis placed on measuring and assessing implementation fidelity (Miller & Miller, 2015). This is exactly what occurred when the described evaluation was conducted. The concepts presented in this chapter were not articulated in the request for proposals, the funding proposal itself, or the evaluator's contract. Moreover, the five factors identified by Miller and Miller support the previous points raised that suggest the need for specialized skills to measure and assess implementation fidelity. Moreover, the five factors demonstrate that information should to be collected from multiple stakeholders. These tasks alone require additional IRB tasks and additional informed consents.

In this example, agency staff were in contact with the evidence-based practice developers. Typically, during implementation, the intervention developer is no longer overseeing implementation of the intervention and training intervention providers resulting in poor implementation fidelity (Welsh et al., 2010).

Time constraints were also relevant. The evaluation was conducted by an external evaluator employed full-time as university faculty without the assistance of a research team. Consequently, the evaluator alone conducted all of the tasks associated with outcome data collection and statistical analysis, in addition to completing written quarterly reports and attending monthly meetings. These tasks were specified in a contractual agreement. Realistically, even if an evaluator had the unique skill set required to measure and assess implementation fidelity, adding the necessary components to complete these tasks would be very time consuming. Further, it would not involve a one-time activity given that implementation fidelity should be measured and assessed at the beginning stage of the evidence-based practice implementation as well as throughout the course of intervention delivery.

The lack of measuring and assessing implementation fidelity during the evidence-based practice implementation process implies that fidelity quality is unknown. Similarly, it is unknown whether the intervention itself or which components of the intervention produced the positive intervention outcomes that were found. After completing the intervention, former female offenders did report increased access to HIV testing, substance abuse treatment, and fewer high-risk behaviors.

SUMMARY

This chapter introduced implementation fidelity, examined several ways fidelity has been defined, and its applications in both clinical interventions and the research process. Unfortunately, in real world settings, and particularly in criminal justice settings, implementation fidelity is rarely assessed using reliable and valid measurement approaches. Chapter 10 further examines implementing evidence-based practices and principles with criminal justice populations and in criminal justice settings.

REFERENCES

Aarons, G. A., Hurlburt, M., & Horwitz, S. M. (2011). Advancing a conceptual model of evidence-based practice implementation in public service sectors. *Administration and Policy in Mental Health and Mental Health Services Research, 38*(1), 4–23.

Beidas, R. S., Maclean, J. C., Fishman, J., Dorsey, S., Schoenwald, S. K., Mandell, D. S., et al. (2016). A randomized trial to identify accurate and cost-effective fidelity measurement methods for cognitive-behavioral therapy: Project FACTS study protocol. *BMC Psychiatry, 16*, 323.

Belenko, S., & Wexler, H. K. (2007). *Implementing evidence-based drug treatment in criminal justice settings: Final conference report.* Retrieved from www.tresearch.org/law_ethics/CEICAFinalReport2006.pdf.

Bellg, A. J., Borrelli, B., Resnick, B., Hecht, J., Minicucci, D. S., Ory, M., & Czajkowski, S. (2004). Enhancing treatment fidelity in health behavior change studies: Best practices and recommendations from the NIH Behavior Change Consortium. *Health Psychology, 23*(5), 443–451.

Blandford, A. M., & Osher, F. C. (2012). *A checklist for implementing evidence-based practices and programs (EBPs) for justice-involved adults with behavioral health disorders.* Delmar, NY: SAMSHA's GAINS Center for Behavioral Health and Justice Transformation.

Bond, G. R., Drake, R. E., Rapp, C. A., McHugo, G. J., & Xie, H. (2009). Individualization and quality improvement: Two new scales to complement measurement of program fidelity. *Administration & Policy in Mental Health & Mental Health Services Research, 36*, 349–357.

Carroll, C., Patterson, M., Wood, S., Booth, A., Rick, J., & Balain, S. (2007). A conceptual framework for implementation fidelity. *Implementation Science, 2*, 40..

Casey, P. M., Elek, J. K., Warren, R. K., Cheesman, F., Kleiman, M., & Ostrom, B. (2014). *Offender risk & needs assessment instruments: A primer for courts.* Retrieved from http://www.ncsc.org/~/media/microsites/files/csi/bja%20rna%20final%20report_combined%20files%208-22-14.ashx.

CrimeSolutions.gov. (n.d.). *About CrimeSolutions.gov: Program review and rating from start to finish.* Retrieved from https://www.crimesolutions.gov/about_starttofinish.aspx.

Emshoff, J. G., Blakely, C., Gottschalk, R., Mayer, J., Dividson, W. S., & Erickson, S. (1987). Innovation in education and criminal justice: Measuring fidelity of implementation and program effectiveness. *Educational Evaluation and Policy Analysis, 9*(4), 300–311.

Fixsen, D. L., Naoom, S. F., Blase, K. A., Friedman, R. M., & Wallace, F. (2005). *Implementation research: A synthesis of the literature.* Tampa, FL: University of South Florida, Louis de la Parte Florida Mental Health Institute, The National Implementation Research Network (FMHI Publication #231).

Gearing, R. E., El-Bassel, N., Ghesquiere, A., Baldwin, S., Gillies, J., & Ngeow, E. (2011). Major ingredients of fidelity: A review and scientific guide to improving quality of intervention research implementation. *Clinical Psychology Review, 31*(1), 79–88.

Mihalic, S. F., & Irwin, K. (2003). Blueprints for violence prevention from research to real-world settings: Factors influencing the successful replication of model programs. *Youth Violence and Juvenile Justice, 1*(4), 307–329.

Miller, J. M., & Miller, H. V. (2015). Rethinking program fidelity for criminal justice. *Criminology & Public Policy, 14*(2), 339–349.

Missett, T. C., & Foster, L. H. (2015). Searching for evidence-based practice: A survey of empirical studies on curricular interventions measuring and reporting fidelity of implementation published during 2004–2013. *Journal of Advanced Academics, 26*(2), 96–111.

Moncher, F. J., & Prinz, F. J. (1991). Treatment fidelity in outcome studies. *Clinical Psychology Review, 11*, 247–266.

Proctor, E., Silmere, H., Raghavan, R., Hovmand, P., Aarons, G., Bunger, A., & Hensley, M. (2011). Outcomes for implementation research: Conceptual distinctions, measurement challenges, and research agenda. *Administration and Policy in Mental Health and Mental Health Services Research, 38*(2), 65–76.

Przybylski, R., & Orchowsky, S. (2015). *Implementing evidence-based practices.* Washington, DC: Justice Research and Statistics Association, Bureau of Justice Statistics, U.S. Department of Justice, National Criminal Justice Association.

Schoenwald, S. K., Garland, A. F., Chapman, J. E., Frazier, S. L., Sheidow, A. J., & Southam-Gerow, M. A. (2011). Toward the effective and efficient measurement of implementation fidelity. *Administration and Policy in Mental Health and Mental Health Services Research, 38*(1), 32–43.

Taxman, F. S., Henderson, C. E., & Belenko, S. (2009). Organizational context, systems change, and adopting treatment delivery systems in the criminal justice system. *Drug and Alcohol Dependence, 103*(1), S1–S6.

Welsh, B. C., Sullivan, C. J., & Olds, D. L. (2010). When early crime prevention goes to scale: A new look at the evidence. *Prevention Science, 11*(2), 115–125.

FURTHER READING

Lowenkamp, C. T., Latessa, E. J., & Smith, P. (2006). Does correctional program quality really matter? The impact of adhering to the principles of effective intervention. *Criminology & Public Policy, 5*(3), 575–594.

CHAPTER 4

Clinical Outcomes for Criminal Justice Populations

George T. Patterson

OUTCOMES AND OUTCOME MEASURES

The term outcome refers to changes in psychological, physiological, and/or behavioral functioning that occur after participating in an evidence-based intervention. Outcomes are expected in the positive direction, or in other words, improved psychological, physiological, and/or behavioral functioning should result.

In order to assess changes in functioning, a consistent approach is required that typically requires measurement. Outcome measures are used to assess the indicators of improved functioning. Typically, reliable and valid standardized instruments are used for these purposes and should be brief in length, relatively easy to score, and connected to the agency or setting mission (Royse & Thyer, 1996). The importance of reliability and validity were discussed in Chapter 2. Also, subjective and objective measures and measurement approaches are important given that subjective and objective information is obtained, and each of these two approaches have both strengths and limitations.

Although risk assessment using actuarial risk assessment instruments as an outcome among criminal justice populations has been discussed extensively throughout the book, other types of outcomes that are assessed using standardized instruments also exist. In order to assess whether an evidence-based practice actually results in positive outcomes on psychological, physiological, and behavioral functioning, it is important to examine the research base that exists for the intervention. It is also important to recognize that bias exists towards publishing studies that demonstrate positive outcome effects, and rejecting for publication those studies that find negative outcome effects, even though rigorous research methodology was employed (McCord, 2003).

Clinical Interventions in Criminal Justice Settings
ISBN 978-0-12-811381-3
http://dx.doi.org/10.1016/B978-0-12-811381-3.00004-4

Public Safety Outcomes

The criminal justice system is characterized by an emphasis on public safety and public health. Public safety issues infer reduced behaviors among offenders and former offenders that place the safety of the public at risk. Thus, public safety focuses on keeping the public safe from victimization and reducing offending behaviors, and public safety outcomes should demonstrate that these results have occurred. Examples include driving while intoxicated or under the influence of drugs, and violent and nonviolent criminal behaviors. In these examples when crimes are committed, victims of crimes are involved. Victims may seek a variety of forms of justice such as incapacitation, retribution, or restitution, which that may not include rehabilitation, which is the form of justice most associated with evidence-based practices. Consequently a major challenge in the criminal justice system is to rehabilitate, reduce victimization and offending behaviors, and provide justice simultaneously. Adding to this challenge is the fact that communities with large numbers of offenders are less likely to provide evidence-based practices to address their needs (Patterson, 2013).

Public Health Outcomes

Public health issues experienced by criminal justice populations are discussed in Chapter 9. Examples of public health issues relevant for criminal justice populations include HIV/AIDS, tuberculosis, and hepatitis, among other health concerns. Public health outcomes should demonstrate decreased risky health behaviors such as sexual and substance use behaviors, and increased testing, knowledge, attitudes, and skills regarding public health issues and behaviors.

Some social problems such as substance abuse are characterized by intersectionality between public safety and public health, consequently evidence-based practices for substance abuse will address both public safety and public health at the same time (Chandler, Fletcher, & Volkow, 2009). As is the case with public safety issues, communities with large number of offenders are less likely to provide evidence-based practices and other services to address their public health needs (Patterson, 2013).

OUTCOMES AMONG CRIMINAL AND JUVENILE JUSTICE POPULATIONS

Clinical outcomes resulting from the treatment of alcohol and substance abuse disorders, mental health, or co-occurring disorders, for example, are not unique to criminal justice settings or populations. Indeed, individuals with no criminal or juvenile justice system involvement can and do experience these disorders and receive treatment.

However, criminal and juvenile justice system involvement present additional considerations. Indeed, varied outcomes are reported in the literature for criminal and juvenile justice populations. The Substance Abuse and Mental Health Services Administration (2010) identified 10 domains, with accompanying outcomes and outcome measures, for mental health and substance abuse treatment, and substance abuse prevention. Mental health outcome measures for mental health prevention are not provided. The 10 domains include: abstinence, education/employment, crime and criminal justice, housing stability, service access/capacity, retention in treatment, social support/connectedness, perception of care received, cost effectiveness, and use of evidence-based practices.

Specifically, the criminal justice domain is characterized by the outcome of decreased criminal and juvenile justice system involvement. An outcome measure associated with mental health treatment is the number of times an offender has experienced criminal justice system involvement. Outcome measures associated with substance abuse interventions include reduced or no changes in the number of arrests that occur during the course of the intervention. Finally, substance abuse prevention outcome measures include criminal offending that is drug-related and car accidents that are alcohol related.

The Criminal Justice-Drug Abuse Treatment Project

To improve reentry among criminal justice populations with substance use disorders, the National Institute on Drug Abuse initiated the Criminal Justice-Drug Abuse Treatment Studies (CJ-DATS) project in 2002. Interventions and intervention outcomes focused on reducing offending behavior, substance use, and high risk sexual behaviors associated with AIDS/HIV. A summary of the following seven research sites illustrates the wide-ranging intervention outcomes that are the focus of the CJ-DATS project (Whitten, 2009):

1. The Southwest Research Center, at Texas Christian University, examined the following outcomes: "motivation to change behavior, anger management, healthier thinking patterns, communication in relationships, social support, and skills and knowledge to reduce risk of sexually transmitted infections" (p. 2).
2. The Rhode Island Research Center, Brown University and Lifespan Hospitals focused on the following behavioral outcomes: "abstinence, employment searches, and counseling attendance" (p. 2).

3. The Midwest Research Center, National Development and Research Institutes examined "adolescent's belief structures underlying criminal activity and drug abuse" (p. 2).
4. The Florida Research Center, University of Miami investigated outcomes associated with adolescent substance abuse.
5. The Pacific Coast Research Center, University of California, Los Angeles examined "post release goals, social support, accomplishments, and skills" (p. 3) during reentry.
6. The Central States Research Center, University of Kentucky investigated the following outcomes among women: "problematic thinking patterns about relationships and reduce their HIV risk" (p. 3).
7. The Mid Atlantic Research Center, University of Delaware studied HIV prevention outcomes among men and women.

Psychological Outcomes

Many of the presenting problems that criminal and juvenile justice populations experience result from underlying psychological, physiological, and behavioral causes. Theoretical frameworks explain the causation, etiology, and interventions of these presenting problems. A behavioral presenting problem can be influenced by a complex interaction of psychological and physiological factors.

In general, psychological outcomes refer to feelings, attitudes, or emotions. Psychological outcomes such as self-esteem, anxiety, and sadness, which are frequently the focus of clinical interventions, are less associated with offending behavior and less relevant for criminal justice populations (Bonta & Andrews, 2017). Common psychological outcomes among criminal justice populations include criminal thinking and motivation, which have greater effects on intervention engagement.

Criminal Thinking

Criminal thinking is a psychological outcome associated with engagement in clinical interventions and offending behavior. Criminal thinking can also be addressed in clinical interventions to improve engagement in clinical interventions and offending behaviors (Best, Day, Campbell, Flynn, & Simpson, 2009; Walters, 2011).

Best et al. (2009) found in a cross-sectional study that higher criminal thinking scores were related to lower levels of motivation to engage in clinical interventions, lower engagement in the clinical intervention process, and lower psychosocial functioning outcomes. Motivation and readiness for clinical interventions were measured using the Client Evaluation of Self and Treatment (Joe, Broome, Rowan-Szal, & Simpson, 2002) and criminal thinking was measured using the Criminal Thinking Scales (Knight, Garner, Simpson, Morey, & Flynn, 2006).

Motivation

Eight evidence-based principles for effective interventions for offenders were identified in 2003 arising from a partnership between the National Institute of Corrections and the Crime and Justice Institute (Domurad & Carey, 2010). The second principle, enhance intrinsic motivation, acknowledges that motivation for psychological, physiological, and behavioral change arises from internal and external factors. Internal factors include relationship difficulties and monetary losses, whereas, external factors include mandated court treatment. Motivation among inmates is associated with institutional misconduct behaviors, the classification of inmates, and their participation in correctional programs (Serin, 2005).

Domurad and Carey (2010) note that motivation outcomes can be increased when practitioner interactions and interventions with offenders include using authority appropriately, showing warmth, and encouraging self-efficacy. Another approach for increasing motivation is the use of motivational interviewing techniques.

Mandated Treatment Outcomes

The goal of mandated treatment is to enforce legal consequences intended to motivate offenders to comply with treatment. Consequences may include loss of benefits, such as loss of pay, or incarceration for treatment noncompliance (Miller & Flaherty, 2000). Among offenders with substance use disorders mandated treatment ordered by a drug court or as a condition of pretrial release is effective for motivating offenders to comply with treatment. Few differences were found between offenders who were mandated and those who were not. Offenders who are mandated to receive treatment also attend more treatment sessions and remain in treatment longer than those who are not mandated. The result is improved intervention outcomes (Fletcher & Chandler, 2006).

Physiological Outcomes

In general, physiological outcomes refer to factors such as blood pressure and heart rate. These factors may be contributing causes to presenting problems experienced by criminal and justice populations, or reactions to interventions. For instance, effective pharmacological interventions for alcohol abuse include the use of disulfiram (Antibuse), which results in the physiological reactions of vomiting and headaches when an individual drinks alcohol, and naltrexone and acamprosate, which reduce physiological craving for alcohol (Bonta & Andrews, 2017).

Behavioral Outcomes

Behavioral outcomes are the most commonly assessed outcomes among criminal and juvenile justice populations. Calsyn, Yonker, Lemming, Morse, and Klinkenberg (2005) examined the following six outcomes: (1) offending behavior associated with substance use such as driving while intoxicated, public intoxication, and drug charges; (2) minor offenses that include probation and parole violations, shoplifting, and burglary; (3) major offenses that include assault, arson, weapons charges, and homicide; (4) arrests; (5) court summonses; and (6) incarcerations.

Focusing on behavioral health issues among juvenile justice involved youth, Kretschmar, Butcher, Flannery, and Singer (2016) examined the outcomes of general psychological functioning, trauma symptoms, and delinquency thereby focusing on both psychological and behavioral outcomes. Caldwell (2011) focused only on behavioral outcomes among youth, such as institutional behavior and post-intervention violent and offending behaviors.

Recidivism

A significant behavioral criminal justice outcome is recidivism. Numerous approaches to measure recidivism exist since it has been defined in various ways. Durose, Cooper, and Snyder (2014) identified six different types of recidivism measures: (1) arrest within 5 years after release from prison; (2) adjudication and arrest within 5 years after release from prison that results in a court adjudication or disposition such as a new conviction, or acquittal; (3) an arrest and conviction within 5 years after release from prison arising from a new court conviction; (4) arrest and incarceration within 5 years after release from prison that results in a jail or prison or jail sentence; (5) arrest and imprisonment within 5 years of release from prison that results in a jail or prison sentence; and (6) an arrest or a technical violation of prison release conditions that results in imprisonment. Similarly, Langan and Levin (2002) described four outcome measures to assess recidivism: (1) rearrest, (2) reconviction, (3) a resentence to prison, and (4) reincarceration either with or without a new sentence.

While these recidivism measurements are behavioral, and can be counted and summated relatively easily, numerous underlying psychological and physiological factors that may contribute to these behaviors are not measured or captured. This is common when assessing outcomes in the criminal and juvenile justice system. While we are not critical of such an approach, we recognize that conducting an assessment that includes these factors is often beyond the scope, training, and expertise of many criminal justice settings and social service organizations that provide evidence-based practices to criminal justice populations.

Some outcome measures assess in multiple domains such as psychological and behavioral within a single instrument. For example, describing the Child and Adolescent Functional Assessment Scale developed by Kay Hodges, Multi-Health Systems, Inc (2017), shows the following eight domains are assessed using the Youth Scale: (1) school, (2) home, (3) community, (4) behavior towards others, (5) moods, (6) self-harm, (7) substance abuse, and (8) thinking; and the Caregiver Scale assesses two domains: (1) material needs and (2) social support. Each scale can be scored individually and treated as a separate outcome, or an aggregated score can be obtained for the Youth Scale and Caregiver Scale.

Case Processing Outcomes

Some studies have examined how individual cases are processed in the criminal justice system, and the case processing results themselves then become an outcome relevant for criminal justice populations. Case processing following an intervention, although the intervention need not necessarily be an evidence-based practice, is also an important criminal justice outcome. Campbell et al. (2014) examined intervention outcomes resulting from the Sexual Assault Nurse Examiner (SANE) program. Using case outcomes related to prosecution rates, the authors found that after victims completed the SANE program, their cases were more likely to result in prosecution than prior to participating in the SANE program.

Donnelly (2017) examined individual case outcomes among juvenile minorities processed in the Pennsylvania juvenile justice system. The purpose of the study was to investigate whether case processing or case outcomes varied among African American and Latino youth during each of the following juvenile case processing phases: petitioning, adjudication, residential program placement, or secure facility placement. Given that federal legislation requires states to implement Disproportionate Minority Contact

(DMC) interventions to reduce DMC within their jurisdictions, examining case processing is a useful approach for determining whether the outcome of reduced DMC resulted from the interventions.

Organizational Outcomes

It is important to recognize that in addition to the numerous types of outcomes relevant for criminal and juvenile justice populations, some outcomes pertain to the organizational setting and are relevant for the implementation of evidence-based practices within social service organizations and criminal justice settings. Organizational outcomes provide important indicators about whether an organization or criminal justice setting has the capacity to implement an evidence-based practice.

Referring to outcomes that are relevant for criminal justice populations as client-level outcomes, Belenko and Wexler (2007) also discuss organizational-level and system-level outcomes. Examples of organizational-level outcomes include "treatment capacity, access to other services, supervision, staff training, professional development, and program costs" (p. 21). Examples of system-level measures include "interagency collaboration, increased capacity of partners, reduce crime, system cost and cost offsets" (p. 21). Among these, numerous outcomes some are more significant to key stakeholders than others.

Bogue et al. (2005) describe the Integrated Model based on the eight evidence-based principles for reducing offender risk and recidivism. While reduced recidivism is the primary outcome, the authors describe two additional outcomes and their measurement; system process measures and program measures. System process measures are those associated with interventions such as dosage, the length of community supervision, and supervision violations. Program measures include factors such as program integrity and quality that are used to determine whether the intervention or program is effective. In summary, organizational outcomes highlight the need to attend to outcomes and outcome measures within the organization that affect the capacity to deliver interventions.

Training and Staff Development Outcomes

Indeed, measuring intervention outcomes and delivering evidence-based practices requires highly skilled and competent practitioners. Practitioner training in core correctional practices is essential to ensure that the delivery of evidence-based practices is effective (Dowden & Andrews, 2004). Thus, training and staff development outcomes are important to assess and ensure that skills and competencies have been acquired. Four quality assurance outcomes are particularly relevant for these purposes: assessment, case planning, cognitive behavioral training, and motivational interviewing and core correctional practices (Domurad & Carey, 2010).

Cost as an Outcome

While evidence-based practice outcomes are important for assessing improved functioning, the costs incurred in implementing an evidence-based practice or program are also important considerations. In Washington State, legislation was enacted that required some State-funded evidence-based practices and programs to demonstrate the cost benefits to taxpayers. The goal was to determine whether the benefits to taxpayers resulting from providing evidence-based practices offset the costs associated with implementing the intervention. Additionally, the employment productivity benefits for intervention participants were also determined.

To determine the cost benefits to taxpayers, monetary value was analyzed by examining factors such as improved work performance, lower health care and associated costs, and lower costs associated with crime. The cost outcome analysis showed that when evidence-based practices are provided to individuals with alcohol, drug, and mental health disorders, Washington State taxpayers receive a benefit of approximately \$3.77 for each dollar spent to provide the evidence-based practice. The cost analyses also showed that 50% of the benefits to the State resulted from lower health care and associated costs, 7% resulted from lower crime costs, 8% resulted from miscellaneous benefits, and 35% of the benefits to intervention participants resulted from increased employment earnings. In 2006, full implementation of evidence-based practices throughout the State was expected to result in \$1.5 billion in net benefits to the State, and \$416 million in taxpayer benefits (Aos, Mayfield, Miller, & Yen, 2006).

Similarly, it is also important to consider the costs that a social service agency or criminal justice setting would incur to implement an evidence-based practice or program for criminal justice populations. Therefore, we provide the most current implementation costs for quite a few common evidence-based practices for criminal and juvenile justice populations. Whereas crimesolutions.gov lists cost benefits to Washington State as determined by the Washington State Institute for Public Policy, we present information obtained from the Substance Abuse and Mental Health Services Administration (SAMSHA) National Registry of Evidence-Based Programs and Practices (NREPP) website. In some instances, costs may not be current. NREPP provides information for locating up-to-date cost information.

Table 4.1 shows a brief summary of nine evidence-based practices, several examples that illustrate the type of implementation materials that are available, the most recently available costs of these materials, and whether the materials are required by the intervention developer or supplier.

CRIMINAL AND JUVENILE JUSTICE SYSTEM OUTCOMES

Legislative Outcomes

Legislative outcomes may include considering the number of jurisdictions that have legislated the use of evidence-based practices and programs for offenders and former offenders, cost analyses that examine expenditures and benefits resulting from enacting legislation for evidence-based practices and programs, and considering a jurisdiction's political climate and readiness to enact legislation.

Law Enforcement Outcomes

Law enforcement outcomes include diversion, referral, and the provision of services such as mediation, crisis intervention, and conflict resolution. These are important functions provided by law enforcement agencies.

Court Outcomes

Court outcomes also include diversion and consideration of alternative sentences, as well as risk assessment and identifying treatment needs. Outcomes that result from specialty court services are essential measures of a court's success.

Corrections Outcomes

As mentioned, the corrections system includes institutional facilities such as jail as prison settings, as well as probation and parole. While outcomes vary based on the nature of the corrections setting, overall risk assessment and reduced recidivism and violation are primary outcomes.

Inmate Classification Outcomes

Serin (2005) describes prison inmate classification as a specialized risk assessment in which the focus is on both static and dynamic factors consistent with the Risk-Need-Responsivity (RNR) model. This approach has the potential to improve public safety and reduce incarceration costs.

Table 4.1 A sample of evidence-based practices implementation materials and costs

Intervention	Sample materials and costs	Required by intervention developer
Adolescent Community Reinforcement Approach (A-CRA/Assertive Continuing Care (ACC) (A-CRA/ACC) – intervention for youth aged 12 to 24 who experience substance use and co-occurring mental health disorders.	A-CRA Training Workshop, 2-days – $950 per person	Required
	ACC Online Training Course, 3 h (no cost information provided)	Required
	A-CRA/ACC Supervisor Coaching Calls (no cost information provided)	Required
Assisted Outpatient Treatment (AOT) – court ordered treatment for adults experiencing severe mental illness	Treatment Implementation Guide – Free	Not Required
	Site visits from the Treatment Advocacy Center – Travel expenses will be charged.	Not Required
Brief Strategic Family Therapy – a family intervention for African American, Latino and White families with adolescent behavioral problems	Unspecified Materials for Implementation, training and quality assurance – (no cost information provided)	Required
Functional Family Therapy for Adolescent Alcohol and Drug Abuse - family therapy treatment for youth ages 13–19 experiencing substance abuse and behavioral health problems and their families	Book – $59.99	Required
	Book Chapter – Free	Required
	PowerPoint Slides – Free	Required
	Stage 1 Training, 2 on-site trainings for 3–8 clinicians – $26,000 – $43,500 in addition to expenses for trainer travel	Required
	Therapist Certification – $500 each	Required
Moral Reconation Therapy – an intervention to enhance moral reasoning and decrease recidivism among juvenile and adult offenders	MRT Client Work – $25 for each participant	Required
	Four day, off-site initial training – $600 for first clinician, $500 for each additional clinician from same agency	Required
	Two day advanced training	Required

Continued

Table 4.1 A sample of evidence-based practices implementation materials and costs —cont'd

Intervention	Sample materials and costs	Required by intervention developer
Motivational Interviewing – focuses on helping individuals to resolve ambivalent feelings and change behaviors	Book – $51.00 each	Not Required
	Two DVD set – $180	Not Required
	On or Off-Site Training – No cost information provided	Not Required
	Quality Assurance Instruments – Free	Not Required
Multisystemic Therapy (MST) for Juvenile Offenders – a family intervention for juvenile offenders aged 6–17 to reduce out of home placements	Program implementation start-up fees – $2000 in addition to travel expenses	Required
	Annual program support fees/services – $19,000–$29,00 in addition to travel expenses	Required
	Annual agency/team licensing fees – $4000 per agency/ plus $2500 per team	Required
Relationship-Based Care – an intervention for homeless adults with criminal justice system involvement focused on improving relationships	Implementation manual – $30 each	Required
	Two day on site training – $500 per clinician for 25 clinicians, in addition to travel expense	Not Required
	Technical support via telephone and e-mail – Free	Not Required
Strengthening Families Program – a family intervention for children ages 3–16 focused on improved family functioning	Two day on-site group leader training – $4,350 in addition to travel expenses for two trainers for no more than 35 clinicians	Not Required
	Basic technical assistance – Free	Not Required
	Advanced technical assistance – $85/h	Not Required
	Evaluation Services – $1,950–$12,000/year based on number of participants and reports produced	Not Required
	Fidelity sit visit – $2,200 in addition to travel expenses	Not Required

Obtained from the substance abuse and mental health services administration (SAMSHA) national registry of evidence-based programs and practices (NREPP).

Serin identified additional benefits to inmate classification that include: (1) managing the inmate population, (2) improving management of the correctional facility, (3) increasing case base knowledge and skills and correctional practitioners, and (4) risk assessment and management for improving the reentry process.

SYSTEMATIC REVIEWS

A convenient and comprehensive approach for determining intervention outcomes among criminal justice populations is to examine systematic reviews. Systematic reviews can also be used to provide information about evidence-based practice effectiveness for criminal and juvenile justice populations.

According to the Campbell Collaboration website: "The purpose of a systematic review is to sum up the best available research on a specific question. This is done by synthesizing the results of several studies... A systematic review must have clear inclusion/exclusion criteria, an explicit search strategy, systematic coding and analysis of included studies, meta-analysis (were possible)" (The Campbell Collaboration, 2017).

As an illustration of the usefulness of systematic reviews, consider the systematic review of outcome measures used in forensic mental health research with consensus panel opinion. Among the 308 studies included in the review, the top six interventions were: (1) cognitive/behavioral interventions, (2) therapeutic community, (3) community supervision/aftercare/mental health services, (4) multisystemic therapy, (5) forensic psychiatric unit/high security hospital, and (6) drug court. The top six outcome domains found among the studies were: (1) recidivism and nonviolent recidivism, (2) substance abuse, (3) service outcomes, (4) violent or sexual assault recidivism, (5) mental state, and (6) cognitive/psychological functioning (Fitzpatrick et al., 2010).

META-ANALYSIS

A major component of a systematic review is data synthesis or meta-analysis. Synthesizing data from multiple studies is useful for summarizing the effects of interventions investigated in rigorous research studies or demonstrating the usefulness of evidence-based practice and policies (Borenstein, Hedges, Higgins, & Rothstein, 2009). Synthesizing data from multiple studies also increases our understanding of what is known about an intervention (Lipsey & Wilson, 2001).

For instance, meta-analysis results show that embracing a therapeutic intervention approach, providing services to high-risk youth offenders, and high quality intervention implementation are the principal factors that underlie effective interventions for justice-involved youth (Lipsey, 2009). Meta-analysis results also show no differences among outcomes between generic and name-brand types of cognitive-behavioral intervention for adults and youthful offenders (Landenberger & Lipsey, 2005). Finally, meta-analysis results also demonstrate the effectiveness of motivational interviewing (Burke, Arkowitz, & Menchola, 2003; Rubak, Sandbaek, Lauritzen, & Christensen, 2005).

MAKING A REFERRAL

Many criminal and juvenile justice settings and social service organizations may not have skilled and competent staff with the expertise to deliver evidence-based practices and programs, or to assess and measure intervention outcomes. In these instances, referrals will need to be made to agencies that are able to provide these services.

A variety of community-based agency models are found that provide interventions to criminal justice populations. Some are national in scope, whereas others are regionally based. Some community-based agencies provide services exclusively to criminal justice populations, others provide services to a diverse client population yet offer special programs for criminal justice populations, and still others provide services to mixed populations of clientele that include criminal justice and non-criminal justice populations.

Referrals can also be treated as an intervention outcome, and therefore be measured. For example, practitioners can track and monitor the number of referrals, reasons for making referrals, and types of social problems, and even track follow-up information regarding whether an offender or former offender followed-up with the referral.

Suggestions for making referrals include:

1. Develop an ongoing list of community-based resources and agencies that provide a range of evidence-based behavioral health and health care interventions. Include eligibility for services criteria. Update the list frequently.
2. Assess offenders' intervention needs and motivation to participate in an intervention.

3. Maintain contact with the agencies to review any changes in service eligibility criteria, and obtain feedback about referrals made to the agency. Maintain a feedback loop.

Case Example

Using Risk Assessment as an Outcomes Among Criminal Justice Populations

Any actuarial risk assessment instrument or evidence-based practice for criminal justice populations must be relevant for the population and attend to specific outcome(s). This case example describes a pilot study supported with funding from the New York Community Trust.

Most research describing the utility of the Level of Service Inventory-Revised (LSI-R) for female offenders has examined its utility compared to male offenders, or its ability to predict recidivism among female offenders. This pilot study examined the feasibility of using the LSI-R among a sample of women of color in a large urban environment, and a basic cost analysis to determine the cost of implementing the LSI-R, training needs among staff to administer the LSI-R and interpret scores, and the feasibility of using the LSI-R among groups receiving different agency services. More specifically, the purpose of the study was to assess the feasibility (administration, scoring, and costs) of using an actuarial risk assessment instrument among a regional population of former female offenders. In Chapter 2, a summary of qualitative data obtained from the two focus groups were described. This case example summarizes the quantitative data.

According to Morash (2009), it is important to examine the purchase cost and ease-of-use of the LSI-R. Such information can contribute to decision-making about its use in gender-responsive social service agencies. Although clinical practitioners express concerns about administering self-reported outcome measures among criminal justice populations due to the uncertainty about trustworthiness, such measures can be useful and accurate (Walters, 2011).

Locating actuarial risk assessment instruments involves much more than merely locating a copy of the instrument itself. Among one of the first steps to accomplish prior to searching for and retrieving information about an instrument is to determine the characteristics of the criminal justice population, intervention goals, and setting. After obtaining a thorough understanding of a criminal justice population's characteristics and intervention goals, subsequent activities include locating and administering the actuarial risk assessment instrument.

When searching for and retrieving an instrument, it is important to recognize that some actuarial risk assessment instruments are in the public domain and readily available from an Internet search, whereas others are copyrighted and must be purchased. Among copyrighted instruments, not all of the questionnaire items are available for examination. This means that copyrighted questionnaire items are not all available for viewing. Permission for use is also required. Each time that an instrument is administered a cost for use is incurred. This case example describes such instruments.

On the other hand, instruments in the public domain can be used without seeking permission. When results are disseminated in reports or published articles, the instrument author(s) should be cited. In other words, these instruments do not require permission to use, although acknowledgement is required.

Numerous actuarial risk assessment instruments are in the public domain such as the Juvenile Sanctions Center (JSC) Boys (2007), the Girls Link (2007), and the Virginia Youth Assessment and Screening Instrument (2008) (Baird et al., 2013). The LSI-R is a copyrighted instrument that was selected for use. The Multi-Health Systems (MHS), Inc. (2017) 2017 catalog contains a forensic and public safety section that contains several actuarial risk assessment instruments. Several are associated with the RNR model such as the Level of Service/Case Management Inventory (Andrews, Bonta, & Wormith, 2004).

The aforementioned issues were all investigated in the pilot study. Among the study participants, basic demographic information was summarized. For example, the race and ethnicity of the population is as follows: African American (N = 39, 65%), White (N = 10, 16.7%), Latina (N = 8, 13.3%) and multiracial (N = 3, 5.0%). The average age of the sample was 39.83 years (SD = 11.10).

Whether an actuarial risk assessment instrument or other type of standardized instrument is administered, a decision needs to be made regarding how these instruments will be scored. Two primary options are hand-scoring or computerized scoring. MHS also provides the option for hand-scoring or the purchase of software for computerized scoring. Obviously for staff, computerized scoring will simplify this task, although hand-scoring will be less expensive. In the pilot study, due to the small sample the LSI-R was hand-scored. This may not be feasible when the LSI-R is administered to large numbers, or busy staff do not have sufficient time to hand-score the 54 items.

Indeed, instrument costs and scoring costs are a consideration for agencies or criminal justice settings considering their implementation. Whether the instrument is in the public domain or copyrighted, administering these instruments requires training and qualifications. Staff who administer the instruments will need to understand their use, scoring procedures, and how to interpret the score.

Among the 20 women participating in the residential program, at pre-test the average score was 25.35 (SD = 5.76). At post-test score the average score decreased to 16.80 (SD = 7.47). Ten women completed the post-test LSI-R. Among the 20 women participating in the outpatient treatment program, the average pre-test score was 24.15 (SD = 5.87), and the average post-test score also decreased to 20.90 (SD = 4.70). Ten women completed the post-test LSI-R. Finally, among the 20 women participating in the alumni/aftercare program their average pre-test score was 23.50 (SD = 6.78). Sixteen women completed the post-test, which yielded an average score of 17.56 (SD = 6.48).

The aggregated LSI-R score of the 60 participants across the three program types at pre-test was 24.33 (SD = 6.10). Among the 36 participants completing the post-test, the average decreased to 18.28 (SD = 6.39).

After scoring the LSI-R and examining the scores for each program type as well as the overall scores, the final step was to interpret the scores. While LSI-R score interpretations can be found in the literature, the LSI-R manual was used to interpret the scores in the pilot study. Using the manual to interpret the scores showed the study participants in the residential program reported scores that were particularly relevant based on the manual given that the high levels of supervision were identified for scoring ranges that demonstrate improvement from pre-test to post-test.

Sustainability was an issue of major concern after the pilot project ended, primarily due to the costs of administering the LSI-R, and decisions centering on how to best use the instrument, for what purposes, and whether it was really necessary to determine whether risk scores decreased. In the end, it was determined that ongoing funding would be required to sustain the use of the LSI-R.

SUMMARY

This chapter provided an overview of the types of psychological, physiological, and behavioral outcomes that are clinically relevant, and result from evidence-based practices and programs for criminal and juvenile justice populations. These outcomes uniquely focus on both public safety and public health risks. Such outcomes should be assessed using reliable and valid outcome measures.

REFERENCES

Andrews, D.A., Bonta, J., & Wormith, J. S. (2004). *The level of service/case management inventory (LS/CMI): User's manual.* Toronto, Canada: Multi-Health Systems.

Aos, S., Mayfield, J., Miller, M., & Yen, W. (2006). *Evidence-based treatment of alcohol, drug, and mental health disorders: Potential benefits, costs, and fiscal impacts for Washington State.* Olympia, WA: Washington State Institute for Public Policy.

Baird, C., Healy, T., Johnson, K., Bogie, A., Dankert, E. W., & Scharenbroch, C. (2013). *A comparison of risk assessment instruments in juvenile justice.* Madison, WI: National Council on Crime and Delinquency.

Belenko, S., & Wexler, H. K. (2007). *Implementing evidence-based drug treatment in criminal justice settings: Final conference report.* Retrieved from www.tresearch.org/law_ethics/CEICAFinalReport2006.pdf.

Best, D., Day, E., Campbell, A., Flynn, P. M., & Simpson, D. D. (2009). Relationship between drug treatment engagement and criminal thinking style among drug-using offenders. *European Addiction Research, 15*(2), 71–77.

Bogue, B., Woodward, B., Campbell, N., Carey, M., Clawson, E., Faust, D., & Wasson, B. (2005). *Implementing effective correctional management of offenders in the community, outcome and process measures.* Washington, DC: National Institute of Corrections, Community Corrections Division.

Bonta, J., & Andrews, D. A. (2017). *The psychology of criminal conduct* (6th ed.). New York: Routledge.

Borenstein, M., Hedges, L.V., Higgins, J. P. T., & Rothstein, H. R. (2009). *Introduction to meta-analysis.* West Sussex, UK: John Wiley & Sons, Ltd.

Burke, B. L., Arkowitz, H., & Menchola, M. (2003). The efficacy of motivational interviewing: A meta-analysis of controlled clinical trials. *Journal of Consulting and Clinical Psychology, 71*(5), 843–861.

Caldwell, M. F. (2011). Treatment-related changes in behavioral outcomes of psychopathy facets in adolescent offenders. *Law and Human Behavior, 35*(4), 275–287.

Calsyn, R. J., Yonker, R. D., Lemming, M. R., Morse, G. A., & Klinkenberg, W. D. (2005). Impact of assertive community treatment and client characteristics on criminal justice outcomes in dual disorder homeless individuals. *Criminal Behaviour and Mental Health, 15*(4), 236–248.

Campbell, R., Bybee, D., Townsend, S. M., Shaw, J., Karim, N., & Markowitz, J. (2014). The impact of sexual assault nurse examiner programs on criminal justice case outcomes: A multisite replication study. *Violence Against Women, 20*(5), 607–625.

Chandler, R. K., Fletcher, B. W., & Volkow, N. D. (2009). Treating drug abuse and addiction in the criminal justice system: improving public health and safety. *JAMA, 301*(2), 183–190.

Domurad, F., & Carey, M. (2010). *Implementing evidence based practices: One in a series of coaching packets designed to assist jurisdictions in the implementation of effective practices that will support successful offender outcomes.* Washington, DC: Center for Effective Public Policy.

Donnelly, E. A. (2017). The disproportionate minority contact mandate: An examination of its impacts on juvenile justice processing outcomes (1997–2011). *Criminal Justice Policy Review, 28*(4), 347–369.

Dowden, C., & Andrews, D. A. (2004). The importance of staff practice in delivering effective correctional treatment: A meta-analytic review of core correctional practice. *International Journal of Offender Therapy and Comparative Criminology, 48*(2), 203–214.

Durose, M. R., Cooper, A. D., & Snyder, H. N. (2014). *Recidivism of prisoners released in 30 states in 2005: Patterns from 2005 to 2010.* Washington, DC: U.S. Department of Justice, Office of Justice Programs, Bureau of Justice Statistics.

Fitzpatrick, R., Chambers, J., Burns, T., Doll, H., Fazel, S., Jenkinson, C., et al. (2010). A systematic review of outcome measures used in forensic mental health research with consensus panel. *Health Technology Assessment, 14*(18).
Fletcher, B. W., & Chandler, R. K. (2006). *Principles of drug abuse treatment for criminal justice populations*. Washington, DC: National Institute on Drug Abuse.
Joe, G., Broome, K., Rowan-Szal, G., & Simpson, D. D. (2002). Measuring patient attributes and engagement in treatment. *Journal of Substance Abuse Treatment, 22*(4), 183–196.
Knight, K., Garner, B. R., Simpson, D. D., Morey, J. T., & Flynn, P. M. (2006). An assessment for criminal thinking. *Crime & Delinquency, 52*(1), 159–177.
Kretschmar, J. M., Butcher, F., Flannery, D. J., & Singer, M. I. (2016). Diverting juvenile justice-involved youth with behavioral health issues from detention: Preliminary findings from Ohio's behavioral health juvenile justice (BHJJ) initiative. *Criminal Justice Policy Review, 27*(3), 302–325.
Landenberger, N. A., & Lipsey, M. W. (2005). The positive effects of cognitive-behavioral programs for offenders: A meta-analysis of factors associated with effective treatment. *Journal of Experimental Criminology, 1*, 451–476.
Langan, P. A., & Levin, D. J. (2002). *Recidivism of prisoners released in 1994*. Washington, DC: U.S. Department of Justice, Office of Justice Programs, Bureau of Justice Statistics.
Lipsey, M. W. (2009). The primary factors that characterize effective interventions with juvenile offenders: A meta-analytic overview. *Victims and Offenders, 4*(2), 124–147.
Lipsey, M. W., & Wilson, D. B. (2001). *Practical meta-analysis*. Thousand Oaks, CA: Sage Publications.
McCord, J. (2003). Cures that harm: Unanticipated outcomes of crime prevention programs. *The Annals of the American Academy of Political and Social Science, 587*(1), 16–30.
Miller, N. S., & Flaherty, J. A. (2000). Effectiveness of coerced addiction treatment (alternative consequences): A review of the clinical research. *Journal of Substance Abuse Treatment, 18*, 9–16.
Morash, M. (2009). A great debate over using the Level of Service Inventory-Revised (LSI-R) with women offenders. *Criminology & Public Policy, 8*(1), 173–181.
Multi-Health Systems, Inc. (2017). *2017 catalog*. North Tonawanda, NY: Author.
Patterson, G. T. (2013). Prisoner reentry: A public health or public safety issue for social work practice? *Social Work in Public Health, 28*, 129–141.
Royse, D., & Thyer, B. A. (1996). *Program evaluation: An introduction* (2nd ed.). Chicago: Nelson-Hall Publishers.
Rubak, S., Sandbaek, A., Lauritzen, T., & Christensen, B. (2005). Motivational interviewing: A systematic review and meta-analysis. *British Journal of General Practice, 55*(513), 305–312.
Serin, R. C. (2005). *Evidence-based practice: Principles for enhancing correctional results prisons*. Washington, DC: U.S. Department of Justice, National Institute of Corrections.
Substance Abuse and Mental Health Services Administration. (2010). *SAMHSA's national outcome measure domains*. Retrieved from http://integratedrecovery.org/wp-content/uploads/2010/08/SAMHSA-National-Outcome-Measures.pdf.
The Campbell Collaboration. (2017). *What is a systematic review?*. Retrieved from https://www.campbellcollaboration.org/research-resources/writing-a-campbell-systematic-review/systemic-review.html.
Walters, G. D. (2011). Predicting recidivism with the psychological inventory of criminal thinking styles and level of service inventory-revised: Screening version. *Law and Human Behavior, 35*(3), 211–220.
Whitten, L. (2009). NIDA at work: Criminal justice-drug abuse treatment studies project. *NIDA Notes, 22*(3). Retrieved from http://www.drugabuse.gov/NIDA_notes/NNvol22N3/nidaatwork.html.

FURTHER READING

Barnoski, R., & Aos, S. (2004). *Outcome evaluation of Washington State's research-based programs for juvenile offenders*. Olympia, WA: Washington State Institute for Public Policy, 460.

Casey, P. M., Warren, R. K., & Elek, J. K. (2011). *Using offender risk and needs assessment information at sentencing: Guidance for courts from a national working group*. Retrieved from http://www.ncsc.org/~/media/Microsites/Files/CSI/RNA%20Guide%20Final.ashx.

Henderson, C. E., Taxman, F. S., & Young, D. W. (2008). A Rasch model analysis of evidence-based treatment practices in the criminal justice system. *Drug and Alcohol Dependence, 93*, 163–175.

CHAPTER 5

The Evidence-Based Rating and Classification Process

George T. Patterson

THE NEED FOR A REVIEW PROCESS

Numerous organizations have established practices and procedures for assessing whether an intervention is evidence-based practice. A sample of these organizations includes the Coalition for Evidence-Based Policy, the What Works Centre for Crime Reduction, the Washington State Institute for Public Policy, the California Evidence-Based Clearinghouse for Child Welfare, the Campbell Collaboration, Cochrane, Department of Education: What Works Clearing House, and Evidence-Based Practices for Substance Use Disorders, among various others.

Prior to be becoming classified and posted on an organization's website as an evidence-based practice, interventions and programs undergo a rigorous review process. It is imperative that interventions or programs be reviewed by external evaluators during the review process when considering classifications as an evidence-based practice. Peer review is an essential part of the rating and classification process. Intervention or program developer involvement in the rating and review can affect the decision making process. For example, Petrosino and Soydan (2005) found in a meta-analysis that among 300 randomized controlled trials investigating crime reduction, program evaluators who were more involved in the intervention or program also reported larger effect sizes than program evaluators who were not involved in the randomized controlled trials or evaluation component.

Bias can result when intervention developers, program developers, or individuals with a conflict of interest or involvement in the intervention or program are engaged in the review, rating, or classification processes (Petrosino & Soydan, 2005; Sherman & Strang, 2009; Welsh, Sullivan, & Olds, 2010). Such involvement, as Petrosino and Soydan point out, can result in the appearance that the intervention or program had a greater effect on intervention outcomes than actually occurred. Clearly, such

Clinical Interventions in Criminal Justice Settings
ISBN 978-0-12-811381-3
http://dx.doi.org/10.1016/B978-0-12-811381-3.00005-6

observations are problematic because the intervention did not actually produce behavioral or other changes. Consequently, peer reviewed and transparent rating and classification procedures are necessary. In fact, in order to become classified as a Model Plus program, a minimum of one rigorous study describing the intervention or program must be produced by an investigator who does not have any involvement in the intervention or program. This includes being part of the research team or having financial interest in the intervention or program (Blueprints for Healthy Youth Development, 2017b).

To illustrate the intervention or program review process, the procedures developed and implemented by three organizations are examined including the Substance Abuse and Mental Health Services Administration (SAMSHA) National Registry of Evidence-Based Programs and Practices (NREPP), the National Institute of Justice, Office of Justice Programs (CrimeSolutions.gov), and Blueprints for Healthy Youth Development. Following a discussion of the procedures used by each organization, the similarities and differences among these procedures are examined.

THE SUBSTANCE ABUSE AND MENTAL HEALTH SERVICES ADMINISTRATION NATIONAL REGISTRY OF EVIDENCE-BASED PROGRAMS AND PRACTICES

SAMSHA's NREPP (SAMSHA's National Registry of Evidence-Based Programs and Practices, 2015) website provides links to several topics providing information about the review process applied to an intervention or program. These links include reviews and submissions, review process, open submission process, resources for dissemination and implementation, reviewer requirements, training and responsibilities, program review criteria, and the submission process. Hennessy, Finkbiner, and Hill (2006) provide a historical and in-depth discussion of NREPP. Here, we discuss only the review process.

The review process first involves *pre-screening and approval for review*. During this initial process, three approaches are used by NREPP to identify an intervention or program: (1) interventions or programs are nominated, (2) SAMSHA and NREPP staff conduct literature searches, focus groups, and other techniques to discover interventions or programs, and (3) SAMSHA identifies interventions or programs based on agency priorities. All evidence-based interventions listed in the NREPP website before September 2015 will be subjected to the *re-review process* based on updates made in the review process.

The next phase involves a *literature search and screening*. During this phase, NREPP staff review nominated studies. The studies are required to be published no earlier than 1995. When multiple studies are nominated for the same review, the most recent study should be published within the past 10 years. NREPP staff also obtain additional materials from the intervention or program developer that can be used for implementation. These materials are not required, but interventions or programs supported with implementation materials such as a training manual receive priority review.

Following the literature search and screening, *expert review* is conducted by two certified reviewers who declare that they have no conflict of interest. The reviewers rate each study according to conceptual framework, study outcomes that are consistent with SAMSHA's mission, research methodology, intervention outcome effects, and program fidelity. The reviewers are also subject matter experts and experienced in research methodology.

Next, *NREPP methodology* is applied, which consists of assessing study components such as research design and attrition, and calculating effect sizes for relevant outcomes based on statistical data reported in the studies. After effects sizes are calculated, evidence classes and outcomes ratings are assigned based on four criteria: (1) study design rigor, (2) calculated effect sizes, (3) fidelity, and (4) conceptual framework. The outcome rating is determined based on summing the outcome score and the conceptual framework rating. Prior to obtaining the outcome score and the conceptual framework rating, an evidence score is calculated, effect class score derived from the confidence interval found among the effect size, and evidence class. A discussion of these statistics is beyond the scope of this book.

Finally, an *outcome score* or outcome rating is assigned to the intervention or program. One of four outcome ratings is assigned: (1) effective, (2) promising, (3) ineffective, and (4) inconclusive. An effective outcome rating suggests that the evidence shows a rigorous research design was employed and a large effect size was found. A promising outcome rating suggests that the research design and effect size were adequate. An ineffective rating suggests the research design was adequate although no effect or negative outcome effects were found. Finally, an inconclusive rating is assigned when a rigorous research design has not been employed and insufficient data are available to calculate effect sizes. SAMSHA makes a determination about which interventions and programs are listed on the NREPP website. When listed, interventions and programs are accompanied by the outcome rating as well as a program profile. Outcome ratings can be appealed using a five-step process.

THE NATIONAL INSTITUTE OF JUSTICE, OFFICE OF JUSTICE PROGRAMS, CRIMESOLUTIONS.GOV

The National Institute of Justice, Office of Justice Programs, CrimeSolutions.gov describes an eight-step review process used to review and rate an intervention or program as evidence-based (National Institute of Justice, Office of Justice Programs, n.d.-a,b). These eight steps are summarized below.

Step 1: Preliminary Program Identification

This step is focused on identifying an intervention or program that will be considered for the review process. Interventions or programs are identified in two ways; database and peer-reviewed journal searches conducted by CrimeSolutions.gov staff or nominations. A link is provided that describes the nomination process and procedures.

Step 2: Initial Program Screening

Interventions or programs are screened by research staff to determine if the aims of the intervention or program are consistent with those of CrimeSolutions.gov. Four areas are identified: (1) the reduction or prevention of crime, delinquency, and other outcomes; (2) prevention or interventions focused on victimization; (3) improving the criminal justice system; and (4) interventions or programs that focus on criminal justice and at-risk populations.

Step 3: Literature Search

If the intervention or program is determined to be consistent with the aims of CrimeSolutions.gov, research staff conduct a literature search to locate and retrieve relevant literature. The primary emphasis is to locate and retrieve quantitative literature describing the intervention or program. Qualitative information or data such as ethnographic or case study methods are used only to provide contextual information, and such information is not included in the evidence rating criteria.

Step 4: Initial Evidence Screening

Upon completion of Step 3, research staff review the retrieved studies and the intervention or program then undergoes an initial evidence screening. Four criteria are applied during this initial screening process: (1) the intervention or program should have been evaluated employing a minimum of one randomized controlled trial or quasi-experimental design; (2) study outcomes are relevant to crime, delinquency, and/or crime victims and obtained from prevention or intervention programs; (3) the evaluation study was published in a peer-reviewed source or submitted as a complete research report; and (4) the evaluation study was published no earlier than 1980.

Step 5: Selection of Evidence Base

A lead researcher, who is required to be a subject matter expert and experienced research methodologist, assumes the tasks of beginning the review process by selecting no more than three research studies summarizing the intervention or program and employing the strongest research methods. Studies are selected according to criteria such as research design rigor, sample size, and the year the study was published, among others.

Step 6: Expert Review

During this step, a minimum of two study reviewers, who are trained and certified in the process, utilize a two-part Program Evidence Rating Instrument to score the intervention or program. Part 1 is focused on the intervention or program's conceptual framework. Part 2 contains scoring criteria for the study design quality, study outcomes, and program fidelity.

Step 7: Study Classification

Based on the study reviewers' scores obtained from the two-part Program Evidence Rating Instrument, reviewed studies are then categorized in one of five classifications. These classification range from Class 1, studies that employ the most rigorous research designs demonstrating intervention or program effectiveness, to Class 5, studies providing insufficient information to receive a classification or employing study designs which do not provide evidence about effectiveness.

Step 8: Program Evidence Rating

In the final step, the intervention or program is assigned one of three evidence ratings: (1) effective, (2) promising, or (3) no effects. An effective rating signifies that the intervention or program has demonstrated rigorous evidence and fidelity. A promising rating signifies that "some" evidence has demonstrated effectiveness, whereas no effects denotes that an intervention or program was implemented with fidelity but either showed no effects or detrimental effects on intervention outcomes. Further, each of the five classifications determined in Step 7 are also applied to the three evidence ratings. In this instance, the study classifications determine the number of studies that are required. For example, an effective rating Class 1 category requires one study that demonstrates strong evidence with positive intervention effects. Conversely, an effective rating Class 5 category is given when studies report insufficient information to rate and classify a study. It is possible to re-review, update, or appeal an evidence rating.

BLUEPRINTS FOR HEALTHY YOUTH DEVELOPMENT

The Blueprints for Healthy Youth Development website maintains several links that describe the review process. We briefly review several of these links including nominate a program, guidelines for becoming a Blueprints certified program, and program criteria.

Interventions or programs are nominated for consideration either by an individual involved with it or through a monthly literature conducted by Blueprints staff. Both articles and reports can be reviewed. Following a nomination, the review process involves seven steps:

1. Blueprints staff complete a critique of the intervention or program's research methodology and intervention outcomes, among others.
2. Two senior Blueprints staff review and edit the critique.
3. A decision is reached to rate and classify the intervention or program as a model program or a promising program.
4. Nominees are informed within 8–10 weeks if an intervention or program does meet Blueprints criteria.
5. Interventions or programs that preliminarily meet Blueprints criteria are submitted to the Blueprints Advisory Board for review and a final decision. The board meets two times each year.
6. Following the board meeting written notification outlining the Board's decision is sent to the intervention or program developer.
7. The Blueprints Advisory Board may seek further information from the nominee and re-review the intervention or program. At this stage, reviews are finalized (Blueprints for Healthy Youth Development, 2017b).

In addition to describing these seven steps involved in the review process, Blueprints also provides a summary of five guidelines that are applied before an intervention or program can become a Blueprints certified program:

1. Interventions or programs are nominated for consideration as previously described. Studies or reports must contain data that can be used to assess effectiveness.
2. Blueprints staff conduct a review of the study/report focusing on methodological rigor and data demonstrating effectiveness, and prepare a summary report. Successful studies/reports are passed on for further review to the Blueprints Advisory Board, each who possess expertise in research methodology and youth development. A 20-item checklist is used to assess studies. Examples of assessed study components include research design, outcome measures, fidelity, and effect sizes (Blueprints for Healthy Youth Development, 2016).

3. The Blueprints Advisory Board examines the Blueprints summary report as well as the nominated studies/reports. At this stage, Blueprints criteria are applied to identify promising programs, model programs, and model plus programs (Blueprints for Healthy Youth Development, 2017a).
4. The Blueprints Director collects additional information and materials about the intervention or program approved by the Blueprints Advisory Board. These materials include manuals, training guidelines, and technical assistance needs, which are necessary for intervention or program implementation. Such materials must be published prior to final approval.
5. Approved interventions or programs are classified as either promising programs, model programs, or model plus programs and posted together with implementation materials on the Blueprints website (Blueprints for Healthy Youth Development, 2017c).

LOCATING AN EVIDENCE-BASED PRACTICE OR PROGRAM

Locating and retrieving information about a specific evidence-based practice can serve several purposes. Prior to implementation such information can provide practitioners with details about training, necessary certifications, costs, and relevant criminal justice populations who will benefit from the evidence-based practice. These advance efforts will save considerable time and expense particularly if an organization is still in the process of making a decision about which evidence-based practice should be implemented. While searching and locating an evidence-based practice it is imperative to understand the characteristics of the criminal justice population that will be participate in the intervention. This stands to reason, given that the intervention should be relevant for the population and have demonstrated effectiveness on outcomes among the population.

For instance, conducting an online search for an evidence-based practice using SAMSHA's NREPP website allows users to search (for recently reviewed intervention only), employing exact search criteria including age of the population, race and ethnicity, gender, special populations such as justice involved adults or youth, older adults, and lesbian, gay, bisexual, transgender, questioning (LGBTQ)/ITS (Intersexual), among other populations, intervention outcomes, program type, geographic locations, and outcome rating, for example (SAMSHA's National Registry of Evidence-Based Programs and Practices, n.d.-b).

To illustrate another example, the CrimeSolutions.gov website also allows users to search for an evidence-based intervention program (only) using specific criteria. The drop down menu provides search options such as race and ethnicity, age, gender, targeted population, setting, program type, topic, and evidence rating (National Institute of Justice, Office of Justice Programs, n.d.-a,b).

Organizations also post relevant information concerning costs associated with intervention implementation, in addition to posting information concerning the studies and materials that were reviewed to rate and classify an intervention or program as an evidence-based practice.

Using functional family therapy (FFT) as an example, FFT is posted on the NREPP and CrimeSolutions.gov websites. NREPP posts the costs of materials required by the intervention developer such as therapist certification ($500 for each therapist) and Stage 1 Training consisting of two on-site trainings with practice guidance ($26,000–$43,000 plus expenses for trainer travel), and other implementation materials such as a free training manual (SAMSHA's National Registry of Evidence-Based Programs and Practices, n.d.-a).

On the other hand, in addition to posting an intervention description and reviewed studies, CrimeSolutions.gov provides direct costs associated with FFT implementation in Washington State ($3134 per youth). These costs such services such as case management and travel, among others. Cost benefits for Washington State crime victims and taxpayers ($36,241 per youth) are also posted (National Institute of Justice, Office of Justice Programs, 2011). In sum, these two examples illustrate the different types of facts associated with intervention costs that are posted on organizational websites. Whereas the NREPP positing may be useful in a social service setting, the CrimeSolutions.gov, although specific to Washington State, may provide State policymakers with FFT cost estimates.

RATING AND CLASSIFYING CRIME PREVENTION PROGRAMS

Sherman et al. (1998) describe a rating and classification schema applied to crime prevention programs. In response to a 1996 Federal law, the U.S. Attorney General was mandated to submit to Congress an independent evaluation describing the efficacy of State and local crime prevention program that received funding from the U.S. Department of Justice. The crime prevention programs were primarily related to juvenile justice. To assess the efficacy of the crime prevention programs, the Maryland Scale of Scientific Methods was developed to rate and classify the programs based on the internal validity reported in the program evaluation studies.

The review process is similar to the process described earlier in this chapter and used by other organizations in which predetermined criteria were applied. Studies are rated on five levels ranging from Level 1 (studies assessed as the weakest in terms of internal validity) to Level 5 (studies assessed as the strongest in terms of internal validity). A detailed description of each of the five levels was presented in Chapter 2.

Following the rating process studies are then categorized into four areas: (1) what works, (2) what doesn't work, (3) what's promising, and (4) what's unknown.

What Works

What works refers to crime prevention programs that are demonstrated by empirical evidence to be effective for crime prevention and reducing the risk factors for crime. This classification is given when a minimum of two Level 3 program evaluation studies with statistically significant results are located and retrieved.

What Doesn't Work

What doesn't work refers to crime prevention programs that are demonstrated by empirical evidence found in program evaluation studies to be ineffective for crime prevention, and do not reduce the risk factors for crime. This classification is given when a minimum of two Level 3 program evaluation studies statistically show ineffectiveness.

What's Promising

This classification is given when the empirical evidence reported in program evaluation studies is insufficient to assess program effectiveness, but supports the belief that further research may demonstrate program effectiveness. Crime prevention program classified as promising require a minimum of one Level 3 program evaluation studies demonstrating effectiveness.

What's Unknown

What's unknown is a classification given to crime prevention program that are not classified as either what works, what doesn't work, or what's promising.

DIFFERENCES AND SIMILARITIES AMONG RATING AND CLASSIFICATION SCHEMAS

The content presented in this chapter is related to other chapters in terms of research concepts, implementing evidence-based practices and principles, and the characteristics of criminal justice populations. The concepts presented in other parts of this book should be integrated with the concepts from this chapter to assess the suitability of using various evidence-based practices. It is so important to understand basic research concepts so that an assessment can be made about implementing the highest quality evidence-based practices that can be provided to criminal justice populations.

The concepts presented in this chapter also demonstrate the need to recognize and understand the similarities and differences found among organizations' rating schemas. In particular, it has demonstrated the need to be able to recognize and understand the differences found among organizations' classification schemas given that such classifications of evidence-based practices are not identical across agencies. These differences have also been reported by Przybylski and Orchowsky (2015).

Perhaps more similar than different, the review process used to rate and classify an evidence-based practice is based on several guiding principles. These guiding principles suggest that in order to be classified as an evidence-based practice, intervention or program efficacy should be based on strong empirical evidence in the form of quantitative data, randomized controlled trials, or rigorous quasi-experimental designs, the use of reliable and valid outcomes measures and positive intervention outcomes. In most instances, more than one program evaluation study are necessary that demonstrate statistical significance.

Organizations post on their website clinical interventions and programs, including crime prevention programs, classified as evidence-based practice using different terminology and different classification schemas. As this chapter has shown, classification terminology range from effective, promising, ineffective, and inconclusive; to promising programs, model programs, and model plus programs; and what works, what doesn't work, what's promising, or what's unknown.

INTERVENTIONS AND PROGRAMS THAT ARE NOT CLASSIFIED AS EVIDENCE-BASED

It is important to note what occurs to clinical practices that do not become classified as evidence-based, or do not become posted on organizations' websites. It would be unwise, and even unethical to use evidence-based principles and practices that have been demonstrated to be ineffective, or to not implement them when empirical evidence shows an intervention is effective. Most professional organizations' code of ethics contain statements about the ethical delivery of interventions.

While it is possible to appeal an organization's rating and classification, Prendergast (2011) noted that SAMSHA's NREPP website is a "decision support tool" (p. 13) because the interventions and programs posted on the website are self-nominated. Because some interventions and programs are not self-nominated, or submitted some interventions and programs may not be classified as evidence-based. Further, all of the interventions and programs submitted to NREPP do not receive a review.

In sum, it is worth repeating how important it is to recognize and understand the different classifications used among organizations that post evidence-based practices on their websites.

Such knowledge can assist clinical practitioners and criminal justice practitioners with selecting and implementing the most effective interventions relevant for specific criminal justice populations.

SUMMARY

This chapter described the procedures utilized by three organizations including the Substance Abuse and Mental Health Services Administration (SAMSHA) National Registry of Evidence-Based Programs and Practices (NREPP), the National Institute of Justice, Office of Justice Programs (CrimeSolutions.gov), and Blueprints for Healthy Youth Development to explain how an intervention or program becomes classified as an evidence-based practice. These descriptions showed the differences and similarities among procedures used among the organizations.

REFERENCES

Blueprints for Healthy Youth Development. (2016). *Guidelines for blueprints checklist.* Retrieved from http://www.blueprintsprograms.com/resources/Guidelines_for_Blueprints_Checklist.pdf.

Blueprints for Healthy Youth Development. (2017a). *Blueprints programs positive youth development, program criteria, Blueprints programs.* Retrieved from http://www.blueprintsprograms.com/criteria.

Blueprints for Healthy Youth Development. (2017b). *Blueprints programs positive youth development, nominate a program, Blueprints programs.* Retrieved from http://www.blueprintsprograms.com/nominate.

Blueprints for Healthy Youth Development. (2017c). *Guidelines for becoming a Blueprints- certified program, Blueprints programs.* Retrieved from http://www.blueprintsprograms.com/guidelines.

Hennessy, K. D., Finkbiner, R., & Hill, G. (2006). The national registry of evidence-based programs and practices. *International Journal of Mental Health, 35*(2), 21–34.

National Institute of Justice, Office of Justice Programs. (2011). *Program: Functional family therapy (FFT): CrimeSolutions.gov*. Retrieved from https://www.crimesolutions.gov/ProgramDetails.aspx?ID=122.

National Institute of Justice, Office of Justice Programs. (n.d.-a). *Advanced search: CrimeSolutions.gov*. Retrieved from https://www.crimesolutions.gov/advsearch.aspx.

National Institute of Justice, Office of Justice Programs. (n.d.-b). *About CrimeSolutions.gov: Practice review and rating from start to finish – CrimeSolutions.gov*. Retrieved from https://www.crimesolutions.gov/about_practicereview.aspx.

Petrosino, A., & Soydan, H. (2005). The impact of program developers as evaluators on criminal recidivism: Results from meta-analyses of experimental and quasi-experimental research. *Journal of Experimental Criminology, 1*(4), 435–450.

Prendergast, M. L. (2011). Issues defining and applying evidence-based practices criteria for treatment of criminal-justice involved clients. *Journal of Psychoactive Drugs*, 7, 10–18.

Przybylski, R., & Orchowsky, S. (2015). *Implementing evidence-based practices*. Retrieved from http://www.jrsa.org/projects/ebp_briefing_paper2.pdf.

SAMSHA's National Registry of Evidence-Based Programs, Practices. (2015). *Review process*. Retrieved from http://nrepp.samhsa.gov/review_process.aspx.

SAMSHA's National Registry of Evidence-Based Programs and Practices. (n.d.-a). *Intervention summary: Functional family therapy for adolescent alcohol, drug abuse*. Retrieved from http://legacy.nreppadmin.net/ViewIntervention.aspx?id=372.

SAMSHA's National Registry of Evidence-Based Programs and Practices. (n.d.-b). *Find an intervention*. Retrieved from http://nrepp.samhsa.gov/AdvancedSearch.aspx.

Sherman, L. W., Gottfredson, D. C., MacKenzie, D. L., Eck, J., Reuter, P., & Bushway, S. D. (1998). *Preventing crime: What works, what doesn't, what's promising*. Washington, DC: U.S. Department of Justice, Office of Justice Programs, National Institute of Justice.

Sherman, L. W., & Strang, H. (2009). Testing for analysts' bias in crime prevention experiments: Can we accept Eisner's one-tailed test? *Journal of Experimental Criminology, 5*(2), 185–200.

Welsh, B. C., Sullivan, C. J., & Olds, D. L. (2010). When early crime prevention goes to scale: A new look at the evidence. *Prevention Science, 11*(2), 115–125.

CHAPTER 6

Risk Assessment and Treatment Levels

George T. Patterson

ASSESSING RISKS FOR REOFFENDING AMONG OFFENDERS AND FORMER OFFENDERS

"The science of predicting criminal recidivism has improved dramatically in the past few decades, and there is far less emphasis on unstructured clinical judgment" (Folsom & Atkinson, 2007, p. 1044). Indeed, decades ago criminal justice practitioners utilized their professional or clinical judgment to assess whether offenders or former offenders would engage in future offending behavior.

Consistent with practice that is evidence-based in which practitioners integrate clinical judgment with research findings (Sackett, Rosenberg, Gray, Haynes, & Richardson, 1996), conducting offender risk assessments involves integrating clinical judgment and research findings. Noting that treatment and supervision of offenders is improved by the use of reliable and valid research data, Schlager and Simourd (2007) call attention to two major methods of collecting such data: clinical judgment, referred to as the traditional approach, which is often subjective; and the use of actuarial risk assessment instruments, which are reliable and valid checklist questionnaires yielding summated scores. Actuarial risk assessment instruments provide an objective assessment for predicting clinical outcomes and offending behavior, and consequently are more effective than clinical judgment. Desmarais and Singh (2013) identified 66 valid actuarial risk assessments, of which 19 instruments were relevant for criminal justice settings, and 47 instruments were relevant for specific jurisdictions. These instruments were administered throughout the United States.

THE HISTORY OF RISK ASSESSMENT

Given the emphasis placed on evidence-based practices and the reduction of recidivism among offenders and former offenders, it is not unexpected that empirical evidence has also been applied to assessing offender's risks for

Clinical Interventions in Criminal Justice Settings
ISBN 978-0-12-811381-3
http://dx.doi.org/10.1016/B978-0-12-811381-3.00006-8

reoffending. Standardized instruments, known as actuarial risk assessment instruments, have been demonstrated to be effective in research studies.

Bonta and Andrews (2007) summarize the history of actuarial risk assessment instruments tracing the advancements made in first generation, second generation, third generation, and fourth generation offender risk assessment. In sum, subsequent generations have been supported by empirical evidence.

First Generation Risk Assessment

First generation risk assessments designed to predict offenders' future offending behaviors were conducted based on professional judgment, in which clinical professionals such as psychologists, psychiatrists, and social workers, correctional practitioners such as probation and parole officers, and jail and prison staff utilized their clinical or professional judgment to make decisions regarding offenders (Bonta & Andrews, 2007). Clearly, these risk assessments were problematic given that they were unsystematic and dissimilar based on clinical and professional background. Moreover, some clinical and professional education or training programs may not provide offender risk assessment skills or experience with criminal justice populations. Among educational programs that provide such skills and training relevant for criminal justice populations, these skills may be more related to providing mental health assessments, mental health services, or other types of assessments and services rather than assessments of risk of reoffending.

Second Generation Risk Assessment

Second generation risk assessment shifted in the 1970s from utilizing clinical and professional judgment to the use actuarial risk assessment instruments. These instruments included factors that were empirically associated with offending behavior, such as a prior history of substance abuse, and yielded a summated score. Higher scores denoted higher risk of reoffending, whereas lower scores denoted lower risk. In spite of these advancements, two major limitations were found among these instruments: the instruments were not grounded in theory, and many of the factors assessed, such as criminal history, were static and therefore did not reflect the changing nature of these factors particularly resulting from participating in an intervention. Examples of second generation risk assessment instruments include the Salient Factor Score (Hoffman & Beck, 1974) and the Statistical Information Scale (Bonta & Andrews, 2007; Nuffield, 1982).

Third Generation Risk Assessment

During the late 1970s and early 1980s, third generation risk assessments appeared. These actuarial risk assessment instruments were evidence-based and assessed both static factors such as criminal history, and dynamic (changeable) risk factors such as employment and social relationships. Moreover, these instruments were grounded in theory and assessed both risks and needs. An example of a third generation risk assessment instrument is the Level of Service Inventory–Revised (LSI-R) (Andrews & Bonta, 1995), which is grounded in social learning theory and assesses risks and needs (Bonta & Andrews, 2007).

Fourth Generation Risk Assessment

Fourth generation risk assessment is the most recent form of assessment, and combines an assessment of risk factors with additional factors such as prison institutional factors together with comprehensive intervention. An example is the Level of Service/Case Management Inventory (LS/CMI) (Andrews, Bonta, & Wormith, 2004), which assesses risk factors and comprehensive intervention. Third and fourth generation risk assessment instruments are an outgrowth of the risk–need–responsivitiy (RNR) model (Bonta & Andrews).

THE RISK–NEED–RESPONSIVITY MODEL

A widely used model to assess risks and intervention or treatment levels is the RNR model (Bonta & Andrews, 2007, 2017).

The RNR model was developed in the 1980s, and was "first formalized" in 1990. Since then, the model has been successfully implemented in numerous countries. The RNR model is based on the General Personality and Cognitive Social Learning (GPCSL) theory. Empirical evidence supports the GPCSL theory, which posits that behaviors, including offending behaviors, are learned. Others in the individual's social environment model or reinforce the rewards and costs associated with behaviors.

Bonta and Andrews (2007) assert that the RNR model is an effective model for assessment and intervention with a variety of offenders including sex offenders, females, youth, Aboriginals, those with mental disorders, and offenders living in poverty as well as those without financial problems. Skeem, Steadman, and Manchak (2015) examined the utility of the RNR model among individuals with mental illness and criminal justice system involvement, and found support for the model as a risk assessment tool. Cognitive-behavioral interventions reduced recidivism among this population when compared to those who only participated in psychiatric interventions. While the RNR model accurately predicted recidivism, the three core principles (risk, need, and responsivity) were not empirically supported as an intervention. Chua, Chu, Yim, Chong, and Teoh (2014) describe implementation of the RNR model in the Singapore juvenile justice system, particularly the use of the Youth Level of Service/Case Management Inventory) (YLS/CMI). Despite implementation challenges, the RNR model and YLS/CMI have become an integrated component of the Singapore juvenile justice system.

Three core principles; the risk principle, the need principle, and the responsivity principle; were initially identified together with the RNR model (Bonta & Andrews, 2007), and in 2017, 12 additional principles were articulated, although the three principles remain the core principles of the RNR model. Consequently, in addition to the three core principles, three overarching principles, six additional core principles, and three organizational principles totaling 15 principles were articulated. Here we review the three core principles: (1) risk, (2) need, and (3) responsivity.

Risk Principle

The risk principle maintains that the level of service or level of intervention that is given to offenders or former offenders should match their level of risk as assessed after administering an actuarial risk instrument such as the LSI-R. Such matching is purported to reduce recidivism. In other words, providing more interventions to high risk offenders, moderate interventions to offenders assessed as moderate risk, and few interventions to low risk offenders, will reduce recidivism among the three groups.

Static Risk Factors

Static risk factors are those factors statistically associated with recidivism that do not change or if they do change, such change only occurs in one direction representing either an increase or a decrease. Examples include the age a former offender was first arrested or criminal history (Casey et al., 2014).

Dynamic Risk Factors

Dynamic risk factors (or dynamic predictors) are those factors that are associated with offending behavior, and a change in dynamic risk factors results in a change in subsequent offending behavior. Among dynamic risk factors behavioral change occurs over a period of time lasting from a few weeks to a few years. For instance, behavioral change that results in fewer interactions with acquaintances involved in offending behavior or improved social relationships at home or work (Bonta & Andrews, 2017).

Need Principle

The need principle maintains that interventions should focus on addressing criminogenic needs. Such interventions include evidence-based practice and principles.

Criminogenic Needs

Criminogenic needs are assessed using third- and fourth-generation actuarial risk assessment instruments, and are dynamic risk factors associated with offending behavior. Because dynamic factors are changeable and not static, criminogenic needs should be reduced after an offender participates in an appropriate intervention (Bonta & Andrews, 2007). Bonta and Andrews (2007, 2017) describe criminogenic needs as the "central eight" risk and need factors. These are the factors that should be addressed in interventions in order to reduce recidivism. Criminal history represents the eighth risk/need factor but because it is a static factor and not dynamic, Bonta and Andrews excluded it from the following list:

1. Antisocial personality pattern.
2. Procriminal attitudes.
3. Social supports for crime.
4. Substance abuse.
5. Family and marital relationships.
6. School and work.
7. Prosocial recreational activities.

Non-Criminogenic Needs

Non-criminogenic needs are factors that are considered "minor risk/need factors" and less associated with offending behavior and recidivism (Bonta & Andrews, 2007). Non-criminogenic needs are not a component of the primary the RNR model risk assessment, although comprehensive risk assessments typically may include one or more of these factors in order to provide comprehensive intervention. These factors include:

1. Self-esteem.
2. Personal distress.
3. Major mental illness.
4. Physical health.

Responsivity Principle

The responsivity principle refers to the process of "how" interventions are delivered. Assuming this definition, two approaches outlining how interventions are delivered are general responsivity and specific responsivity.

General Responsivity

General responsivity suggests that structured cognitive social learning interventions are effective for reducing offending behavior irrespective of the type of offense or behavior, and helping offenders to learn new adaptive behaviors and attitudes. Moreover, cognitive social learning interventions should focus on establishing a therapeutic relationship with an offender or former offender that emphasizes such strategies as modeling or social learning to support prosocial behaviors (Bonta & Andrews, 2007, 2017).

Specific Responsivity

Specific responsivity requires modifying cognitive social learning interventions and cognitive–behavioral interventions so that they are culturally relevant or relevant for other offender characteristics such as gender, personality, and cognitive abilities. These characteristics can facilitate or prevent intervention outcomes if not integrated as components of the intervention (Bonta & Andrews, 2007, 2017). Specific responsivity is recommended for offenders with a high level of functioning in many areas. Offenders and former offenders who do not demonstrate these characteristics, or when practitioners are unsure of an offender's level of functioning, the general responsivity approach structured cognitive social learning interventions should be provided (Bonta & Andrews, 2017).

THE RISKS–NEEDS–RESPONSIVITY SIMULATION TOOL

The Center for Advancing Correctional Excellence! (2015) in partnership with the Bureau of Justice Administration, the Substance Abuse and Mental Health Administration, and the Public Welfare Foundation developed the *risk-need-responsivity simulation tool* which is available online at https://www.gmuace.org/research_rnr.html. The tool was created based on the need to help practitioners implement the RNR model. Three user-friendly portals help practitioners to achieve these aims and include: (1) The RNR Program Tool for Adults, (2) Assess an Individual, and (3) Assess Jurisdiction's Capacity.

Among the many examples provided on the website are the RNR program tool feedback report for a reentry program, and the RNR simulation tool individual assessment.

THE DESISTANCE, GOOD LIVES MODEL

Just as the RNR model has been put forward as a model of offender rehabilitation and applicable for a range of offenders, the Good Lives Model (GLM) has been proposed as a model of offender rehabilitation. The GLM was developed to supplement the strength of the RNR model while at the same time strengthening the RNR model by considering offender's goals as part of a strength-based risk assessment. Placing clinical emphasis on offender and former offender's well-being instead of criminogenic needs is theorized to result in effective rehabilitation (Ward & Stewart, 2003). Suggesting that the GLM has been embraced by clinical practitioners, Andrews, Bonta and Wormith (2011) counter that by clinically focusing on criminogenic needs first will subsequently enhance offender and former offender's well-being.

CRIMINAL JUSTICE POPULATIONS AND RISK ASSESSMENT INSTRUMENTS

It is important that actuarial risk assessment instruments yield reliable and valid risk of reoffending information among criminal justice populations. Certainly, given the considerable numbers of racial and ethnic minorities and women involved in the criminal justice system accurately predicting risks of reoffending among these groups is an essential undertaking.

Numerous differences have been found between male and female offending patterns; women commit fewer violent offenses, have better treatment outcomes to correctional programs than men, are more likely to be mothers of young children, are more likely to have histories of sexual and physical abuse, and have higher conviction rates for offenses related to drugs and alcohol, and property offense offenses. Therefore, gender responsive interventions are necessary to address the social problems of drug and alcohol use, mental disorders, and poverty (Covington, 2001). It stands to reason that such differences may affect risk assessment.

The LSI-R, one of the primary risk assessment instruments associated with the RNR model, has been the focus of considerable research examining its reliability and validity among female and racial and ethnic minority populations (Coulson, Ilacqua, Nutbrown, Giulekas, & Cudjoe, 1996; Holsinger, Lowenkamp, & Latessa, 2003; Holtfreter & Cupp, 2007; Smith, Cullen, & Latessa, 2009). The LSI-R was also the focus of a case example presented in Chapter 2, exploring its implementation among minority female former offenders receiving interventions from a social service agency. Though research studies have focused on prediction, recidivism, and establishing reliability and validity, Ferguson, Ogloff, and Thomson (2009) argued that risk assessment and making predicting recidivism and reoffending behavior are but one essential use of the LSI-R. Another use of the LSI-R to determine intervention and community supervision needs among offenders.

Gender differences should be considered when conducting correctional assessments since females should be assessed for less restrictive criminal justice settings, and participate in gender responsive interventions that focus on criminogenic needs relevant for women (Rettinger & Andrews, 2010). The LSI-R reliably predicts recidivism among both males and females convicted of serious violent offenses (Manchak, Skeem, Douglas, & Siranosian, 2009). Agreeing that recidivism rates can be decreased by addressing criminogenic needs, Ferguson et al. (2009) suggested that interventions be adapted to the needs of individual offenders.

Observing the research investigating the validity of the LSI-R is obtained from studies utilizing predominantly Caucasian samples, Schlager and Simourd (2007) examined the psychometric properties among African-American and Hispanic male offenders. They found that reliability and validity data were similar between African-American and Hispanic study participants, although the differences in the LSI-R scores between the two groups were not statistically significant. Also, African-American males reported higher LSI-R scores than found in prior research studies. Although their sample was too small to identify racial differences, Folsom and Atkinson (2007) found among a Canadian sample of 100 female offenders that were incarcerated for 2 years or more, that while the LSI-R scores varied from the scores found another studies, the LSI-R was a reliable predictor of recidivism particularly the subscale items that assessed criminal behavior.

The LSI-R has also been examined in terms of its utility among offenders with mental disorders. Ferguson et al. (2009) assessed the validity of the Level of Service Inventory–Revised: Screening Version (LSI-R: SV) among a sample of mentally ill offenders in Australia and found that it was a reliable predictor of recidivism among the sample, but did not reliably predict recidivism for those experiencing a dual diagnosis.

Additional criminal justice populations for which actuarial risk assessment instruments have been developed and or tested include violent offenders (Quinsey, Harris, Rice, & Cormier, 1998) and sex offenders (Barbaree, Seto, Langton, & Peacock, 2001).

RISK ASSESSMENT IN THE JUVENILE JUSTICE SYSTEM

In addition to administering actuarial risk assessment instruments to adults to assess future offending behavior, these instruments are also administered to juveniles in juvenile justice settings to assess future juvenile delinquency behavior and supervision and intervention needs among youth. Asserting that the use of actuarial risk assessment instruments among youth to predict future juvenile delinquency began in the juvenile justice system in the 1970s, Baird et al. (2013) described the results obtained from seven sites that evaluated six actuarial risk assessment instruments.

Baird et al. (2013) identified the following instruments including also identifying the practitioners who administered the instrument as well as its purpose: (1) the Positive Achievement Change Tool was administered by probation officers to assess supervision and service levels; (2) the Comprehensive Risk/Needs assessment was administered by probation officers and commitment services specialists to assess supervision levels, and decisions regarding commitment and placement; (3) the YLS/CMI was administered by juvenile justice service evaluation coordinators to assess supervision levels and decisions regarding commitment; and probation officers to assess supervision levels and case planning efforts; (4) the Juvenile Crime Prevention assessment was administered by probation officers, and detention and prevention workers with the purpose of case planning and service supervision; (5) the gender specific risk assessment, which is part of the Juvenile Assessment and Intervention System, was administered by probation officers with the purpose of assessing supervision levels; and finally (6) the Youth Assessment and Screening Instrument (YASI) was administered by probation officers and institutional staff to assess case planning needs, supervision levels, and the amount of contacts with probation. Results show that while these instruments effectively assessed risks among youth, some instruments performed better than others.

A meta-analysis conducted to examine the predictive validity of actuarial risk assessment instruments employed in the juvenile justice system and the characteristics of these instruments comprised 28 instruments found in 28 studies. The total sample size was comprised of 53,405 youth. Results showed good predictive validity among the instruments, although third generation instruments demonstrated higher predictive validity than second generation instruments (Schwalbe, 2007).

Case Example

In real world criminal justice and community based social service settings, the implementation and administration of actuarial risk assessment instruments can present numerous challenges. Some of these challenges center on obtaining staff buy-in regarding the purpose of the instrument, its theoretical underpinnings, and implications for assessment and intervention. To facilitate learning and discussion around the challenges associated with the use of these instruments in real world settings, students enrolled in an MSW graduate social work course elective titled *Evidence-Based Practices in the Criminal Justice System*, completed a class assignment that examined the implementation of actuarial risk assessment instruments, and evidence-based practices and principles in their educational field placements (Patterson & Sullivan, 2012).

These second year graduate students addressed the following questions: (1) "does your agency use actuarial risk assessment instruments?", (2) "are the instruments reliable and valid?", and (3) "identify the staff who administer the instruments." One student intern described the use of the New York State (NYS) COMPAS-Probation risk and needs assessment system in a social service agency providing services to juvenile justice involved youth. The NYS COMPAS-Probation is used by each of the 57 NYS probation departments except those located in New York City. The instrument also follows the three core principles of the RNR model (Lansing, 2012).

The assignment results revealed that the reliability and validity of the NYS COMPAS-Probation was unknown by the student intern since it was not discussed in the agency. The instrument was administered by each staff member who provided services to a client. Since the instrument was computer scored, it was relatively easy for staff to ask questions when responses were computerized. Scores were not interpreted nor used for risk classification or interventions consistent with the RNR model. It was discovered that only low scores or low risk offenders' scores were submitted to the courts.

It was also discovered that staff did not realize the significance of the use of the instrument. Staff did not "like" the instrument; they did not perceive the questions as relevant for youth and often disagreed with the risk assessment scores. As mentioned in Chapter 5, some standardized instruments assess risk, while others classify and screen. These varied uses of standardized instruments are greatly dependent upon the criminal justice setting and purpose for which they are used. It is unknown how the court system responded to receiving risk assessments from low risk youth only, or how the courts used the scores in decision-making. It appears that while the social service agency obtained risk scores consistent with the RNR model, these scores were not interpreted to provide interventions.

Casey et al. (2014) suggested several guidelines for the implementation of actuarial risk assessment instruments; staff should be knowledgeable about use of the instrument, trained and skilled to administer the instrument, and receive administrative oversight to administer the instrument appropriately and reliably.

RISK ASSESSMENT IN CRIMINAL JUSTICE SETTINGS

Consistent with a theme presented throughout the book, evidence-based practices are relevant for specific components of the criminal justice system. Likewise, assessing offender and former offenders' risks for reoffending, and the use of actuarial risk assessment instruments are relevant for specific components of the criminal justice system. Risk assessments and subsequent interventions should be relevant for a specific criminal justice setting or component. For instance, while the LSI-R can be administered to assess high risk and low risk offenders, thereby suggesting more interventions or fewer interventions, the LSI-R can also be used to classify supervision and intervention needs relevant for prison, probation, and halfway house settings (Andrews & Bonta, 1995).

Among the four components of the criminal justice system, actuarial risk assessment instruments are less likely to be implemented in the legislative and law enforcement components, and more likely to be implemented in the courts and correction components. Therefore, the latter are examined in detail.

Legislation

As previously discussed, the legislative component can authorize the implementation of evidence-based practices. Similarly, the implementation and use of actuarial risk assessment instruments can be legislated.

The NYS Division of Criminal Justice Services (DCJS), Office of Probation and Correctional Alternatives has made available a practitioner guide for probation officers and community corrections practitioners. The purpose of the guide is to describe the New York Correctional Offender Management Profiling for Alternative Sanctions (NYCOMPAS) risk and needs assessment instrument, and the NYS legislation that supports it use. Use of the NYCOMPAS is consistent with implementing evidence-based practices, and the RNR model given its attention to criminogenic needs among other factors (New York State Division of Criminal Justice Services, Office of Probation and Correctional Alternatives, 2015).

DCJS' Probation State Aid Block Grant rule, 9 New York Codes, Rules and Regulations (NYCRR) Part 345 mandates that NYS probation departments administer empirically valid risk and needs instruments to both youth and adults. In addition, 9 NYCRR Part 341 mandates that empirically valid risk and needs instruments be used to assess supervision levels for individuals placed on probation. The levels range from minimal level supervision or low risk, to high supervision level or high risk. A Supervision Recommendation Matrix is described, which guides the use of scoring and risk assessment.

While legislation can mandate the use of actuarial risk assessment instruments to assess risk needs, legislation or court rulings can prohibit the use of such instruments. Reporting on the significance of cultural and ethnic diversity for clinical intervention as well as the need for valid and reliable assessment instruments that consider these factors, Shepard and Lewis-Fernandez (2016) describe a Canadian federal court ruling against the use of five actuarial risk assessment instruments with Canadian Aboriginal prisoners.

Courts

As the previous example has shown, support for the use of actuarial risk assessment instruments can be legislated and backed by court rulings. Similar to the use of such instruments to assess risk and needs among probationers, other uses of actuarial risk assessment instruments include court sentencing decisions.

Due to the assortment of sentencing functions such as rehabilitation, retribution, deterrence, and restitution, among others, the use of actuarial risk assessment instruments is multifaceted when compared to other criminal justice system components (Casey, Warren, & Elek, 2011). Consequently, Casey et al. proposed nine guiding principles to assist judges with effectively implementing risk assessment instruments and using the results to inform sentencing decisions. The guiding principles include the following:

1. Focus on public safety and risk management purpose.
2. Willingness to be placed on probation.
3. Effective probation conditions and responding to probation violations.

4. Stakeholder training.
5. Use of offender assessments.
6. Evidence-based infrastructure.
7. Risk and need assessment instruments.
8. Assessment reporting.
9. Monitoring and evaluation.

In their publication *Offender risk & needs assessment instruments: A primer for courts*, Casey et al. (2014) discuss numerous pertinent topics for judges implementing actuarial risk assessment instruments and using results during the sentencing phase. Included among these topics is the importance of using these instruments, examples showing differences among the various instruments, instrument descriptions, and selecting and implementing appropriate instruments. Notably, the authors describe six frequently administered instruments:

1. Correctional Assessment and Intervention System (CAIS)
2. Correctional Offender Management Profile for Alternative Sanctions (COMPAS)
3. The Level of Service Inventory-Revised (LSI-R) and Level of Service/ Case Management Inventory (LS/CMI)
4. Offender Screening Tool (OST)
5. Ohio Risk Assessment System (ORAS)
6. Static Risk and Offender Needs Guide (STRONG)

Corrections

Previous examples in this chapter have discussed how probation departments administer empirically valid risk and needs instruments to both youth and adults to assess supervision levels. Probation is subcomponent of the corrections component within the criminal justice system.

Parole is also a subcomponent of the corrections component within the criminal justice system. Parole boards are increasingly relying on the use of actuarial instruments as the basis for their release and other decisions (Ostermann, 2011). The U.S. Board of Parole has used a salient factor score, an actuarial instrument, to assess parolee risks and make parole decisions (Hoffman & Beck, 1974). Osterman examined the validity of the LSI-R for predicting recidivism among a sample of 450 parolees and found at the LSI-R was a valid predictor of recidivism in terms of rearrests, re-convictions, and parole violations. The LSI-R was a valid predictor of recidivism following a period of long-term incarceration of 10 years or more (Manchak, Skeem, & Douglas, 2008).

Indeed, in prisons risk assessment instrument have been used to assess the risk for violence among prisoners (Cunningham & Sorensen, 2006). The National Governors Association (2005) recommends that risk assessment instruments be used in prisons to assess high-risk prisoners, provide evidenced-based practices for substance abuse and mental disorders, and improve reentry.

SAMPLE RISK ASSESSMENT INSTRUMENTS

The Level of Service Inventory–Revised

The LSI-R is a quantitative survey of offender attributes and their situations relevant to level of supervision and treatment decisions. Designed for ages 16 and older, the LSI-R helps predict parole outcome, success in correctional halfway houses, institutional misconducts, and recidivism. The 54 items are based on legal requirements and include relevant factors needed for making decisions about risk and treatment by measuring scales specific to criminal history, education/employment, financial, family/marital, accommodation, leisure/recreation, companions, alcohol/drugs problems, emotional/personal, and attitudes/orientation.

The Youth Assessment and Screening Instrument

In 2000, New York State began implementation of a new assessment tool for juvenile probation, the YASI. Through the efforts of the New York State Division of Probation and Correctional Alternatives, the implementation of YASI has now extended to 54 counties across the State of New York. The YASI is a comprehensive risk, need, and protective factor assessment instrument designed for use in juvenile probation and other high-risk youth service settings. The instrument is based on an assessment model first developed for juveniles in the State of Washington where it is used in all 33 juvenile courts in that state. The Washington tool was selected by NYSDPCA to serve as a model for risk, needs, and strengths assessment in juvenile probation in New York State. The model was selected for adaptation with both juvenile delinquents and persons in need of supervision (Orbis Partners, 2007).

Juvenile probation services are an enormous operational component of the juvenile justice system. Probation services are provided at all stages of juvenile justice processing and to a diverse range of youth and their families. A major component of this role involves the work of assessing and screening youth as they are referred for services (Office of Juvenile Justice and Delinquency Prevention, 1996).

The YASI instrument has two assessment components: a pre-screen to identify risk, and a full assessment to identify risk, criminogenic need areas, and protective factors (New York State Division of Probation and Correctional Alternatives, 2007).

Global Appraisal of Individual Needs

The Global Appraisal of Individual Needs (GAIN) is a standard biopsychosocial instrument designed to integrate the assessment for both clinical (e.g., diagnosis to APA's DSM 5, placement to ASAM's PPC-2, treatment planning to JCAHO, and program planning to CARF) and program evaluation (needs assessment, clustering, fidelity, outcomes, and benefit-cost) purposes. The GAIN family of instruments is appropriate for use with adolescents, young adults, and adults from a variety of populations in various levels of care, including outpatient/intensive outpatient programs; short-term/long-term residential programs; therapeutic communities; justice programs; and drug courts (Chestnut Health Systems, 2017).

Child and Adolescent Functional Assessment Scale

Designed for youth aged 5 to 19 years, the Child and Adolescent Functional Assessment Scale (CAFAS) is the gold standard instrument for assessing a youth's day-to-day functioning and for tracking changes in functioning over time. The CAFAS is backed by over 20 years of research supporting its validity and sensitivity to detecting change in behaviors. It is widely used to inform decisions about type and intensity of treatment, level of care, placement, and need for referral. The CAFAS assesses functioning across eight critical life subscales assessing the youth as well as two scales to assess caregiver functioning. The CAFAS yields both a total score and 10 individual subscales scores. The total score represents the total level of dysfunction and can be used to recommend intensity of treatment required. The individual subscale scores can be used to inform the focus of treatment and to monitor change in behavior over time (MHS, 2017).

SUMMARY

The current use of fourth generation actuarial risk assessment instruments that integrate offender risk assessments together with comprehensive intervention represents a significant advancement over using clinical judgment. Selecting an appropriate instrument is dependent upon many factors such as the criminal justice population characteristics, criminal justice or social service setting, theoretical relevance, and reliability and validity. It is worth emphasizing that changing the items contained in any instrument by omitting, deleting, or otherwise significantly changing the meaning may compromise the reliability and validity or scoring of the instrument. It may also compromise the subsequent intervention levels based on risk scores. This also means compromised intervention and supervision levels. Therefore, any modifications should be made with caution, and always considering the developers' recommendations.

REFERENCES

Andrews, D. A., & Bonta, J. (1995). *The level of service inventory - revised user's manual*. Toronto: Multi-Health Systems.

Andrews, D. A., Bonta, J., & Wormith, J. S. (2004). *The level of service/case management inventory*. Toronto: Multi-Health Systems.

Andrews, D. A., Bonta, J., & Wormith, J. S. (2011). The risk-need-responsivity (RNR) model: Does adding the good lives model contribute to effective crime prevention? *Criminal Justice and Behavior, 38*(7), 735–755.

Baird, C., Healy, T., Johnson, K., Bogie, A., Dankert, E. W., & Scharenbroch, C. (2013). *A comparison of risk assessment instruments in juvenile justice*. Madison, WI: National Council on Crime and Delinquency.

Barbaree, H. E., Seto, M. C., Langton, C. M., & Peacock, E. J. (2001). Evaluating the predictive accuracy of six risk assessment instruments for adult sex offenders. *Criminal Justice and Behavior, 28*(4), 490–521.

Bonta, J., & Andrews, D. A. (2007). Risk-need-responsivity model for offender assessment and rehabilitation. *Rehabilitation, 6*(1), 1–22.

Bonta, J., & Andrews, D. A. (2017). *The psychology of criminal conduct* (6th ed.). New York: Routledge.

Casey, P. M., Elek, J. K., Warren, R. K., Cheesman, F., Kleiman, M., & Ostrom, B. (2014). *Offender risk & needs assessment instruments: A primer for courts*. Retrieved from http://www.ncsc.org/~/media/microsites/files/csi/bja%20rna%20final%20report_combined%20files%208-22-14.ashx.

Casey, P. M., Warren, R. K., & Elek, J. K. (2011). *Using offender risk and needs assessment information at sentencing: Guidance for courts from a national working group*. Retrieved from http://www.ncsc.org/~/media/Microsites/Files/CSI/RNA%20Guide%20Final.ashx.

Center for Advancing Correctional Excellence!. (2015). *Risk-need-responsivity (RNR) simulation tool*. Retrieved from https://www.gmuace.org/research_rnr.html.

Chestnut Health Systems. (2017). *The Global Appraisal of Individual Needs (GAIN) progressive approach to assessment*. Retrieved from http://gaincc.org/about/.

Chua, J. R., Chu, C. M., Yim, G., Chong, D., & Teoh, J. (2014). Implementation of the risk-need-responsivity framework across the juvenile justice agencies in Singapore. *Psychiatry, Psychology and Law, 21*(6), 877–889.

Coulson, G., Ilacqua, G., Nutbrown, V., Giulekas, D., & Cudjoe, F. (1996). Predictive utility of the LSI for incarcerated female offenders. *Criminal Justice and Behavior, 23*(3), 427–439.

Covington, S. (2001). Creating gender-responsive programs: The next step for women's services. *Corrections Today, 63*(1), 85–87.

Cunningham, M. D., & Sorensen, J. R. (2006). Actuarial models for assessing prison violence risk: Revisions and extensions of the risk assessment scale for prison (RASP). *Assessment, 13*(3), 253–265.

Desmarais, S., & Singh, J. (2013). *Risk assessment instruments validated and implemented in correctional settings in the United States*. Retrieved from https://aupa.wrlc.org/bitstream/handle/11204/4006/Risk%20Assessment%20Instruments%20Validated%20and%20Implemented%20in%20Correctional%20Settings%20in%20the%20United%20States.pdf?sequence=3.

Ferguson, A. M., Ogloff, J. R., & Thomson, L. (2009). Predicting recidivism by mentally disordered offenders using the LSI-R: SV. *Criminal Justice and Behavior, 36*(1), 5–20.

Folsom, J., & Atkinson, J. L. (2007). The generalizability of the LSI-R and the CAT to the prediction of recidivism in female offenders. *Criminal Justice and Behavior, 34*(8), 1044–1056.

Hoffman, P. B., & Beck, J. L. (1974). Parole decision-making: A salient factor score. *Journal of Criminal Justice, 2*(3), 195–206.

Holsinger, A. M., Lowenkamp, C. T., & Latessa, E. J. (2003). Ethnicity, gender, and the level of service inventory-revised. *Journal of Criminal Justice, 31*(4), 309–320.

Holtfreter, K., & Cupp, R. (2007). Gender and risk assessment: The empirical status of the LSI-R for women. *Journal of Contemporary Criminal Justice, 23*(4), 363–382.

Lansing, S. (2012). *New York State COMPAS-Probation risk and need assessment study: Examining the recidivism scale's effectiveness and predictive accuracy*. New York: Division of Criminal Justice Services, Office of Justice Research and Performance.

Manchak, S. M., Skeem, J. L., & Douglas, K. S. (2008). Utility of the revised level of service inventory (LSI-R) in predicting recidivism after long-term incarceration. *Law and Human Behavior, 32*(6), 477–488.

Manchak, S. M., Skeem, J. L., Douglas, K. S., & Siranosian, M. (2009). Does gender moderate the predictive utility of the Level of Service Inventory - Revised (LSI-R) for serious violent offenders? *Criminal Justice and Behavior, 36*(5), 425–442.

Multi-Health Systems, Inc.. (2017). *2017 catalog*. North Tonawanda, NY: Author.

National Governors Association. (2005). *Improving prisoner reentry through strategic policy innovation*. Retrieved from https://www.nga.org/files/live/sites/NGA/files/pdf/0509PRISONER-REENTRY.PDF.

New York State Division of Criminal Justice Services, Office of Probation, Correctional Alternatives. (2015). *New York State correctional offender management profiling for alternative sanctions (NYCOMPAS) risk and needs assessment instrument: Practitioner guidance for probation and community corrections agencies*. Retrieved from https://apps.criminaljustice.ny.gov/opca/pdfs/2015-5-NYCOMPAS-Guidance-August-4-2015.pdf.

New York State Division of Probation and Correctional Alternatives. (2007). *Youth assessment and screening instrument*. Retrieved from http://ccf.ny.gov/files/5813/8074/7416/YASIDescription.pdf.

Nuffield, J. (1982). *Parole decision-making in Canada: Research towards decision guidelines*. Ottawa: Solicitor General of Canada.

Office of Juvenile Justice and Delinquency Prevention, U.S. Department of Justice. (1996). *State responses to serious and violent juvenile crime*. Washington, DC: Author.

Orbis Partners. (2007). *Long-term validation of the Youth Assessment and Screening Instrument (YASI) in New York state juvenile probation*. Ottawa, Ontario. Retrieved from http://criminaljustice.state.ny.us/opca/pdfs/nyltyasifullreport20feb08.pdf.

Ostermann, M. (2011). Parole? Nope, not for me: Voluntarily maxing out of prison. *Crime & Delinquency, 57*(5), 686–708.

Patterson, G. T., & Sullivan, K. (Spring/Summer 2012). *From the field: A class project examining evidence-based practices and principles in the criminal justice system*. Section Connection - NASW Social Work & the Courts Newsletter, 5–6.

Quinsey, V. L., Harris, G. T., Rice, M. E., & Cormier, C. A. (1998). *Violent offenders: Appraising and managing risk*. Washington, DC: American Psychological Association.

Rettinger, L. J., & Andrews, D. A. (2010). General risk and need, gender specificity, and the recidivism of female offenders. *Criminal Justice and Behavior, 37*(1), 29–46.

Sackett, D. L., Rosenberg, W. M., Gray, J. A., Haynes, R. B., & Richardson, W. S. (1996). Evidenced based medicine: What it is and what it isn't. *Bmj: British Medical Journal, 312*, 71–72.

Schlager, M. D., & Simourd, D. J. (2007). Validity of the Level of Service Inventory—Revised (LSI-R) among African American and Hispanic male offenders. *Criminal Justice and Behavior, 34*(4), 545–554.

Schwalbe, C. S. (2007). Risk assessment for juvenile justice: A meta-analysis. *Law and Human Behavior, 31*(5), 449.

Shepard, S. M., & Lewis-Fernandez, R. (2016). Forensic assessment and cultural diversity: Contemporary challenges and future directions. *Psychology, Public Policy, and Law, 22*(4), 427–438.

Skeem, J. L., Steadman, H. J., & Manchak, S. M. (2015). Applicability of the Risk-Need-Responsivity model to persons with mental illness involved in the criminal justice system. *Psychiatric Services, 66*(9), 916–922.

Smith, P., Cullen, F. T., & Latessa, E. J. (2009). Can 14,737 women be wrong? A meta-analysis of the LSI-R and recidivism for female offenders. *Criminology & Public Policy, 8*(1), 183–208.

Ward, T., & Stewart, C. (2003). Criminogenic needs and human needs: A theoretical model. *Psychology, Crime & Law, 9*(2), 125–143.

FURTHER READING

Dowden, C., & Andrews, D. A. (2004). The importance of staff practice in delivering effective correctional treatment: A meta-analytic review of core correctional practice. *International Journal of Offender Therapy and Comparative Criminology, 48*(2), 203–214.

Fazel, S., Singh, J. P., Doll, H., & Grann, M. (2012). Use of risk assessment instruments to predict violence and antisocial behaviour in 73 samples involving 24,827 people: Systematic review and meta-analysis. *British Medical Journal, 345*, e4692.

Hanson, R. K., & Morton-Bourgon, K. E. (2009). The accuracy of recidivism risk assessments for sexual offenders: A meta-analysis of 118 prediction studies. *Psychological Assessment, 21*(1), 1–21.

Looman, J. (2006). Comparison of two risk assessment instruments for sexual offenders. *Sexual Abuse: a Journal of Research and Treatment, 18*(2), 193–206.

Rice, M. E., Harris, G. T., & Lang, C. (2013). Validation of and revision to the VRAG and SORAG: The Violence Risk Appraisal Guide - revised (VRAG-R). *Psychological Assessment, 25*(3), 951.

CHAPTER 7

Evidence-Based Practices for Juveniles in the Juvenile Justice System

Warren K. Graham

THE SCOPE OF THE PROBLEM

Many individuals who come into contact with law enforcement and the criminal or juvenile justice systems have a mental and/or substance use disorder. Studies have found that for youth in the juvenile justice system, 50%–70% met criteria for a mental disorder, and 60% met criteria for a substance use disorder. Of those youth with co-occurring mental and substance use issues, almost 30% experienced severe disorders that impaired their ability to function (SAMHSA, 2017).

With those involved in the system at a significantly higher rate for experiencing mental health issues, interventions need to be clinically sound to address underlying issues in order to moderate issues of risk, public safety, and mitigate recidivism. Not only is attending to issues of clinical significance of vital importance, addressing institutional barriers to functioning is as well. For most juveniles, that means intensive clinical work on the family system, with interventions speaking to strengthening the family unit, while simultaneously addressing topics of clinical significance like trauma, abuse, and neglect.

THE JUVENILE JUSTICE SYSTEM

Youth involved in the criminal justice system are involved/processed in a separate system known as the juvenile justice system. Within this system, there exists juvenile probation officers, juvenile detention centers, and separate categories of criminal behavior such as status offenses and juvenile delinquency. By definition, the standard juvenile age range is considered 12–17 years (US DOJ, 2017). In 2010, the U.S. Census Bureau estimated that 74,181,500 persons in the United States were under the age of 18; the age group commonly referred to as juveniles. The juvenile population reached a low point

Clinical Interventions in Criminal Justice Settings
ISBN 978-0-12-811381-3
http://dx.doi.org/10.1016/B978-0-12-811381-3.00007-X

in 1984, at 62.5 million, then grew each year through 2010, increasing 19% (Sickmund & Puzzanchera, 2014). The age of the youth is one of many important factors for selecting the type of evidence-based practice to use.

Since the inception of the juvenile justice system, juvenile justice philosophies have cycled between restorative and punitive approaches depending on the public and government officials' beliefs about juvenile crime rates and juvenile offenders (Howell & Lipsey, 2004). Note that this has resulted in the implementation of many different policies and programs such as boot camps, "Scared Straight" programs, and detention and residential centers during punitive times and various treatment programs during rehabilitative times (McKee & Rap, 2014).

JUVENILE DETENTION EFFORTS

The utilization of an evidence-based practice (EBP) is contingent on the appropriateness of models for various milieus, as professionals must now differentiate between a model better suited for inpatient versus outpatient practice, young versus old, and multiple layered considerations. Based on the needs at the point of engagement, various models may be better suited for residential settings like juvenile detention centers and prisons, or outpatient systems like probation, parole, and court-based programs. Detention remains a critical point of inquiry within the juvenile justice system. It is a consequential decision point in juvenile justice because of the impact it has on later decisions; youth who are detained are likely to experience harsher consequences at later points in the system (Rodriguez & Eells, 2013).

For example, Moral Reconation Therapy (MRT) is a peer-supported EBP shown to be highly effective when facilitated in various settings including with a prison population or outpatient setting. That same model effective with criminal and juvenile justice populations is not appropriate for certain transient settings. In juvenile detention centers, where the length of stay is minimal, the inability to work with a consistent population prevents the MRT practitioner the opportunity to engage adolescents. So as heralded as this approach may be, generally speaking, it is not the best model for the entire population it was designed for.

In a 2000 study of 16,770 youth from Florida, length of stay and treatment efficacy were examined. For institutionalized juveniles, only two measures were strong positive predictors of effect size; integrity of treatment implementation and total weeks of treatment, both of substantive significance to policymakers and juvenile justice professionals when considering the varied effects of practical intervals of lengths of stay in juvenile justice facilities (Winokur, Cass, & Blankenship, 2002). In this same study, it is youth identified as a moderate risk to public safety and requiring close supervision that are placed in secure detention facilities. Among the residential facilities, mean lengths of stay ranged from a low of a little more than 3 months for low-risk programs, to a high of 19 months for maximum-risk, juvenile facilities.

Vermont's Woodside Juvenile Detention Center, while not a treatment program, offers some services including crisis counseling/intervention, psychological evaluations, and education. According to Woodside's Description of Programs, their Detention Program is a temporary placement with a maximum stay of 60 days. In a 2003 study, youth admitted for being at-risk had the longest average stay; 23.2 days, while those admitted for procedural reasons, such as a psychological evaluation or to wait for space at another facility, had the shortest average stay; 3.6 days (Bellas & Clements, 2004).

A detention center is designed to be a short-term facility and houses youths until final dispositions of their cases. Based upon the dispositions made, the youths are returned to their communities, placed on probation, or referred to agencies that provide longer-term care. For example, the average length of stay at a center is approximately 14 days (Nassau County, 2017). The Nassau County Juvenile Detention facility has staff trained in MRT, and are ready and available to administer the intervention, yet length of stay is a determinant for effective implementation with not having youth institutionalized for the average length of time that MRT requires for successful completion.

Understanding that interventions that engage the family are more effective, it may be cost-prohibitive to secure funds for training staff, and contrary to the need for secure detention, to administer.

The Juvenile Detention Center Statistics reported through June 30, 2011 for Ramsey County and Saint Paul Public School, Minnesota yielded an average stay of 6.9 days (Juvenile Detention Center Statistics, 2011).

Staff described different types of barriers to implementing each EBP. For motivational interviewing, the majority of barriers involved staff resistance or organizational setting. For adolescent community reinforcement approach (A-CRA), the majority of barriers involved specific characteristics of the EBP or client resistance. For cognitive behavioral therapy (CBT), the majority of barriers were associated with client resistance, and for assertive community treatment, the majority of barriers were associated with resources. EBP designers, policymakers who support EBP dissemination, and funders should include explicit strategies to address such barriers (Amodeo, 2011).

JUVENILE SUBSTANCE ABUSE

For youths in the United States aged 12–17, over 1.7 million persons (7% of this population) met DSM-IV criteria for an alcohol or illicit drug disorder in 2009 (SAMHSA, 2010a, 2010b), yet many adolescents who need substance abuse treatment never receive it (SAMHSA, 2010b). Only 27% percent of facilities offered programming for adolescents (National Survey of Substance Abuse Treatment Services (N-SSATS), 2016). Considering that higher levels of involvement with substance use increase the rate of offending, the severity of the committed offense, and the duration of antisocial behavior (Young, Dembo, & Henderson, 2007), this begs the questions of why those with an identified problem influencing functioning are denied the opportunity to receive care.

The largest referral source for adolescents to substance use treatment in the United States is the juvenile justice system. Alcohol and drug use is illegal, and some youth have legal issues because they use or sell alcohol or drugs, yet many adolescents also become involved in the juvenile justice system because of poor decisions they make under the influence of alcohol or drugs (Chestnut Health Systems, 2017). At this point of entry, it is important to adequately and thoroughly screen and assess juveniles to develop comprehensive treatment aimed at ameliorating patterns of usage, developing coping mechanisms, and educating them about better life choices.

In October 2006, approximately 2658 facilities in the United States held 92,093 juvenile offenders on the day of the census. The number of facilities declined since 2000, when 3061 facilities housed 110,284 juvenile offenders (Read & O'Cummings, 2010). Even with statistics over a decade old, we can see the trend of increased need and decreased ability to service. According to the Office of National Drug Control Policy, only 4 in 10 offenders needing treatment reported receiving treatment services while incarcerated. Among those who do receive treatment, the quality of those services varies from state to state (SAMHSA, 2017). Evidence-based practices and promising practices need to be systematically uniform in order to address the growing national problem facing this vulnerable population, and models mainstreamed to allow access to these services while institutionalized.

The 2014 National Report of Juvenile Offenders and Victims, compiled by the National Center for Juvenile Justice and Office of Juvenile Justice and Delinquency Prevention (2014), states, "the juvenile justice system must react to the law-violating behaviors of youth in a manner that not only protects the community and holds youth accountable but also enhances youth's ability to live productively and responsibly in the community. The system must also intervene in the lives of abused and neglected children who lack safe and nurturing environments (pp. iii)."

Picard-Fritsche and Kralstein (2012) identified that a growing body of research suggests that substance abuse interventions for adolescents must be uniquely tailored to their needs in order to be effective (Belenko & Logan, 1998; Marlowe, 2010; Muck et al., 2001; SAMSHA 1999). More specifically, the evaluation literature has found that some interventions designed for adults are less successful with adolescents (Alford, Koehler, & Leonard, 1991; Melnick, De Leon, Hawke, Jainchill, & Kressel, 1997). In particular, adolescents respond well to CBT and multi-system interventions, such as family therapy models like Functional Family Therapy (FFT) and Multisystemic Therapy (MST). Both CBT and family therapy models of intervention have been shown to yield positive impacts on an array of adolescent behavioral outcomes, including substance use, educational outcomes, future criminality, and family relationships (Azrin, Donohue, Besalel, Kogan, & Acierno, 1994; Borduin, 1999; Henggeler et al., 1991, 2006). In addition to the use of evidence-based treatment modalities, components of the adult drug court model, such as intensive judicial monitoring and certain non-detention sanctions for noncompliance, have been independently found effective with juvenile offenders (Marlowe, 2010).

It is important to note that while we between adult and juvenile models of clinical intervention, structures that support these practices, like the drug court model, can operate in similar fashion without minimizing the fidelity of the actual treatment delivered, but add layers of successful intervention already shown to be effective in correcting maladaptive behavior.

While the aforementioned evidence-based models are more widely known, other types of lesser-known evidence-based models for adolescent service delivery like "psychosocial rehabilitation-type" services delivered consumer to consumer, are also viable. These peer-led models are promising and cost-effective.

JUVENILE JUSTICE OUTCOMES

Chapter 4 provided an overview of common outcomes in the criminal justice system. Some of the same outcomes are desirable in the juvenile justice system, although additional outcomes include truancy and school performance.

Developing policy and practices based on best available scientific evidence is the most efficient way to demonstrate taxpayer dollars have been spent on programs producing significant reductions in juvenile delinquency and recidivism. With that being said, juvenile justice organizations throughout the country have felt increasing pressure to use evidence-based practices within their programs and services (McKee & Rap, 2014). One million American adolescents are processed by juvenile courts each year, and approximately 160,000 are referred to residential placements. Therefore, it is imperative that "what works" and "what doesn't work" in reducing criminal behavior is identified (Henggeler & Schoenwald, 2011).

There are significant theoretical frameworks that outline the underpinnings of a life course perspective that speak to the necessity of treating juveniles differently than adults as it relates to crime and delinquency. According to Hutchison (2014), "the life course perspective recognizes the importance of timing of lives not just in terms of chronological age, but also in terms of biological age, psychological age, social age, and spiritual age. The life course perspective recognizes the linkages between early life experiences and later experiences in adulthood (pp. 2)" As referenced in Hutchison (2014, pp.14), this perspective "is stage-like because it proposes that each person experiences a number of transitions, or changes in roles and statuses that represent a distinct departure from prior roles and statuses (Elder & Kirkpatrick, Johnson, 2003; Hagestad, 2003; Hseret al., 2007)." Each transition has the propensity of bringing with it negative experiences that may introduce issues relating to adjustment and lack of appropriate coping strategies.

This is an especially important consideration since the cognitive, emotional, and physiological changes affecting juveniles at this life stage will help shape their adult life. Recent studies report that adolescent brain development continues through the age of 26 (National Institutes of Health, 2016), well into the years previously thought to be early adulthood. The inability to cope with the multiple transitions and events for juveniles is key to understanding juvenile crime, delinquency, and its practice implications.

In a meta-analysis that examined the characteristics of effective interventions for juvenile offenders, Lipsey (2009) found that among 361 research studies an intervention approach that was therapeutic, providing interventions to high-risk juvenile offenders, and better intervention implementation. The analysis included "very few model programs or even named programs of any generally recognized sort" (p. 145). Lipsey concluded that most interventions provided to youth in real world settings "are not name brand model programs" (p. 145), but are more similar to those found among the retrieved studies included in the analysis.

SCARED STRAIGHT PROGRAMS

Programs such as "Scared Straight" involve organized visits to prison facilities by juvenile delinquents or at-risk youth to deter them from delinquency (Petrosino, Turpin-Petrosino, & Buehler, 2003). In their article, "Scared Straight and Other Juvenile Awareness Programs for Preventing Juvenile Delinquency," Petrosino et al. describe similar prison exposure programs used in several other nations. It is called the "day in prison" or "day in gaol" in Australia (O'Malley, Coventry, & Walters, 1993), "day visits" in the United Kingdom (Lloyd 1995), and the "Ullersmo Project" in Norway (Storvall & Hovland, 1998). Hall (1999) reported positively on a program in Germany designed to scare straight young offenders with ties to neo-Nazi and other organized hate groups. The program has been also implemented in Canada (O'Malley et al., 1993). In a different variation in the United Kingdom, a program was initiated that employed ex-prison guards to re-create a prison atmosphere in public schools, with the goal of deterring any potential lawbreakers (Middleton, Lilford, & Hyde, 2001; Petrosino et al., 2003).

The presentations usually depicted life in adult prisons and often included exaggerated stories of rape and murder (Finckenauer, 1982). The premise is to expose these youths to the reality of incarceration without glorifying criminal behavior popularized in the media and among peer groups. Being able to experience being in a secure, with dangerous felons, was intended to discourage juveniles from continuing offending behaviors and reduce further involvement in the juvenile justice system, by the use of fear. In recent years, these programs have been shown to be not only ineffective at preventing delinquency, but promoting negative behavior and even "increasing crime between 1% and 28% when compared to a no-treatment control group" (Petrosino et al., 2003, p.44). Despite several research studies and reviews questioning their effectiveness, they remain in use and have now been implemented in at least six nations (Petrosino et al., 2003).

BOOT CAMPS

Used for decades for juveniles, the intention of boot camps is to shock juveniles into complying and exhibiting more prosocial behaviors (Jeter, 2010). Boot camp programs are short-term residential programs modeled after military basic training facilities (MacKenzie, 2006) and were first introduced in the 1980s. They became increasingly popular as a correctional sanction, and were widely adopted and implemented throughout the United States (Meade & Steiner, 2010). Juvenile participants are typically assigned to platoons and housed in military style barracks. They are exposed to rigorous daily routines that emphasize discipline, physical labor, exercise, and drills that are supervised by program staff who function as drill instructors and are often addressed by military titles (MacKenzie & Armstrong, 2004). Understanding the need for clinical interventions above and beyond behavioral modification, some programs also incorporate rehabilitative elements such as substance abuse or group counseling, and aftercare (MacKenzie & Rosay, 2004).

In 2000, 27 boot camps and 22 traditional facilities were examined in a national study of juvenile correctional facilities, which found that boot camp environments were more structured and most incorporated military basic training components (Gover, MacKenzie, & Styve, 2000). In addition, evidence has suggested that juvenile offenders found boot camps to be safer and more therapeutic than traditional facilities (Steiner & Giacomazzi, 2007). Unfortunately though, this method of rehabilitation is not based on empirical evidence nor supported by research (Jeter, 2010) and a survey of the literature shows boot camps are considerably less effective than the public believes (Tyler, Darville, & Stalnaker, 2001). Boot camps, by themselves, typically do not have an effect on participants' odds of recidivism. Boot camps do seem to improve individuals' attitudes and other behaviors within programs. Boot camps also appear to reduce the number of confinement beds jurisdictions require, often resulting in cost savings (Meade & Steiner, 2010).

Also, as it relates to implementation, there exists considerable variation between programs in terms of the emphasis, availability, and quality of programming which is the antithesis of implementation science (MacKenzie & Rosay, 2004), as discussed in Chapter 10. This model of intervention, although widely popular, operates in a manner inconsistent with the literature that suggests keeping juveniles in their environment and building resources in their support system/network is the most effective, as is the case with other evidence based models such as FFT, MST, and Strengthening Families.

MULTIDIMENSIONAL TREATMENT FOSTER CARE

The Oregon Multidimensional Treatment Foster Care (MTFC) model was originally developed for adolescents with severe and chronic problems with delinquency, and interventions are implemented using multiple methods (e.g., family and individual therapy, skills training, and academic supports) in a number of key settings (Chamberlain, 2003). The model was designed in the 1980s to address serious and violent juvenile offenders who would otherwise need to be placed in a group or residential program (Green et al., 2014; SAMHSA, 2011).

As a program for intensive parenting, family, support, and skill building, MTFC is a proactive approach to creating and maintaining a consistent and reinforcing environment for the participating youth (Chamberlain & Fisher, 2000). In a randomized evaluation of this model in 2007, MTFC was found to be an empirically validated intervention for child welfare and juvenile justice populations, with demonstrated efficacy in reducing arrest rates in delinquent boys and girls (Leve & Chamberlain, 2007).

Because of its high success rate, MTFC has become a model of interest internationally, also being implemented and evaluated in Sweden and Britain (Green et al., 2014; Hansson & Olsson, 2012).

MORAL RECONATION THERAPY

MRT is a systematic treatment strategy that seeks to decrease recidivism among juvenile offenders by increasing moral reasoning. Developed in 1985 by Gregory Little, Ed.D., and Kenneth Robinson, Ed.D., this model was initially developed as the CBT component in a prison-based therapeutic community, and more than 120 published reports have documented that MRT-treated offenders show significantly lower recidivism for periods as long as 20 years after treatment (Correctional Counseling, 2017). This intervention can be facilitated in community-based organizations while under supervision in the community, schools, jails, and prisons, so it has multiple applications, and use is not predicated on a specific type of setting (Little & Robinson, 1997).

Based on the developer's website, "MRT is a cognitive-behavioral counseling program that combines education, group and individual counseling, and structured exercises designed to foster moral development in treatment-resistant clients. Clients must be confronted with the consequences of their behavior and the effect that it has had on their family, friends and community. MRT addresses beliefs and reasoning and is a systematic, step-by-step group counseling treatment approach for treatment-resistant clients. The program is designed to alter how clients think and make judgments about what is right and wrong. MRT research has shown that as clients complete steps moral reasoning increases in juvenile offenders" (Correctional Counseling, 2017).

MRT systematically focuses on seven basic treatment issues, which guide practice:

1. confrontation of beliefs, attitudes and behaviors;
2. assessment of current relationships;
3. reinforcement of positive behavior and habits;
4. positive identity formation;
5. enhancement of self-concept;
6. decrease in hedonism and development of frustration tolerance; and
7. development of higher stages of moral reasoning (Correctional Counseling, 2017).

This is done by utilizing a step method consisting of 12 individual steps, all designed to elicit certain behavioral responses and foster critical thinking and self-awareness. The steps are progressive, and peers must achieve consensus in order for individual members to move from one step to the next. Detailed in the MRT Facilitator's Handbook (Little & Robinson, 2009), the steps include:

1. honesty;
2. trust;
3. acceptance;
4. awareness;
5. healing relationships;
6. helping others;
7. goal setting and identity formation;
8. consistency between short and long term goals;
9. never give up;
10. maintaining positive change;
11. backsliding and firm commitments; and
12. setting appropriate goals.
13. steps 13 through 16 are optional and focus on moral refinements.

The importance of peer-led support groups which often target a mutually significant recovery experience has been emphasized by consumers (Stout & Hayes, 2005), and has been shown to deliver compassionate and empathetic services. Peer-led models of support have been in use for many years since the introduction of Alcoholics Anonymous.

As clients move through the program and address group content specific to the topics and stages, peers must develop consensus to decide whether a peer graduates to the next stage based on their presentation, thoughtfulness, sincerity, and moral reasoning. If a transgression is identified, clients can step down to one or more previous stages until they can successfully navigate the program and resume upward mobility. One of the reasons for the success is the level of accountability to the group and ones' community using a systems perspective to guide behavioral intervention.

FUNCTIONAL FAMILY THERAPY

As a family-systems approach that focuses on the functions that problems serve within the family and for individual family members, the assumption is that the child's problem behaviors are a means of meeting some interpersonal needs and functions among family members (Alexander & Parsons, 1982). FFT is an integrated family system and cognitive behavioral intervention model that has been shown to be efficacious with drug-using and/or delinquent youth. The FFT model changes adolescent substance use by replacing maladaptive behaviors with new and more adaptive behaviors that serve to maintain family members' relational functions. Interventions are implemented in a phase-based manner, from engagement in treatment and building alliances to more sophisticated motivation and behavior change strategies (Waldron, Brody, Robbins, & Alexander, 2013).

In addition to behavioral-based interventions, cognitive interventions are incorporated into FFT. Cognitive interventions focus on altering attributions, attitudes, expectations, and emotions within the family. Families work with a therapist to improve communication skills, increase reciprocity and positive reinforcement among family members, clarify behaviors that are desired between family members, and negotiate and generate solutions to interpersonal problems (Mulford & Redding, 2008).

As a dynamic model of engagement, FFT is best utilized in a community-based setting to facilitate ease of attendance and participation of family members. Settings restricted due to safety and risk considerations may prove to be more challenging in implementing this model due to the nature of interaction from family necessary, and referral to pro-social community activities to strengthen newly acquired behavior change approaches.

ADOLESCENT COMMUNITY REINFORCEMENT APPROACH

A-CRA is a behavioral treatment that is among the most effective and most cost-effective substance use treatments for adolescents (Dennis et al., 2004). As an intervention, it is an operant behavioral approach that attempts to make an alcohol- and drug-free lifestyle more rewarding than continued use (Godley et al., 2001). A-CRA is an adaptation of the Community Reinforcement Approach (CRA), a behavioral treatment for adults that uses "community" (i.e., familial, social, recreational, occupational) reinforcers to support change in an individual's substance using behaviors (Hunt & Azrin, 1973; Meyers & Smith, 1995). CRA in general has a strong evidence base for its effectiveness (Meyers, Smith, Serna, & Belon, 2013; Smith, Crotwell, Simmons, & Meyers, 2015). A-CRA has been found effective in randomized clinical trials (Dennis et al., 2004; Godley, Godley, Dennis, Funk, & Passetti, 2007; Godley & Godley, 2013; Henderson et al., 2016; Slesnick, Prestopnik, Meyers, & Glassman, 2007).

A-CRA consists of a total of 17 A-CRA procedures; however, clinicians are trained to deliver procedures based on individual needs, so some clients may receive certain procedures multiple times (e.g., problem-solving or communication skills) and may never receive other procedures (e.g., medication adherence and monitoring; Garner, Hunter, Funk, Griffin, & Godley, 2016). Receiving 10 or more unique procedures during a treatment episode has been found to maximize client outcomes (Garner et al., 2009).

Findings showed that participation in A-CRA treatment predicted significant decreases in future substance use, which in turn, led to significant reductions in illegal activity and juvenile justice involvement (Chestnut Health Systems, 2017).

MULTISYSTEMIC THERAPY

MST is an intensive family- and community-based treatment that has proven effectiveness for substance-abusing juvenile offenders, in addition to a range of other serious clinical problems that place youth at risk for out-of-home placement (e.g., chronic and violent criminal behavior, sexual offending, and psychiatric emergencies). The empirical evidence for MST has led numerous federal entities to recognize it as one of the most extensively validated evidence-based psychosocial treatments for youth antisocial behavior, including substance abuse (Sheidow & Houston, 2013).

It is a highly individualized family- and community-based therapeutic approach that views behavior as the end product of the interactions between individuals and their interconnected systems (family, school, peer group, and community). Treatment plans, developed in collaboration with the family, integrate family, school, community, peer, and individual level interventions (Henggeler, Melton, & Smith, 1992).

STRENGTHENING FAMILIES

The Strengthening Families Program (SFP) (Molgaard, Spoth, & Redmond, 2000) is another more universal strategy, designed to prevent substance use and antisocial behavior, which targets the general population of 10- to 14-year-old children and their parents (Mulford & Redding, 2008). The program's 7-week curriculum includes parent-only sessions, child-only sessions, and family sessions. Four booster sessions are provided at between 3 months and 1 year following completion of the curriculum. The child sessions address issues such as handling stress, emotions and peer pressure; the development of social problem-solving skills; and the development and strengthening of prosocial goals and activities. Parent sessions address parental expectations, effective discipline practices, the setting and communicating of rules, and effective parent–child communication (Mulford & Redding, 2008).

"During family sessions, parents and youth practice listening and communicating with respect, identify family strengths and family values, learn how to use family meetings to teach responsibility and solve problems, and learn how to plan enjoyable family activities" (Molgaard et al., 2000, pp. 3). An important element of the model is community-building among parents and juveniles alike, and for that reason, evening meetings to accommodate working parents and include family-style meals, allowing parents to take part in their "process." There is precedent for mealtime interventions with various other populations to support best practices (Nevins, Weddle, & Luis, 1996; Wen, Jooyoung, & Thomas, 2014).

PROBLEM-SOLVING SKILLS TRAINING

During the past three decades, considerable progress has been made in the development, implementation, and evaluation of psychosocial treatments focused on alleviation of risk factors of delinquency, reduction of juvenile crime, and prevention of recidivism.

Youth-focused treatments such as anger control training and problem-solving skills training (PSST) have demonstrated efficacy for reducing relatively mild forms of antisocial behavior and improving a child's psychosocial functioning (Sukhodolsky & Ruchkin, 2006). PSST addresses cognitive processes, such as perception and decision-making, which are involved in social interaction. For example, hostile attribution bias or inability to generate alternative solutions may contribute to aggressive behavior. Participants of PSST are taught to analyze interpersonal conflicts, to develop nonaggressive solutions, and to think about the consequences of their actions in problematic situations. The efficacy of PSST has been demonstrated in several controlled studies (Hudley & Graham, 1993; Camp, Blom, & Hebert, 1977).

The juvenile justice system is often the only source of mental health services for many youths who have serious emotional and behavioral disturbances (Burns, Costello, & Angold, 1995). High rates of psychiatric disorders and substance abuse in juvenile offenders require that these problems also be addressed in treatments provided through juvenile justice services. Opportunities for delivery of mental health services including psychotherapy and counseling are available during mandated residential treatment, during aftercare, or as part of services alternative to incarceration (Sukhodolsky & Ruchkin, 2006).

Based on the review of empirical support for PSST, this treatment modality has been recommended as one of the likely efficacious treatments for child conduct problems (Chambless & Ollendick, 2001; Eyberg, Boggs, & Algina, 1995).

DISPROPORTIONATE MINORITY CONTENT

As referenced in the "Impact Evaluation of Three Strategies Created to Reduce Disproportionate Minority Contact and the Detention Population" submitted to the Office of Juvenile Justice and Delinquency Prevention by Dr. Nancy Rodriguez and Dr. Elizabeth Fells (2013), studies continue to find that race and ethnicity play a significant role in juvenile court outcomes. The study's findings outline general themes that:

1. race and ethnicity directly and indirectly influences court outcomes (through gender, age, and community context);
2. racial/ethnic biases are more common in front-end court processes like referral and detention than adjudication and disposition;

3. racial/ethnic disparities accumulate as youth are processed further into the system; and
4. we know much more about the effect of race than ethnicity in juvenile court outcomes (Engen, Steen, & Bridges, 2002; Leiber & Johnson, 2008).

In light of this empirical evidence, the Office of Juvenile Justice and Delinquency Prevention (OJJDP) has been instrumental in efforts to reduce disproportionate minority contact (DMC). According to OJJDP, reduction in DMC can only come with comprehensive assessments that include five important phases: Identification, Assessment/Diagnosis, Intervention, Evaluation, and Monitoring of the problem (Rodriguez & Eells, 2013). This is an especially important consideration for program developers to ensure their clinical methods of intervention are culturally appropriate, and that their initial engagement strategies that predicate assessment are culturally sound.

Evidence-based practices must be scrutinized to ensure their viability in communities of color so as not to create structural barriers to implementation, and to afford all juvenile offender populations the opportunity for rehabilitation with a clinical tool designed for inclusivity. As an example, A-CRA has been evaluated as such, and found effective with a variety of populations of adolescent substance users, including ethnically and regionally diverse samples (Godley, Hedges, & Hunter, 2011).

SUMMARY

Implementation of evidence-based practices in juvenile justice shares the challenges of transporting treatments from research settings into real-world contexts and adds its own unique practical considerations. Although a plethora of treatment manuals, clinical resources, and therapy guides are commercially available, the principles of effective implementation of these resources in juvenile justice are not well examined (Sukhodolsky & Ruchkin, 2006). The clinical exercise of evaluating practices must be significantly and well thought out, in real world applications to ensure implementation considering all the nuances and confounding variables present in everyday life.

To summarize interventions for juvenile justice, the consensus of the research is to include parents and peer groups in treatment modalities. Parent training is consistently highlighted as one of the most effective means of preventing delinquency and treating young children with conduct problems, and it has proven to be one of the most cost-effective interventions for doing so (Mulford & Redding, 2008). During adolescence, the influence of the peer group is considerably stronger than familial connections (Hutchison, 2014), necessitating the utilization of those networks to facilitate clinical intervention. Model programs including FFT, MST, and SFP have been highlighted to provide examples of promising programs that include parent-training components with adolescents (Mulford & Redding, 2008). The theoretical frameworks supporting parent training to address delinquency are based on a social development approach that integrates social control and social learning theories (Hawkins & Weis, 1985). The model is based on the idea that youths who are attached to pro-social peers, parents, and others are less likely to engage in delinquent acts (Mulford & Redding, 2008).

Moving away from systems-based interventions, there are available treatments that narrowly focus often on the child alone. They do not address the multi-dimensional and changing nature of the problems faced by these youths (Borduin, 1994), and they often are not delivered in the natural environment where the youth lives (Mulford & Redding, 2008). This should be considered more of a consequence of the concern for risk and safety mandating removal from the home or custodialization, than a function of inadequate clinical services available. As will be discussed in Chapter 10, there is a difference between implementing evidence-based practices in a private practice setting, human service agency, or criminal justice setting. Each has its own challenges due to physical setting or agency limitations, structural barriers, and fiscal considerations.

With summaries of evidence-based models being readily available, effective implementation is best served by not just understanding the intervention itself, but the system within which the model will be disseminated. Understanding the limitations, scope of special programmatic boundaries, and depth of resources is integral for an intervention to be successful. That success can be skewed by extraneous factors outside of the evidence-based model itself, but related to facilitation, fidelity, and maintenance. Reviewing an agency's or organization's ability to support an evidence-based or promising practice is paramount before moving forward to identifying a model, especially when considering fiscal considerations. An under-discussed concern with agencies adopting these methods of intervention has to do with staff retention efforts. Staff turnover is a significant issue with social services and the delivery of consistent, professional services. It may be subject to market considerations, yet affects ability to implement intervention strategies. There is no mechanism to account for staff that receive training in a community-based organizational setting, then leave that organization with an upgraded skill-set and newer employment prospects. Administratively, organization personnel need to evaluate staff satisfaction to determine the viability of service delivery using valid and tested means.

REFERENCES

Abuse, S. (2016). *National Survey of Substance Abuse Treatment Services (N-SSATS): 2009 (Data on substance abuse treatment facilities.* DASIS Series: S-39, DHHS Publication No. SMA 07-4296).

Alexander, J. F., & Parsons, B. V. (1982). *Functional family therapy: Principles and procedures.* Carmel, CA: Brooks & Cole.

Alford, G. S., Koehler, R. A., & Leonard, J. (1991). Alcoholics Anonymous - Narcotics Anonymous model inpatient treatment of chemically dependent adolescents: A 2-year outcome study. *Journal of Studies on Alcohol, 52,* 118–126.

Amodeo. (2011). Barriers to implementing evidence-based practices in addiction treatment programs: Comparing staff reports on motivational interviewing, adolescent community reinforcement approach, assertive community treatment, and cognitive-behavioral therapy. *Center for Addictions Research and Services, Boston University, 34*(4), 382–389.

Azrin, N. H., Donohue, B., Besalel, V. A., Kogan, E. S., & Acierno, R. (1994). Youth drug abuse treatment: A controlled outcome study. *Journal of Child & Adolescent Substance Abuse, 3*(3), 1–16.

Belenko, S., & Logan, T. K. (1998). Delivering more effective treatment to adolescents: Improving the juvenile drug court model. *Journal of Substance Abuse Treatment, 25,* 189–211.

Bellas, M. L., & Clements, W. H. (2004). *Determinants of length of stay at woodside juvenile detention center.* VA: Vermont Center for Justice Research. Retrieved from http://www.jrsa.org/pubs/juv-justice/reports/vermont-juvenile-detention.pdf.

Borduin, C. M. (1994). Innovative models of treatment and service delivery in the juvenile justice system. *Journal of Clinical Child Psychology.*

Borduin, C. M. (1999). Multisystemic treatment of criminality and violence in adolescents. *Journal of the Academy of Child and Adolescent Psychiatry, 38,* 242–249.

Burns, B. J., Costello, E. J., & Angold, A. (1995). Children's mental health service use across service sectors. *Health Affinity (Millwood), 14*(3), 147–159.

Camp, B. W., Blom, G. E., & Hebert, F. (1977). "Think aloud": A program for developing self- control in young aggressive boys. *Journal of Abnormal Child Psychology, 5*(2), 157–169.

Chamberlain, P. (2003). The Oregon multidimensional treatment foster care model: Features, outcomes, and progress in dissemination. *Cognitive and Behavioral Practice, 10,* 303–312.

Chamberlain, P., & Fisher, P. A. (2000). Multidimensional treatment foster care: A program for intensive parenting, family, support, and skill building. *Journal of Emotional and Behavioral Disorders, 8*(3), 155–164.

Chambless, D. L., & Ollendick, T. H. (2001). Empirically supported psychological interventions: Controversies and evidence. *Annual Review of Psychology, 52,* 685–716.

Chestnut Health Systems. (2017). *ACRA.* Retrieved from http://ebtx.chestnut.org/Treatments-and-Research/Juvenile-Justice.

Dennis, M., Godley, S. H., Diamond, G., Tims, F. M., Babor, T., Donaldson, J., et al. (2004). The cannabis youth treatment (CYT) study, 1016 the cannabis youth treatment (CYT) Study: Main findings from two randomized trials. *Journal of Substance Abuse Treatment, 27*, 197–213. http://dx.doi.org/10.1016/j.jsat.2003.09.005.

Engen, R. L., Steen, S., & Bridges, G. S. (2002). Racial disparities in the punishment of youth: A theoretical and empirical assessment of the literature. *Social Problems, 49*(2), 194–220.

Eyberg, S. M., Boggs, S. R., & Algina, J. (1995). Parent-child interaction therapy: A psychosocial model for the treatment of young children with conduct problem behavior and their families. *Psychopharmacology Bulletin, 31*(1), 83–91.

Finckenauer, J. O. (1982). *Scared straight and the panacea phenomenon*. Englewood Cliffs, NJ: Prentice Hall.

Garner, B. R., Godley, S. H., Funk, R. R., Dennis, M. L., Smith, J. E., & Godley, M. D. (2009). Exposure to Adolescent Community Reinforcement Approach treatment procedures as a mediator of the relationship between adolescent substance abuse treatment retention and outcome. *Journal of Substance Abuse Treatment, 36*, 252–264. http://dx.doi.org/10.1016/j.jsat.2008.06.007.

Godley, M. D., Godley, S. H., Dennis, M. L., Funk, R. R., & Passetti, L. L. (2007). The effect of assertive continuing care on continuing care linkage, adherence and abstinence following residential treatment for adolescents with substance use disorders. *Addiction, 102*, 81–93. http://dx.doi.org/10.1111/j.1360-0443.2006.01648.x.

Godley, S. H., & Godley, M. D. (2013). Behavioral treatments for adolescents with substance use disorders. *Interventions for Addiction: Comprehensive Addictive Behaviors and Disorders, 3*.

Garner, B. R., Hunter, S. B., Funk, R. R., Griffin, B. A., & Godley, S. H. (2016). Toward evidence-based measures of implementation: Examining the relationship between implementation outcomes and client outcomes. *Journal of Substance Abuse Treatment, 67*, 15–21.

Godley, S. H., Hedges, K., & Hunter, B. (2011). Gender and racial differences in treatment process and outcome among participants in the adolescent community reinforcement approach. *Psychology of Addictive Behaviors, 25*(1), 143.

Godley, S. H., Meyers, R. J., Smith, J. E., Karvinen, T., Titus, J. C., & Godley, M. D. (2001). *The adolescent community reinforcement approach for adolescent cannabis users, cannabis youth treatment (CYT) series* (Vol. 4). Silver Spring, MD: Substance Abuse and Mental Health Services Administration.

Gover, A. R., MacKenzie, D. L., & Styve, G. J. (2000). Boot camps and traditional correctional facilities for juveniles: A comparison of the participants, daily activities, and environments. *Journal of Criminal Justice*, 53–68.

Green, J. M., Biehal, N., Roberts, C., Dixon, J., Kay, C., Parry, E., et al. (2014). Multidimensional treatment foster care for adolescents in english care: Randomized trial and observational cohort evaluation. *British Journal of Psychiatry, 204*, 214–221.

Hall, A. (October 26, 1999). Jailhouse shock aims to scare youths straight. *The Scotsman*, 12.

Hansson, K., & Olsson, M. (2012). Effects of multidimensional treatment foster care (MTFC): Results from a RCT study in Sweden. *Children and Youth Services Review, 34*(9), 1929–1936.

Hawkins, J. D., & Weis, J. G. (1985). The social development model: An integrated approach to delinquency prevention. *The Journal of Primary Prevention, 6*(2), 73–97.

Henderson, C. E., Wevodau, A. L., Henderson, S. E., Colbourn, S. L., Gharagozloo, L., North, L. W., et al. (2016). An independent replication of the adolescent-community reinforcement approach with justice-involved youth. *American Journal on Addictions, 25*, 233–240. http://dx.doi.org/10.1111/ajad.12366.

Henggeler, S. W., Borduin, C. M., Melton, G. B., Mann, B. J., Smith, L. A., Hall, J. A., et al. (1991). Effects of multisystemic therapy on drug use and abuse in serious juvenile offenders: A progress report from tow outcome studies. *Family Dynamics of Addiction Quarterly, 1*, 40–51.

Henggeler, S. W., Halliday-Boykins, C. A., Cunningham, P. B., Randall, J., Shapiro, S. B., & Chapman, J. E. (2006). Juvenile drug Court: Enhancing outcomes by integrating evidence- based treatments. *Journal of Consulting and Clinical Psychology, 74*(1), 42–54.

Henggeler, S. W., Melton, G. B., & Smith, L. A. (1992). Family preservation using multisystemic therapy: an effective alternative to incarcerating serious juvenile offenders. *Journal of Consulting and Clinical Psychology, 60*(6), 953.

Henggeler, S. W., & Schoenwald, S. K. (2011). *Evidence-based interventions for juvenile offenders and juvenile justice policies that support them*. Social Policy Report. Volume 25, Number 1. Society for Research in Child Development.

Howell, J. C., & Lipsey, M. W. (2004). A practical approach to evaluating and improving juvenile justice programs. *Juvenile and Family Court Journal, 55*(1), 35–48.

Hudley, C., & Graham, S. (1993). An attributional intervention to reduce peer-directed aggression among African-American boys. *Child Development, 64*(1), 124–138.

Hunt, G. M., & Azrin, N. H. (1973). A community-reinforcement approach to alcoholism. *Behaviour Research and Therapy, 11*, 91–104. http://dx.doi.org/10.1016/0005-7967(73)90072-7.

Hutchison, E. D. (2014). *Dimensions of human behavior: The changing life course* (5th ed.). Thousand Oaks: Sage Publications.

Jeter, L.V. (2010). Conduct disorders: Are boot camps effective? *Reclaiming Children and Youth, 19*(2), 32–36.

Juvenile Detention Center Statistics. (2011). Retrieved from http://ramseyjdai.org/pdf/statistics-reports/qtr-2-2011.pdf.

Leiber, M. J., & Johnson, J. D. (2008). Being young and black: What are their effects on juvenile justice decision making? *Crime & Delinquency, 54*(4), 560–581.

Leve, L. D., & Chamberlain, P. (2007). A randomized evaluation of multidimensional treatment foster care: Effects on school attendance and homework completion in juvenile justice girls. *Research on Social Work Practice, 17*(6), 657–663.

Lipsey, M. W. (2009). The primary factors that characterize effective interventions with juvenile offenders: A meta-analytic overview. *Victims and Offenders, 4*(2), 124–147.

Little, G. L., & Robinson, K. D. (1997). *Juvenile MRT: How to escape your prison*. TN: Eagle Wing Books.

Little, G. L., & Robinson, K. D. (2009). *MRT: Moral reconation therapy facilitator's handbook*. TN: Eagle Wing Books.

MacKenzie, D. L. (2006). *What works in Corrections: Reducing the criminal activities of offenders and delinquents*. New York, NY: Cambridge University Press.

MacKenzie, D. L., & Armstrong, G. S. (Eds.). (2004). *Correctional boot camps: Military basic training or a model for corrections* (pp. 16–25). Thousand Oaks, CA: Sage Publications, Inc.

MacKenzie, D. L., & Rosay, A. B. (2004). Correctional boot camps for juveniles. In D. L. MacKenzie, & G. S. Armstrong (Eds.), *Correctional boot camps: Military basic training or a model for corrections?* (pp. 26–45). Thousand Oaks, CA: Sage Publications, Inc.

Marlowe, D. B. (2010). *Research update on juvenile drug treatment courts*. Washington, DC: National Association of Drug Court Professionals.

McKee, E. C., & Rapp, L. (2014). The current status of evidence-based practice in juvenile justice. *Journal of Evidence-Based Social Work, 11*(4), 308–317.

Meade, B., & Steiner, B. (2010). The total effects of boot camps that house juveniles: A systematic review of the evidence. *Journal of Criminal Justice, 38*(5), 841–853.

Melnick, G., De Leon, G., Hawke, J., Jainchill, N., & Kressel, D. (1997). Motivation and readiness for therapeutic community treatment among adolescents and adult substance abusers. *The American Journal of Drug and Alcohol Abuse, 23*(4), 485–506.

Meyers, R. J., & Smith, J. E. (1995). *Clinical guide to alcohol treatment: The community reinforcement approach*. New York, NY: Guilford Press.

Meyers, R. J., Smith, J. E., Serna, B., & Belon, K. E. (2013). Community reinforcement approaches: CRA and CRAFT. In P. Miller (Ed.). P. Miller (Ed.), *Interventions for addiction: Comprehensive addictive behaviors and disorders:* (*Vol. 3*). San Diego, CA: Academic Press.

Middleton, J., Lilford, R., & Hyde, C. (2001). Applying Campbell Principles. Letter to the editor. *British Medical Journal, 323*, 1252.

Molgaard, V. K., Spoth, R. L., & Redmond, C. (2000). *Competency training—the strengthening families program: For parents and youth 10–14.* Juvenile Justice Bulletin (NCJ-182208). Washington, DC: U.S. Dept. of Justice, Office of Juvenile Justice & Delinquency Prevention.

Muck, R., Zempolich, K. A., Titus, J. C., Fishman, M., Godley, M., & Schwebel, R. (2001). An overview of the effectiveness of adolescent substance abuse treatment models. *Youth and Society, 33*, 133.

Mulford, C., & Redding, R. (2008). Training the parents of juvenile Offenders: State of the art and recommendations for service delivery. *Journal of Child and Family Studies, 17*(5), 629–648.

Nassau County Government. (2017). *Juvenile detention center statistics.* Retrieved from https://www.nassaucountyny.gov/3437/Juvenile-Detention-Center.

National Center for Juvenile Justice (2014).

National Institutes of Health. (2016). *The teen brain: 6 things to know.* NIH Publication No. OM 16–4307. Retrieved from https://www.nimh.nih.gov/health/publications/the-teen-brain-6-things-to-know/om-16-4307_153233.pdf.

Nevins, A., Weddle, D. O., & Luis, M. (1996). Alzheimer's disease - mealtime interventions. *The Gerontologist, 36*(5), 718.

O'Malley, P., Coventry, G., & Walters, R. (1993). Victoria's "Day in Prison Program": an evaluation and critique. *Australian & New Zealand Journal of Criminology, 26*(2), 171–183.

Petrosino, A., Turpin-Petrosino, C., & Buehler, J. (2003). Scared Straight and other juvenile awareness programs for preventing juvenile delinquency: A systematic review of the randomized experimental evidence. *The Annals of the American Academy of Political and Social Science, 589*(1), 41–62.

Picard-Fritsche, S., & Kralstein, D. (2012). *The nassau juvenile treatment court: Program outcomes and impact evaluation.* Center for Court Innovation.

Read, N., & O'Cummings, M. (2010). *Fact Sheet: Juvenile Justice Facilities.* Washington, DC: National Evaluation and Technical Assistance Center for the Education of Children and Youth Who Are Neglected. Delinquent, or At Risk (NDTAC). Online at http://www.neglected-delinquent.org/nd/docs/factSheet_facilities.pdf.

Rodriguez, N., & Eells, E. (2013). An impact evaluation of three strategies created to Reduce Disproportionate minority contact and the detention population. *Office of Juvenile Justice and Delinquency Prevention*, 47.

SAMHSA. (2010a). National Survey on Drug Use and Health, 2009 [Data file]. *Inter-university Consortium for Political and Social Research [Distributor].*

SAMHSA. (2010b). *Results from the 2009 National Survey on Drug Use and Health: Volume I. Summary of National Findings*, 10–4586. Office of Applied Statistics; Rockville, MD. NSDUH Series H-38A, HHS Publication No. SMA.

SAMHSA. (2017). *Criminal and juvenile justice.* Retrieved from https://www.samhsa.gov/criminal-juvenile-justice.

Sheidow, A. J., & Houston, J. L. (2013). Multisystemic therapy for adolescent substance use. *Interventions for Addiction: Comprehensive Addictive Behaviors and Disorders, 3.*

Sickmund, M., & Puzzanchera, C. (2014). *Juvenile offenders and victims: 2014 national report.*

Storvall, A. E., & Hovland, A. (1998). The Ullersmo Project: Scared Straight in Norway 1992–1996 [Ullersmoprosjecktet: "Scared Straight" I Norge 1992–1996]. *Nordisk Tiddskrift for Kriminalvidenskab, 85*(2), 122–135.

Slesnick, N., Prestopnik, J. L., Meyers, R. J., & Glassman, M. (2007). Treatment outcome for street-living, homeless youth. *Addictive Behaviors, 32*, 1237–1251. http://dx.doi.org/10.1016/j.addbeh.2006.08.010.

Smith, J. E., Crotwell, S. M., Simmons, J. D., & Meyers, R. J. (2015). CRA and CRAFT: Behavioral treatments for both motivated and unmotivated substance abusing individuals. In N. el-Guebaly, G. Carra, & M. Galanter (Eds.), *Textbook of addiction treatment: International perspectives* (pp. 941–959). Berlin, Germany: Springer. http://dx.doi.org/10.1007/978-88-470-5322-9_110.

Steiner, B., & Giacomazzi, A. L. (2007). Juvenile waiver, boot camp, and recidivism in a Northwestern state. *The Prison Journal, 87*(2), 227–240.

Stout, C. E., & Hayes, R. A. (2005). *The evidence based practice: Methods, models, and tools for mental health professionals*. New Jersey: Wiley.

Substance Abuse and Mental Health Services Administration. (2011). *Evidence based and promising practices: Interventions for disruptive behavior disorders*. U.S. Department of Health and Human Services.

Substance Abuse and Mental Health Services Administration (SAMSHA). (1999). *Treatment of adolescents with substance use disorders.* Treatment Improvement Protocol (TIP) Series, no. 32 Rockville, MD: SAMSHA. Available at http://www.ncbi.nlm.nih.gov/books/NBK64350/.

Sukhodolsky, D. G., & Ruchkin, V. (2006). Evidence-based psychosocial treatments in the juvenile justice system. *Child Adolescent Psychiatric Clinical North America, 15*, 501–516.

Tyler, J., Darville, R., & Stalnaker, K. (2001). Juvenile boot camps: A descriptive analysis of program diversity and effectiveness. *The Social Science Journal, 38*(3), 445–460.

US Department of Justice. (2017). *Criminal resource manual. Definition of juvenile*. Retrieved from https://www.justice.gov/usam/criminal-resource-manual-38-juvenile-defined.

Waldron, H. B., Brody, J. L., Robbins, M. S., & Alexander, J. F. (2013). Functional family therapy for adolescent substance use disorders. *Interventions for Addiction: Comprehensive Addictive Behaviors and Disorders, 3*.

Wen, L., Jooyoung, C., & Thomas, S. A. (2014). Interventions on mealtime difficulties in older adults with dementia: A systematic review. *International Journal of Nursing Studies, 51*(1), 14–27.

Winokur, K. P., Cass, E., & Blankenship, J. (2002). *Juvenile recidivism and length of stay*. FL: Justice Research Center. Retrieved from https://www.ncjrs.gov/pdffiles1/Digitization/202932NCJRS.pdf.

Young, D. W., Dembo, R., & Henderson, C. E. (2007). A national survey of substance abuse treatment for juvenile offenders. *Journal of Substance Abuse Treatment, 32*(3), 255–266.

FURTHER READING

Crawford, G. (April 2013). To be young, criminalized, and black: How the black church matters for young, black men in the 21st century. *Journal of Race, Ethnicity, and Religion, Vol. 4*(3).

Dennis, M. L., Funk, R., Godley, S. H., Godley, M. D., & Waldron, H. (2004). Cross-validation of the alcohol and cannabis use measures in the Global Appraisal of Individual Needs (GAIN) and Timeline Followback (TLFB; Form 90) among adolescents in substance abuse treatment. *Addiction, 99*(Suppl. 2), 120–128. http://dx.doi.org/10.1111/j.1360-0443.2004.00859.x.

Merriam-Webster. (October 12, 2016). *Definition of juvenile*. retrieved from http://www.merriam-webster.com/dictionary/juvenile.

Office of the United States Attorneys. (2016). *Criminal resource manual*. Retrieved from https://www.justice.gov/usam/criminal-resource-manual-38-juvenile-defined.

Office of the United States Attorneys. (2017). *Juvenile definition*. Retrieved from https://www.justice.gov/usam/criminal-resource-manual-38-juvenile-defined.

The Sentencing Project. (2000). *Reducing racial disparity in the criminal justice system: A manual for practitioners and policymakers*. Washington, DC: Author.

The Sentencing Project. (2014). *Disproportionate minority contact in the juvenile justice system*. Washington, DC: Author.

United States Census Bureau. (2015). *State and county quick facts. United states Department of Commerce*. Author.

Van Ryzin, M. J. (2012). Affiliation with delinquent peers as a mediator of the effects of multidimensional treatment foster care for delinquent girls. *Journal of Consulting and Clinical Psychology*, *80*(4), 588–596.

CHAPTER 8

Evidence-Based Practices for Adults in the Criminal Justice System

Warren K. Graham

Important to note is the distinction between what evidence-based practices are, and good clinical practice related to positive outcomes. Evidence-based practice more broadly "applies the principles and techniques of evidence-based decision making to all interventions intended to improve, or ameliorate, the social or clinical problems of affected individuals" (Prendergast, 2011, p. 11). There are elements of evidence-based principles central to many standardized practices and those elements need to be identified, since foundational. For example, drug courts are considered a legitimate evidence-based model, when "combining drug treatment with the legal and moral authority of the court in an effort to break the cycle of drug use and drug related crime... The practice was rated." Promising for reducing recidivism and promising for reducing alcohol and drug-related offenses, according to the National Institute for Justice (2017). And with this "promising" designation, drug courts in and of themselves use varying elements of principles to enhance the overall judicial supervision to be effective, rather than employing specific treatment modalities themselves.

As with the juvenile population from Chapter 7, treatment modalities for an adult population also balance risk, public safety, and recidivism. A significant difference between the two may focus on the conception of systemic integration supporting treatment. The successful utilization and implementation of evidence-based interventions is most noticeable for family-oriented interventions for substance abusing adolescents, those experiencing delinquency, and associated problem behaviors. This is a critical distinction as thousands of therapists have been trained to provide empirically based family services, discussed in Chapter 7, such as brief strategic family therapy (Szapocznik, Hervis, & Schwartz, 2003), functional family therapy (Alexander, Pugh, Parsons, & Sexton,

Clinical Interventions in Criminal Justice Settings
ISBN 978-0-12-811381-3
http://dx.doi.org/10.1016/B978-0-12-811381-3.00008-1

2000), multidimensional family therapy (Liddle, 2002), multidimensional treatment foster care (Chamberlain & Mihalic, 1998), and multisystemic therapy (Henggeler & Borduin, 1990).

Assessing risk, need, and intervention scope, practice, and effectiveness continues to be a challenge for criminal justice populations. The evidence-based practices movement is premised on an accumulation of evidence showing that specific treatment and practices lead to better outcomes (Henderson, Taxman, & Young, 2008). The criminal justice system is often the point of convergence for clients with simultaneous clinical needs, like mental health, substance abuse, and chronic health issues. More importantly:

> *Approximately 80% of criminal offenders are substance abusers and nearly one-half are addicted to drugs or alcohol. Traditionally, the criminal justice system failed to address the clinical needs of these individuals in sentencing and supervision practices, and the treatment system failed to address their supervisory and management challenges. Historically, the court system was seen as adversarial, where the inherent conflict between defense and prosecution teams often meant the sacrificing of client needs within a system which balances safety, risk, and clinical attention. Recently, evidence-based practices have begun to be applied in sentencing, treatment, and criminal justice supervision, with the goal of matching drug-involved offenders to the most effective and cost-effective programs given their clinical and supervision requirements.*
>
> ***Marlowe (2013)***

In Friedmann, Taxman, and Henderson's (2007) article, "Evidence-based treatment practices for drug-involved adults in the criminal justice system," best practices were identified to support the most adjunctive ways to implement strong intervention models with the most promising research; treatment orientations that employ therapeutic community (TC), cognitive-behavioral, or standardized behavioral modification techniques; comprehensive services that address co-occurring medical and psychosocial disorders; family involvement in treatment; treatment duration of 90 or more days; systems integration and a continuum of care (including aftercare); routine drug testing to monitor treatment progress; and use of sanctions and incentives to improve program retention or use of reinforcement schedules (Friedmann, Taxman, & Henderson, 2007).

Significant points of entry for the adult offender have created alternative sentencing and court-based programs tailored to specific clinical needs, like mental health courts, drug courts, sex-offender programs, and community courts, speaking to legislative need for a court-based response. Drug courts offer addicted defendants who plead guilty to drug charges the opportunity to have their cases dismissed if they successfully complete drug treatment. Their progress in treatment is rigorously monitored by the drug court judge and by court-based case managers. Drug courts seek to halt the revolving door of addiction and arrest, using a graduated system of rewards and sanctions to help substance abusers attain—and maintain—sobriety (Lang & Belenko, 2000).

The close relationship between drug use and crime is widely documented (Prendergast, Hall, Wexler, Melnick, & Cao, 2004) as a large percentage of inmates have long histories of involvement with drug use contributing to recidivism. According to the National Institute for Justice, between 25% and 50% of all adult male arrestees demonstrate that they were at risk for alcohol and other drug dependence (Scott, 2008).

Increased access to treatment needs to be supported by policies and procedures that incorporate EBP into daily life, and frameworks need to be created that strengthen the systems ability to create, maintain, and support new modes of intervention as they become available (Taxman, Henderson, & Belenko, 2009). That level of incorporation may need to be the inclusion of evidence-based principles for effective interventions that overlap between specific evidence-based practices. Elements like assessing actuarial risk/need, enhancing internal motivation, targeted interventions, skill training, increased positive reinforcement, and engaging social support (Bogue, 2004) cross the boundaries of specific modalities, but can be added to policies to create additional programmatic support.

Ensuring that the totality of the criminal justice system; legislation, law enforcement, courts, and corrections; is represented as we move toward adopting evidence-based practices and principles for adults in the criminal justice system may be daunting. Legislative efforts to allow the dissemination of evidence-based protocols may be subject to the social climate in a way that prevents those that need help most from receiving it. For instance, The Rockefeller Drug Laws "still require punishments for the possession or sale of heroin, cocaine, and other hard drugs that.rank among the most severe in the nation" (Women in Prison Project, 1999, p. ii). Finally, these sentences have a fundamentally negative effect on the administration of justice as mandatory sentencing in the adversarial criminal justice system stacks the deck in favor of one side (Correctional Association of New York, 2001). With programs addressing substance abuse in prisons/jails being staggered according to sentencing, those experiencing addiction or dual diagnosis issues may not receive adequate treatment until a significant portion of their sentence is completed.

Coordinated efforts to streamline every aspect of the criminal justice system need to be advocated for smooth transitions between entry into the system, assessment of the need, and the delivery of clinical services, throughout.

COGNITIVE BEHAVIORAL THERAPY

There is a high prevalence of drug problems among offenders (Wexler & Fletcher, 2007), yet considering varied interventions available, evidence-based practices such as cognitive behavioral therapy (CBT), TCs, and manualized treatment shown to be effective with this population, were the least used (Henderson et al., 2008). Two of the top three programs that resulted in the most reduction in recidivism rates in adult correctional settings were cognitive and behavioral treatment (Aos, Miller, & Drake, 2006). Multiple systems have created variations of these treatments, tailored for specific programs and settings. For example, the National Institute of Corrections (NIC) has developed a manualized version titled, "Thinking for a Change," which has been shown to reduce recidivism among offenders. Manualized treatments are helpful in chronicling specific intervention steps offered to clients in the criminal justice system. Material presented to client inmates includes how thinking controls behavior; paying attention to thinking, recognizing risk, using new thinking, problem solving skills, and goal settings among others (Bush, Glick, & Taymans, 2011). Not just for use with incarcerated offenders, this adaptive model has also been used with other areas of the system, like Suffolk County Department of Probation's Criminal Thinking Group, which mirrors the NIC content. Their Criminal Thinking Groups, as a cognitive behavioral intervention, have been used with offender populations for the last 30 years (Suffolk County Probation Department, 2011).

Cognitive behavioral interventions are based on the simple principle that thinking (an internal behavior) precedes and controls overt action (external behavior). Teaching new ways of thinking that will ultimately correct maladaptive criminal behavior, enhanced decision-making, and problem solving are the goals of the interventions (Suffolk County Probation Department, 2011).

As an outgrowth of the National Institute on Drug Abuse's (NIDA) Criminal Justice Drug Abuse Treatment Studies qualitative information has been introduced to influence the trajectory of services for the addicted offender population. McCarty and Chandler (2009) identified the need for CBT to shape an offender's understanding of criminal thinking to support, enhance, and reinforce addiction treatment.

THERAPEUTIC COMMUNITIES

TCs are typically drug-free residential settings that treat drug abuse and addiction in various predetermined stages. The ultimate goal of a TC is to help individuals recognize the dangers of addiction by identifying, expressing, and managing feelings while learning personal and social responsibility (Ulsperger, 2005). Although a variety of approaches have been implemented to address the issue of substance abuse within the criminal justice population, the approach most widely studied by researchers is the TC modified for the prison environment (Prendergast et al., 2004).

The ultimate goal of a TC is to help individuals recognize the dangers of addiction by identifying, expressing, and managing feelings while learning personal and social responsibility (Ulsperger, 2005). Similar to cognitive behavioral models, where the acknowledgement of thought processes that influence action are central to behavioral change, the TC model has been shown to be effective in residential settings.

Prison environments, though, can make addiction rehabilitation difficult. The availability of drugs, violence related to inmate gangs divided along racial lines, and the frustration that accompanies confinement can hinder personal change and reform. Unlike other prison drug treatment programs, on-site TCs offer an escape from the typical prison subculture by providing an area where individuals are isolated from the general inmate population (Vanderplasschen et al., 2013). That isolation translates into longer time spent in treatment, understanding that there is a consistent relationship between retention in treatment and positive post-treatment outcomes in all modalities (DeLeon, 2015).

Outside of a prison-based setting, high dropout and relapse rates (Ulsperger, 2005; Vanderplasschen et al., 2013) have created scrutiny of this program's effectiveness. In the move towards the proliferation of evidence-based intervention and culturally sensitive treatment, the confrontational nature of TC's has also been questioned as being antithetical to more mainstream clinical methods of ensuring the diverse and intersecting needs of the prison population.

AMITY PRISON BASED THERAPEUTIC COMMUNITY

The Amity In-Prison TC was originally established as a demonstration project funded by the California Department of Corrections in 1990, and the program provides intensive treatment to male inmates who reside in a dedicated housing unit during the last 9–12 months of their prison term (Wexler, De Leon, Thomas, Kressel, & Peters, 1999).

All of the major evaluations of prison-based TCs have examined outcomes at 1, 2, or 3 years following release. Studies have found that positive results for treatment (compared with no treatment), in terms of various measures of recidivism, are observable at 1 or 2 years. At 3 years, however, the differences between treatment and comparison groups tend to disappear. The Amity TC was evaluated over the course of 5 years, and with a response rate of 81% post-release, the Amity treatment group had significantly lower rates of reincarceration than the control group. Those who attended after-care had lower levels of reincarceration, longer time to reincarceration, and higher levels of employment (Prendergast et al., 2004). So in essence, the favorable effects of incarcerated treatment were connected to and subject to post-release care, suggesting the need for "more treatment, better treatment, and moving beyond treatment," hallmarks of the Reclaiming Futures Initiative model of youth engagement (Reclaiming Futures, 2017).

MOTIVATIONAL INTERVIEWING

Motivational Interviewing (MI) is a counseling technique that enables people to get beyond their reluctance to change problem behaviors. MI is directive (focused on goals), client-centered, and non-confrontational (Bogue & Nandi, 2012). MI is considered to be a direct method of helping, focusing on discrete, specific changes rather than on underlying psychological patterns. Instead of presuming pathology, deficits, or inability, MI practitioners assume that clients are probably stuck, confused, or unclear (Hayes & Levin, 2012).

The five principles of MI have significant and useful properties for implementation in a criminal justice context. Clinical strategies that include confrontation have not been successful in the overall therapeutic process. The NIC urges use of MI techniques by its workforce, and it is incumbent on criminal justice organizations to find effective methods of personnel training in this evidence-based practice (Hartzler & Espinosa, 2011).

A criticism of MI is that the model can be difficult to learn and often requires several training exposures for skill change (Doran, Hohman, & Koutsenok, 2011).

MI has many applications for any population for which resistance may be inherent or present. For example, in correctional settings, which involve the use of coercive power and authority that tend to increase client defensiveness and lead to conflict with corrections staff, MI can help by reflecting, rather than reacting to statements, help improve communication by providing feedback about perceived resistance, and explore ambivalence about changing behavior (Bogue & Nandi, 2012, p. 3).

RACE RELATIONS

Overt and subtle forms of racism exist in the United States; specifically, it exists in many structural institutions such as law enforcement and the justice system (Otuyelu, Graham, & Kennedy, 2016). According to the National Association of the Advancement of Colored People (NAACP) (2015) Criminal Justice Fact sheet, African Americans constitute nearly 1 million of the total 2.3 million incarcerated populations with an incarceration rate nearly six times the rate of whites. Together, African American and Hispanics comprised 58% of all prisoners in 2008, even though African Americans and Hispanics make up approximately one quarter of the U.S. population.

There is a consensus amongst activist and research and advocacy groups that substantial racial inconsistencies exist in the sentencing decisions of black males in the United States Federal Court system (American Civil Liberties Union, 2014; Hagan & Bumiller, 1983; Spohn & DeLone, 2000). These racial inconsistencies reflect that the sentencing imposed on black males are approximately 20% longer than those of their white male counterparts convicted of similar crimes (American Civil Liberties Union, 2014; Spohn & DeLone, 2000).

The impact of racial micro-aggression in the delivery of services can be detrimental to service provision and staff development (Otuyelu et al., 2016). This was confirmed in a study by Constantine (2007) where the findings showed that perceived racial micro-aggression were negatively associated with African American clients' perceptions of the therapeutic working alliance. Sue (2010) identify that micro-aggressions "assail the mental health of recipients, create hostile climates, perpetuate stereotype threat, and create physical health problems, and lower productivity and problem solving abilities" (p. 183).

Specific to self-efficacy, and in normal settings, the affected person of color can terminate services when feeling marginalized or oppressed, however, those involved in the criminal justice system may feel less choice when considering terminating their services received via that system. These issues highlight the need for evidence-based practices and principles that are culturally relevant.

SUMMARY

The practice of MI has gained acceptance as an effective approach to support behavior change in various therapeutic contexts. In recent years, MI has been extended to clients within less traditional therapeutic settings including prisons and probation departments (Hayes & Levin, 2012). Despite the known strengths of MI for positively affecting behavioral change in therapeutic contexts, the extent to which probation officers are able to effectively utilize MI remains unknown. A significant element of the under-utilization of EBP may be the premise that the criminal justice system does not generally include service provision as a primary goal, even though individuals along the continuum have unmet clinical needs (Taxman, Henderson, & Belenko, 2009). So, even with its ability to be an effective tool, MI, as well as other EBP models, may not be proliferated within organizations due to this basic ideology.

The ever-present balance of therapeutic jurisprudence and safety and risk is all the more important when considering the implementation of EBPs in prisons and with probation. While incarcerated, corrections administrations primary goal is overall safety, while the secondary may be clinical need. Expanding the paradigm used to oversee prison administration is crucial to extend the range of services offered while incarcerated to integrate treatment, like hiring corrections personnel with a background in human services, and garnering support from state and federal administrators for resources.

Therapeutic evaluation studies have shown that treatment density and length of time in.treatment are all determinant factors for positive outcomes (Wexler et al., 1999) so developing mechanisms to allow more access to treatment upon entry to prison/jail would lend to increased treatment success. The focus on treatment as a precursor to rehabilitative efforts may mean the utilization of validated screening tools upon admissions rather than focusing clinical efforts for re-entry. Frontloading clinical services while utilizing MI to address treatment ambivalence will alleviate the pressure to connect prisoners to services pending release and allow increased time in treatment, shown as a precursor to positive outcomes.

Whether treatment interventions are encouraged concurrent to prison/jail admissions, or continue to be facilitated at set intervals pending release, legislation needs to be drafted to support staff training and culture change allowing for a more therapeutic perspective for those identified with a substance use disorder or mental health issue. The delivery of evidence-based models need to be considered as part of a continuum of services designed to reduce recidivism by addressing clinical needs.

Perhaps the distinguishing feature of adapting evidence-based practices and principles in the criminal justice system is the importance of interventions that enhance public safety and public health (Patterson, 2013) at a time when most necessary. Offenders are in need of evidence-based treatment while incarcerated and after diversion, and former offenders who reenter communities are in need of a wide variety of services such as vocational training, housing, and drug and mental health treatment (Wheeler & Patterson, 2008).

REFERENCES

Alexander, J. F., Pugh, C., Parsons, B., & Sexton, T. L. (2000). *Blueprints for violence prevention, Book Three: Functional family therapy*. Boulder, CO: Center for the Study and Prevention of Violence.

American Civil Liberties Union. (2014). Racial disparities in sentencing: Hearing on reports of racism in the justice system of the United States. In *Submitted to the Inter-American Commission on Human Rights 153rd session submitted October 27, 2014*.

Aos, S., Miller, M., & Drake, E. (2006). *Evidence-based adult corrections programs: What works and what does not*. Olympia: Washington State Institute for Public Policy.

Bogue, B. M. (2004). *Implementing evidence-based practice in community corrections: The principles of effective intervention*. Washington, DC: National Institute of Corrections.

Bogue, B., & Nandi (2012). *Motivational interviewing in corrections: A comprehensive guide to implementing MI in corrections*. US Department of Justice.

Bush, J., Glick, B., & Taymans, J. (2011). *Thinking for a change: Integrated cognitive behavior change program*. National Institute of Corrections Academy, 3. December 10, 2011.

Chamberlain, P., & Mihalic, S. F. (1998). *Multidimensional treatment foster care. Center for the Study and Prevention of Violence*. Institute of Behavioral Science, University of Colorado at Boulder.

Constantine, M. G. (2007). Racial micro aggressions against African American clients in cross- racial counseling relationships. *Journal of Counseling Psychology*, *54*(1), 1–16.

Correctional Association of New York. (2001). *Stupid and irrational and barbarous: New York judges speak against the Rockefeller drug laws*.

DeLeon, G. (2015). "The Gold standard" and related considerations for a maturing science of substance abuse treatment. Therapeutic communities; a case in point. *Substance Use & Misuse*, *50*, 1106–1109.

Doran, N., Hohman, M., & Koutsenok, I. (2011). Linking basic and advanced motivational interviewing training outcomes for juvenile correctional staff in California. *Journal of Psychoactive Drugs*, *43*(S1), 19–26.

Friedmann, P. D., Taxman, F. S., & Henderson, C. E. (2007). Evidence-based treatment practices for drug-involved adults in the criminal justice system. *Journal of Substance Abuse Treatment*, *32*(3), 267–277.

Hagan, J., & Bumiller, K. (1983). Making sense of sentencing: A review and critique of sentencing research. *Research on Sentencing: The Search for Reform*, *2*, 1–54.

Hartzler, B., & Espinosa, E. (June 2011). Moving criminal justice organizations toward adoption of evidence-based practice via advanced workshop training in motivational interviewing: A research note. *Criminal Justice Policy Review*, *22*(2), 235.

Hayes, S. C., & Levin, M. (2012). *The context press mindfulness and acceptance practica series: Mindfulness and acceptance for addictive behaviors: Applying contextual CBT to substance abuse and behavioral addictions*. Reno, NV: Context Press.

Henderson, C. E., Taxman, F. S., & Young, D.W. (2008). A Rasch model analysis of evidence-based treatment practices used in the criminal justice system. *Drug and Alcohol Dependence*, *93*(1), 163–175.

Henggeler, S.W., & Borduin, C. M. (1990). *Family therapy and beyond: A multisystemic approach to treating the behavior problems of children and adolescents*. Pacific Grove, CA: Thomson Brooks/Cole.

Lang, M. A., & Belenko, S. (2000). Predicting retention in a residential drug treatment alternative to prison program. *Journal of Substance Abuse Treatment*, *19*(2), 145–160.

Liddle, H. A. (2002). Multidimensional Family Therapy for Adolescent Cannabis Users. *Cannabis Youth Treatment (CYT) Series, Volume 5*.

Marlowe, D. B. (2013). *Criminal justice interventions. Interventions for addiction: Comprehensive addictive behaviors and disorders* (Vol. 3).

McCarty, D., & Chandler, R. K. (2009). Understanding the importance of organizational and system variables on addiction treatment services within criminal justice settings. *Drug and Alcohol Dependence*, *103*, 91–93.

National Association of the Advancement of Colored People (NAACP). (2015). *Criminal justice fact sheet*. Retrieved from http://www.naacp.org/pages/criminal-justice-fact-sheet.

Otuyelu, F., Graham, W., & Kennedy, S. A. (2016). The death of Black males: The unmasking of cultural competence and oppressive practices in a micro-aggressive environment. *Journal of Human Behavior in the Social Environment*, *26*(3–4), 430–436.

Patterson, G. T. (2013). *Social work practice in the criminal justice system*. New York: Routledge.

Prendergast, M. L. (2011). Issues defining and applying evidence-based practices criteria for treatment of criminal-justice involved clients, treatment of criminal-justice involved clients. *Journal of Psychoactive Drugs*, 7, 10–18.

Prendergast, M. L., Hall, E. A., Wexler, H. K., Melnick, G., & Cao, Y. (2004). Amity prison-based therapeutic community: 5 year outcomes. *The Prison Journal*, *84*(1), 36–60.

Reclaiming Futures Initiative. (2017). The model. Retrieved from http://reclaimingfutures.org/model/model-solution.

Scott, W. (2008). *Effective clinical practices in treatment clients in the criminal justice system*. National Institute of Corrections.

Spohn, C., & DeLone, M. (2000). *When does race matter? In Sociology of crime, law and deviance*. Emerald Group Publishing Limited, 3–37.

Sue, D. W. (2010). *Microaggressions in everyday life: Race, gender, and sexual orientation*. Hoboken, NJ: John Wiley & Sons.

Suffolk County Probation Department. (2011). *Criminal Thinking(Unpublished manuscript)*.

Szapocznik, J., Hervis, O., & Schwartz, S. (2003). *Therapy Manuals for Drug Addiction: brief strategic family therapy for adolescnet drug abuse. Manual 5* (No. 3). US Department of Health and Human Services, National Institutes of Health, National Institute on Drug Abuse.

Taxman, F., & Henderson, C., Belenko, S. ((Suppl. 1), 2009, S1–S6). Organizational context, systems change, and adopting treatment delivery systems in the criminal justice system. *Drug and Alcohol Dependence*.

Ulsperger, J. S. (2005). Therapeutic communities. In M. Bosworth (Ed.), *Encyclopedia of prisons and correctional facilities* (Vol. 2) (pp. 955–959) Thousand Oaks, CA: SAGE Reference, 2005.

Vanderplasschen, W., Colpaert, K., Autrique, M., Rapp, R. C., Pearce, S., Broekaert, E., et al. (2013). Therapeutic communities for addictions: A review of their effectiveness from a recovery-oriented perspective. *The Scientific World Journal, 2013*.

Wexler, H. K., De Leon, G., Thomas, G., Kressel, D., & Peters, K. (1999). The Amity prison TC evaluation. *Criminal Justice and Behavior*, *26*(2), 147–167.

Wexler, H., & Fletcher, B. (March 2007). National criminal justice drug abuse treatment studies (CJ-DATS) overview. *The Prison Journal, 87*(1), 9–24.

Wheeler, D. P., & Patterson, G. (March 2008). Prisoner reentry. *Health & Social Work, 33*(2), 145.

Women in Prison Project of the Correctional Association of New York. (1999). *Mandatory injustice: Case histories of women convicted under New York's Rockefeller drug laws*. New York State Division of Criminal Justice Services.

FURTHER READING

Armstrong, G. S., Atkin-Plunk, C., & Gartner, N. (2016). Perceptions of motivational interviewing. *Criminal Justice and Behavior, 43*(8), 1095–1106.

Berman, G., & Anderson, D. (1999). *Drugs, Courts and Neighborhoods: Community Reintegration and the Brooklyn Treatment Court*. Center for Court Innovation.

Blandford, A. M., & Osher, F. C. (2012). *A checklist for implementing evidence-based practices and programs (EBPs) for justice-involved adults with behavioral health disorders*. Delmar, NY: SAMSHA's GAINS Center for Behavioral Health and Justice Transformation.

Constantine, M. G., & Sue, D. G. (2007). Perceptions of racial micro aggressions among black supervisees in cross racial dyads. *Journal of Counseling Psychology, 54*(2), 142–153.

Newport, F. (2014). *Gallup review: Black and white attitudes toward police*. Retrieved from http://www.gallup.com/poll/175088/gallup-review-black-white-attitudes-toward-police.aspx.

Tafrate, R. C., & Mitchell, D. (2013). *Forensic CBT: A handbook for clinical practice*. Wiley-Blackwell.

Wolff, N., Hueninga, J., Shi, J., Fruehc, C., Hoover, D. R., & McHugo, G. (2014). Implementation and effectiveness of integrated trauma and addiction treatment for incarcerated men. *Journal of Anxiety Disorders, 30*, 66–80.

CHAPTER 9

Evidence-Based Practice With Special Criminal Justice Populations

George T. Patterson and Warren K. Graham

Considerable diversity is found among criminal justice populations. Indeed, offenders and former offenders vary in terms of demographic characteristics such as age, race and ethnicity, gender, income and education, among other characteristics. Actuarial risk assessment instruments and subsequent interventions should be relevant for a specific special population.

Undoubtedly, special populations with criminal justice system involvement are identified in different ways depending upon the organization. The Center for Substance Abuse Treatment (1998) identified seven "special populations" with criminal justice system involvement: women, elderly offenders, offenders with mental illness, offenders with mental retardation, sex offenders, offenders with long-term medical conditions, and offenders with physical disabilities. These special populations are characterized by special needs based on culture, age, gender, and medical needs, in addition the need for substance abuse disorder interventions. The Substance Abuse and Mental Health Administration (SAMSHA) (2016) supports the use of early interventions and evidence-based practices instead of incarceration for adults and youth involved in the criminal justice system. Referring to these youth and adults as "specific population groups," SAMSHA identified the behavioral health problems experienced by these groups as co-occurring disorders or serious mental illness (SMI). Finally, the Office for Victims of Crime (2013) identified "special populations" as victims with disabilities, young men of color, the elderly, and survivors of homicide.

However, more information and research is needed concerning the types of effective interventions and services provided to special populations. Although the data were collected from substance abuse treatment programs, and not criminal justice settings, Olmstead and Sindelar (2004) examined the 2000 National Survey of Substance Abuse Treatment Services, which included 13,749 substance abuse treatment agencies. The 2002 Area

Clinical Interventions in Criminal Justice Settings
ISBN 978-0-12-811381-3
http://dx.doi.org/10.1016/B978-0-12-811381-3.00009-3

Resources File was also used to determine population characteristics. Services and interventions were determined using practice and clinical guidelines, and research indicating best approaches for special populations. Olmstead and Sindelar identified the following "special populations" and essential interventions:

- Gays and lesbians (tests for HIV, sexually transmitted diseases, and hepatitis; and HIV education, counseling and support services).
- Persons living with HIV/AIDS (HIV testing, education, counseling, and support services).
- Co-occurring disorders (mental health assessment and pharmacotherapy).
- Women (child care, transportation, housing, domestic violence, and employment counseling).
- Youth (family and aftercare interventions, mental health assessment).

Special populations, which include offenders and former offenders with criminal justice involvement, are affected by concerns about public safety and public health risks. Public safety is maintained by a variety of approaches such as legislation defining what constitutes offending behavior, police patrol and other law enforcement procedures, court sentences that involve sanctions such as incapacitation, probation and parole, and corrections which oversees community supervision. Individuals who experience social problems such as substance abuse or mental disorders may engage in offending behavior to obtain drugs, those with a mental disorder may be involved in public disorder offenses, or individuals with a drinking problem may drive while intoxicated. It stands to reason that these criminal justice system issues will affect the evidence-based practices in terms of expected outcomes that address these issues.

Public health issues such as chronic and infectious diseases, mental disorders, and substance abuse disorders also characterize special populations. Particularly among former offenders transitioning from incarceration back into the community, behavior that increases the risk of infectious disease, including HIV, hepatitis C, and other chronic illnesses, can adversely affect the community's public health and, for those who are re-incarcerated, burden criminal justice health care resources as well (Wexler & Fletcher, 2007).

According to the Centers for Disease Control and Prevention (CDC) (2017):

> *Public health is the science of protecting and improving the health of families and communities through promotion of healthy lifestyles, research for disease and injury prevention and detection and control of infectious diseases. Overall, public health is concerned with protecting the health of entire populations. These populations can be as small as a local neighborhood, or as big as an entire country or region of the world...A large part of public health is promoting healthcare equity, quality, and accessibility.*

Intersectionality exists between the individual person's characteristics and the social problems they experience. However, as a result of the emphasis in the criminal justice system on public safety and public health, it is important to understand these distinctions in relationship to evidence-based practices and principles. For a review of evidence-based practices that consider the intersectionality between substance abuse and criminal justice involvement, such as substance abuse and HIV and pharmacotherapy issues, see the *Handbook of evidence-based substance abuse treatment in criminal justice settings* (Leukefeld, Gullotta, & Gregrich, 2011).

Clearly, the evidence-based practice should focus on improving public safety, public health, or both. Therefore, we categorize the clinical intervention needs of special populations based on public safety and public health issues.

PUBLIC SAFETY AND SPECIAL POPULATIONS

Sex Offenders

Sex offender is a legal term and does not refer to a diagnostic or clinical category. The Center for Sex Offender Management (CSOM, 1999) defines sexual offender as "the term most commonly used to define an individual who has been charged and convicted of illegal sexual behavior" (p. 20). Illegal sexual behaviors include rape and sexual assault, among other types of behaviors (U.S. Department of Justice, 2005).

Sex offenders are managed in the criminal justice system using several approaches. Some of these approaches include incarcerating offenders, extending incarceration after an offender's original sentence ends through the use of civil commitments or other processes, and sex offender registration and notification laws (Grady, 2009).

In their systematic review examining effective interventions for sex offenders, Aos, Miller, and Drake (2006) found that psychotherapy, counseling, and/or behavioral therapy interventions were not effective for reducing recidivism. Cognitive behavioral treatment provided in prison effectively reduced recidivism by 14.9%, and cognitive behavioral treatment provided to low-risk offenders on probation effectively reduced recidivism by 31.2%

Violent Offenders

Most of the focus on violent offenders has concentrated on assessing risks for future violent behavior among offenders with mental disorders as well as incarcerated offenders. Such activities require considering public safety risks as well as the offender's civil rights (Quinsey, Harris, Rice, & Cormier, 1998).

It appears that more efforts have been conducted to validly and reliability predict the risks of future violent behaviors, or compare the ability among several actuarial risk assessment instruments to accurately predict violent recidivism among violent offenders (Glover, Nicholson, Hemmati, Bernfeld, & Quinsey, 2002; Rice, Harris, & Lang, 2013), than the development and implementation of evidence-based practices aimed at reducing violence. A meta-analysis was conducted to examine the predictive validity of actuarial risk assessment instruments developed to assess risks for violent, sexual offending and criminal offending behaviors. The analysis included 73 samples, and 24,847 study participants from 13 countries. Findings suggest that these instruments accurately predicted intervention decisions, risks for future violence, and reoffending behavior among high-risk offenders. The instruments were less effective when they were used as the only basis for sentencing and/or release decisions (Fazel, Singh, Doll, & Grann, 2012).

However, numerous evidence-based practices for violent offenders have been developed. For instance, the Duluth Model is described as an effective intervention for reducing violent recidivism among batterers, and promising for reducing intimate partner victimization (CrimeSolutions.gov, n.d.a). On the other hand, cognitive behavioral therapy had no effects on violent offenses among batterers, or domestic/intimate partner victimization (CrimeSolutions.gov, n.d.b).

Victims of Crime

A key objective of public safety is the reduction of crime and victimization. This objective also includes keeping individuals and communities safe. This objective is often at odds with the provision of evidence-based practice to offenders and former offenders due to concerns about recidivism and victimization, which can result from violent or nonviolent offenses.

The violent crime rate in 2014 was 20.1 victims per 1000 individuals. Violent crimes were defined as rape or sexual assaults, robbery, and aggravated and simple assault. The rate of property crime in 2014 was 118.1 victims per 1000 individuals. Property crimes include house burglaries, theft, and car theft. Although these data show that more victimizations are reported for property crimes, only 12% of victims of violent crimes and 28% who experienced intimate partner victimization received interventions from a victim service agency (Truman & Langton, 2015).

CrimeSolutions.gov describes effective evidence-based practices for a variety of specialized populations who are victims of crime. The list of effective interventions include:

1. Advocacy interventions for women who experience intimate partner violence.
2. Psychotherapies for victims of sexual assault.
3. School-based bullying prevention programs.
4. School-based child sexual abuse prevention programs.
5. School-based interventions to reduce dating and sexual violence.
6. Sexual assault nurse examiners for forensic examinations in cases of sexual assault/rape.
7. Therapeutic approaches for sexually abused children and adolescents.

Driving While Intoxicated/Driving Under the Influence

Drunk driving and driving under the influence of alcohol pose serious risks to public safety. It has been estimated that each day, 28 individuals in the United States are killed in car crashes in which alcohol has impaired a driver (CDC, 2017). The last available estimates show that in 1997, 513,300 offenders were incarcerated or on probation following a driving while intoxicated (DWI) conviction. Offenders convicted of DWI represented approximately 14% of individuals on probation, 7% of inmates incarcerated in jails, and 2% prisoners in State prisons. The demographic characteristics of DWI offenders when compared to other special populations show that the majority of these offenders are male, white, older, and have more education (Maruschak, 1999).

Brief interventions are effective for treating individuals who experience alcohol use in the mild to moderate range. Cognitive behavioral therapy and motivational enhancement therapy are effective interventions for individuals who have been diagnosed with alcohol use disorders or alcohol dependence (Center for Substance Abuse Treatment, 2004). Evidence-based practices provided for alcohol disorders have been shown to reduce the rate of these disorders by 15% (Aos, Mayfield, Miller, & Yen, 2006).

Specific to drunk driving, a quasi-experimental study found that the New South Wales Sober Driver Programme (SDP) reduced DWI recidivism by 43% over a two-year follow-up period. SDP participants also reported increased knowledge, attitudes, and skills in relation to drunk-driving (Mills, Hodge, Johansson, & Conigrave, 2008). In another quasi-experimental study using a matched group design, Quinn and Quinn (2015) found that after completing a 16-week cognitive behavioral therapy intervention, offenders with prior DWI offenses reported lower DWI recidivism rates 3 years after completing the intervention. Sobriety checkpoints and ignition locks are effective nonclinical interventions (Centers for Disease Control and Prevention, 2017).

Two interventions with effective evidence ratings (Checkpoint Tennessee, LifeSkills Training (LST)), and three interventions with promising evidence ratings (Alcohol Misuse Prevention Study (AMPS), Cass County/Leech Lake Band of Ojibwe Wellness Court, Clarke County (GA) Victim Impact Panels) have been developed as interventions for drunk driving (CrimeSolutions.gov, n.d.d).

PUBLIC HEALTH AND SPECIAL POPULATIONS

Human Immunodeficiency Virus

Significant overlaps have emerged between the fields of criminal justice and public health. The more risk factors that are present, the greater the risk, and interventions that minimize risk factors are central to reducing involvement in negative behaviors (Sanders, Deeds, & Thomas, 2013, p. vii). People with both HIV and alcohol use disorders are disproportionately concentrated within the U.S. criminal justice system; approximately one-quarter of all persons living with HIV cycle through the system each year (Hammett, Gaiter, & Crawford, 1998; Springer, Azar, & Altice, 2011).

Health strategies to manage utilization of substance use disorder (SUD) treatment may impact treatment access and delivery (Merrick et al., 2015). While a great deal of attention has been given SUDs, HIV risk and criminal justice populations, alcohol dependence and HIV risk are also significant among criminal justice populations (Springer et al., 2011).

Meyer, Cepeda, and Altice (2015) found that gender-based differences existed, which determined treatment outcomes and highlighted varied gender-related health disparities that need to be addressed. The higher prevalence of non-violent offenses and increased comorbidities of women, especially treatable SUDs, supports alternatives to incarceration strategies. Interventions for HIV-positive criminal justice populations should be gender-specific to effectively align health and justice goals (Meyer et al., 2015).

In addition to creating gender-specific services for criminal justice populations, immediate policies need to be implemented to reduce HIV infection in prisons and jails. Rape and coercive sexual relationships must be addressed by taking steps to end sexual violence in prison and ensuring the provision of basic necessities to prisoners in accordance with international standards (Todrys & Amon, 2012). In prisons, opioid substitution therapy, testing, condom distribution, programs to learn tattoo safety, needle-exchange programs, and drug-free housing units are among a list of effective interventions for prisoners who experience SUDs and HIV risks (Underhill, Dumont, & Operario, 2014).

The CDC provides resources for HIV treatment including acute HIV infection. Testing, counseling and referral recommendations are also provided. Prior to individuals leaving the HIV testing site, the CDC suggests the following four best practices recommendations for referral to behavioral health and other interventions:

1. Persons who test positive for HIV should be counseled, either on-site or through referral, concerning the behavioral, psychosocial, and medical implications of HIV infection.
2. Healthcare providers should assess the need for immediate medical care and psychosocial support.
3. Providers should link persons with newly diagnosed HIV infection to services provided by healthcare personnel experienced in the management of HIV infection. Additional services that might be needed include substance abuse counseling and treatment, treatment for mental health disorders or emotional distress, reproductive counseling, risk-reduction counseling, and case management. Providers should follow up to ensure that patients have received services for any identified needs.
4. Persons with HIV infections should be educated about the importance of ongoing medical care and what to expect from these services (Centers for Disease Control and Prevention, 2017).

Tuberculosis

In the early 1990s, a task force headed by New York City's Health Commissioner recommended measures to help control the spread of tuberculosis (TB) in jails and holding cells throughout the criminal justice system. The task force recommended that workers "with extensive training in communicable diseases" be assigned to identify symptoms like chronic coughing among those arrested and held for arraignment in central booking areas and court pens (Navarro, 1992). From New York to sub-Saharan Africa, the prevalence of TB is higher in prison than in non-prison populations due, in part, to on-going transmission related to overcrowding and a lack of adequate prevention and treatment services (Todrys & Amon, 2012). Indeed, the Alabama Department of Corrections recently experienced a severe TB outbreak due to prisoners living in close, overcrowded housing units (Collins, 2014).

The CDC indicates that among individuals who become infected with TB, not all of these individuals will become sick from the disease. Consequently, two forms of TB have been identified: latent TB infection and TB disease. Effective treatments exist for both forms of TB. However, due to the lack of treatment, TB disease may develop from latent TB infection. It is possible that without effective treatment TB disease can result in fatalities. The CDC provides recommendations for treating latent TB infection and TB disease, and special populations such as persons living with HIV, pregnant women, and children (Centers for Disease Control and Prevention, 2016).

Hepatitis

Based on the CDC website, of the three forms of viral hepatitis; hepatitis A, hepatitis B, and hepatitis C; it appears that hepatitis C is of most concern in correctional settings. According to the website, the hepatitis C virus is also "the most common chronic bloodborne infection in the U.S.". Nearly 3.2 million Americans are infected. The primary risk for exposure to the virus results from exposure to contaminated blood typically through sharing needles or works when injecting drugs. Individuals at risk for hepatitis C should also be tested for HIV. Counseling and testing should be provided in both instances. To reduce individual and public health risks, the CDC provides nine recommendations for actions to be taken by individuals who use illegal intravenous drugs:

1. Never reuse or share syringes, water, or drug preparation equipment.
2. Only use syringes obtained from a reliable source (e.g., pharmacies).
3. Use a new, sterile syringe to prepare and inject drugs.
4. If possible, use sterile water to prepare drugs; otherwise, use clean water from a reliable source (e.g., fresh tap water).
5. Use a new or disinfected container (i.e., cooker) and a new filter (i.e., cotton) to prepare drugs.
6. Clean the injection site before injection with a new alcohol swab.
7. Safely dispose of syringes after one use.
8. Get vaccinated for hepatitis A and B if non-immune.
9. Get tested for HIV infection (Centers for Disease Control and Prevention, 2011).

Substance Abuse

Although substance use is common among individuals involved in the U.S. criminal justice system, treatment initiation remains an ongoing problem (Spohr, Taxman, Rodriguez, & Walters, 2016). Little is known about the implementation of evidence-based practices for substance abuse in criminal justice systems (Friedmann, Taxman, & Henderson, 2007). A recent survey of correctional agencies (National Criminal Justice Treatment Practices Survey) found that alcohol and drug education programs were offered in 61% of jails, 74% of prisons, and 53% of community corrections agencies, making education the most widespread form of substance abuse treatment, while more intensive services such as intensive outpatient counseling, therapeutic community, and other programs are infrequently available (Taxman, Young, Wiersema, Rhodes, & Mitchell, 2007). This is especially important considering this special population of offenders "has clearly been identified as having serious substance use disorders that are four times that of the general population" (Taxman et al., 2007).

Evidence-based practices for substance abuse disorders have been shown to reduce the rate of these disorders by 22% (Aos et al., 2006). A national survey which yielded 384 programs providing substance abuse treatment to adult offenders in 2004 reported the availability of 13 specified intervention models, yet most programs actually offered fewer than 60% of the specified evidence-based programs to drug involved offenders (Friedmann et al., 2007). This under-utilization is especially important, as recidivism for substance abusers is also very high. High recidivism rates are also related to violations of parole or other conditional release, and many of these violations are related to relapse as the lack of effective treatment may contribute to relapse and return to incarceration (Taxman, Young, & Fletcher, 2007). The National Criminal Justice Treatment Practices (NCJTP) survey indicated a need to expand intensive treatment modalities for offenders in community corrections settings.

It is becoming apparent that organizational interventions can promote the adoption of more effective treatment and better quality of care (McCarty & Chandler, 2009), so initiatives to disseminate evidence-based practice might target institutions and environmental domains (Friedman et al., 2007). As an outgrowth of National Institute on Drug Abuse's (NIDA) Criminal Justice Drug Abuse Treatment Studies, qualitative information has been introduced to influence the trajectory of services for persons experiencing addictions, offender population. McCarty and Chandler (2009) identified the need for cognitive behavioral therapy to shape an offender's understanding of criminal thinking to support, enhance, and reinforce addiction treatment.

Medication-Assisted Treatment

Special criminal justice populations may require medications in addition to evidence-based practices that are clinically focused, as well as other types of services such as housing, employment, and transportation. Medication-assisted treatment (MAT) refers to interventions that link medication and behavioral therapy, typically for the treatment of substance use disorders.

Combining medication with behavioral interventions is effective for treating alcohol and opioid dependence (Substance Abuse and Mental Health Services Administration, 2016b). Indicating that MAT for opioid dependence is regulated by federal legislation and guidelines, SAMSHA provides resources such as an opioid treatment program directory, a MAT mobile app for opioid disorder, descriptions of opioid treatment medications such as buprenorphine, methadone, and naltrexone, and the medication naloxone for opioid overdose.

Methadone maintenance treatment, a practice of MAT for individuals who experience opioid dependence, received an evidence rating of "effective." Positive intervention outcomes are reported including longer treatment retention and fewer drug use related HIV risk behaviors (CrimeSolutions.gov, 2011). As of 2004, two drugs available by prescription, Disulfiram and Naltrexone, were identified and approved by the Food and Drug Administration as an effective medication treatment for alcohol dependence (Center for Substance Abuse Treatment, 2004).

While MAT is an effective evidence-based practice, its use in criminal justice settings continues to be challenging. An expert panel was formed to examine the use of MAT in criminal justice settings. The panel was organized by and included the following agencies: the U.S. Department of Health and Human Services, SAMHSA, Center for Substance Abuse Treatment, and the Center for Health and Justice located at Treatment Alternatives for Safe Communities (TASC). The panel identified six challenges associated implementing MAT in criminal justice settings:

1. The difficulty encountered when articulating the benefits of medication, and the linkages between public safety and treatment among key stakeholders.
2. Health care funding for criminal justice populations.
3. Staff training on the topic of medications for alcohol and substance abuse disorders.
4. The lack of continuity of care throughout each of the components of the criminal justice system resulting in gaps in services.

5. The lack of standards, education, best practices, and research to inform the use of MAT in criminal justice settings.
6. The implementation of policies in many jurisdictions that function to limit access to MAT for criminal justice populations (SAMSHA, 2013).

Mental Disorders

The prevalence of SMI in the criminal justice system is between three and six times the rate for individuals with SMI in the general U.S. population (Blanford & Osher, 2012). Evidence-based practices provided for SMI have been shown to reduce the rate of SMI by 22% (Aos et al., 2006). Assisted Outpatient Treatment is a common evidence-based intervention for individuals experiencing mental illness and criminal justice system involvement, and has received an "effective" rating (CrimeSolutions.gov, 2012). In addition to evidence-based practices to divert individuals experiencing SMI from the criminal justice system, policy and legislative initiatives are needed, particularly those that focus on the provision of health care (Kennedy-Hendricks, Huskamp, Rutkow, & Barry, 2016).

Not all offenders and former offenders who experience SMI receive evidence-based interventions. Numerous factors affect the quality of care received among these former offenders during reentry. These factors include service gaps, lack of continuity of service from jails and prison to the community, deinstitutionalization, inadequate mental health training for probation and parole officers, and lack of coordination between criminal justice and mental health agencies (Lurigio, Rollins, & Fallon, 2004). Decarceration, which refers to reducing or decreasing the number of offenders incarcerated in jails and prisons, has implications for the SMI population given their special population status and need for specialized interventions (Lamb & Weinberger, 2014).

Epperson, Wolff, et al. (2014) proposed a comprehensive intervention for individuals experiencing SMI with criminal justice system involvement that could be beneficial for addressing these needs. The intervention is comprised of several modules that include medication adherence, criminogenic risks, addiction risk, trauma risk, stress risk, and social and environmental disadvantage risk.

Given the difficulty that probationers who experience SMI have with complying with the conditions of their probation supervision, some research has focused on the use of specialty and standard probation officers and agencies as an approach to supervision (Skeem, Emke-Francis, & Louden,

2006; Skeem & Louden, 2006). In a qualitative study that examined differences in perceptions among specialty and standard caseload probation officers concerning probationers with SMI, Epperson, Canada, Thompson, and Lurigio (2014) found that probation officers reported several differences in their approaches to supervising individuals with SMI based on their caseload assignments. Specialty probation officers more often reported utilizing a social service perspective and emphasizing mental interventions.

Co-occurring Disorders

Co-occurring disorders, previously dual diagnosis, refers to the occurrence of both a mental disorder and a SUD. Individuals diagnosed with mental disorders experience more alcohol and substance use disorders than individuals who are not diagnosed with mental disorders. It is estimated that in 2014, nearly 7.9 million adults in the U.S. experienced a co-occurring disorder (Substance Abuse and Mental Health Services Administration, 2016a). Further, in jails, of the approximately 17 percent of inmates with SMI, an estimated 72% experienced a co-occurring disorder (Blanford & Osher, 2012).

However, due to the presence of a mental disorder and a SUD and accompanying symptoms, diagnosing co-occurring disorders is not a simple undertaking. Such efforts require training, and the use of effective screening and assessment instruments. Undiagnosed and untreated co-occurring disorders can result in incarceration or death, among other outcomes (Substance Abuse and Mental Health Services Administration, 2016a). As the result of living with a co-occurring disorder, individuals are likely to become involved in the criminal justice system due to behaviors associated with their illness. These individuals, as a result of their behaviors and illness, are also likely to be exposed to a wide range of public health risks.

Five recommendations for effectively screening co-occurring disorders among criminal justice populations have been proposed:

1. Routine screening at entry points to criminal justice settings.
2. Use of standardized instruments that include cut-off points to determine whether a person should be referred for a follow-up assessment.
3. Trained staff to administer the screening instruments and refer people for assessment.
4. A response for incarcerated people experiencing a behavioral health crisis, such as intoxication or drug use that requires medical attention, or if an individual is experiencing suicidal thoughts.
5. Health care records being maintained by the agency conducting the screening (Substance Abuse and Mental Health Services Administration, 2016a).

The 259-page report titled *Screening and assessment of co-occurring disorders in the justice system* provides a number of invaluable resources. First, screening and assessment issues for co-occurring disorders in the law enforcement, courts, and corrections components of the criminal justice system are examined. Second, risk factors for co-occurring disorders are examined. Third, innovative approaches to screening and assessment including risk assessment are presented. Finally, screening, diagnostic, and assessment instruments are provided (Substance Abuse and Mental Health Services Administration, 2015).

Homelessness

Homelessness is approximately 7.5–11.3 times higher among jail inmates than the general population, and homeless inmates comprise 15.3% of the U.S. jail population (Greenberg & Rosenheck, 2008). Individuals who experience co-occurring disorders are also more likely to experience homelessness (Substance Abuse and Mental Health Services Administration, 2016a).

A critical need that former offenders have upon reentry from jails and prisons is housing. Housing is a central need, because it can disrupt interventions if individuals lack stable housing. When former offenders move without a forwarding address or collateral contact information that can be used to locate the individual, former offenders can experience serious service disruptions or even disengage from services. This highlights the need for stable housing. Indeed, when criminal justice populations, particularly those who experience substance use and mental disorders, are involved in interventions, multiple contact numbers and addresses should be obtained to maintain contact.

Several evidence-based practices have been developed to treat homelessness. For instance, Behavioral Day Treatment and Contingency Managed Housing and Work Therapy, developed in 1991, is a six-month evidence-based practice for adults aged 26–55. The intervention integrates behavioral day treatment and contingency managed housing and work therapy components. Intervention outcomes are alcohol and drug abstinence, and homelessness (Substance Abuse and Mental Health Services Administration, 2017).

SPECIAL POPULATIONS WITH JUVENILE JUSTICE SYSTEM INVOLVEMENT

Latino Youth

Latino and other minority youth are well-represented among those admitted to substance abuse treatment during the past two decades (Szapocznik,

Prado, Burlew, Williams, & Santisteban, 2007). The goal of reaching culturally diverse groups through psychotherapy interventions is consistent with the multicultural guidelines set forth by the American Psychological Association, and to engage in culturally adapting interventions, ethical researchers must be culturally sensitive and particularly attuned to the manner in which clinical interventions are introduced and conducted in ethnocultural communities (Trimble, Scharrón-del-Río, & Hill, 2012). However, among the 12 existing evidence-based interventions for adolescent substance abuse, only Brief Strategic Family Therapy (BSFT) has been designated as a model program for Hispanic adolescents by SAMSHA (Santisteban, Suarez-Morales, Robbins, & Szapocznik, 2006; Szapocznik, Lopez, Prado, Schwartz, & Pantin, 2006).

BSFT targets substance use, conduct problems, association with antisocial peers, and problematic family relations (Valdez, Cepeda, Parrish, Horowitz, & Kaplan, 2013). This evidence-based approach systematically improves family functioning, and is delivered in phases, starting with joining with individual family members and the family system and building to structured and directive interventions intended to facilitate new behaviors and family interactions (Robbins et al., 2011). The Hispanic family protects its members through its support structure, close-knit family systems, and community networks (Marsiglia, Miles, Dustman, & Sills, 2002), which make this model ideal for addressing issues of acculturation stress and intergenerational conflict (Valdez et al., 2013).

Gangs

CrimeSolutions.gov (n.d.c) identifies youth gangs as comprised of three or more group members who are between the ages of 12–24 and involved in offending or delinquent behaviors. Definitions of what constitutes a gang varies according to jurisdiction. The website identifies five evidence-based practices that have an evidence rating of "effective." In general, these interventions have demonstrated reduced gang violence:

1. Group Violence Reduction Strategy
2. Operation Ceasefire
3. Operation Cul-de-Sac
4. Operation Peacemaker
5. Project BUILD (Broader Urban Involvement and Leadership Development, currently known as the BUILD Violence Intervention Curriculum)

Individual, family, peer group, school, and community systems are risk factors for becoming a gang member, and in turn each of these factors can be negatively affected by gang membership. Interventions to reduce gang involvement and activity include public health approaches, law enforcement, individual and family clinical interventions, and community involvement (Office of Justice Programs, 2016).

SPECIAL POPULATIONS WITH CRIMINAL JUSTICE SYSTEM INVOLVEMENT

Women

The number of women in prison increased by 587% between 1980 and 2011, rising from 15,118 to 111,387, and including women in local jails, more than 200,000 women are now incarcerated in the United States (Sentencing Project, 2012). Roughly two-thirds of women in prison are women of color, representing the fastest growing prison population (Fact Sheet, Women in Prison Project, 2017). Nationally, there are more than 120,000 incarcerated mothers and 1.1 million incarcerated fathers who are parents of minor children (ages 0–17) (Glaze & Maruschak, 2011).

As it relates to services for incarcerated, substance-abusing women, "it is imperative to examine organizational level contextual factors that shape the availability of wraparound services for female offenders" (Oser, Knudsen, Staton-Tindall, & Leukefeld, 2008).

Given that men constitute more than 90% of the U.S. prison population, the majority of policies in most prison systems have been designed to manage the behavior of male prisoners. The contemporary criminal justice system has placed a low priority on the gender-related treatment needs of female offenders. The lives of female offenders are shaped by socioeconomic status as well as by women's experiences of trauma and substance abuse and their relationships with partners, children, and family (Bosworth, 2005a, 2005b). Research indicates that women in prisons are often at risk of sexual abuse by prison staff (Bosworth, 2005a, 2005b).

Nearly one-third of those admitted to therapeutic communities are women, and mixed-gender and women-only communities exist. Research suggests that therapeutic communities exclusively for women have specific benefits because they focus on services that only women need. Some women's programs also let children stay in the facilities with their mothers. When women feel as though their needs are being met, they are more likely to stay and finish the program (Vanderplasschen et al., 2013).

New mothers at Bedford Hills live with their infant children in the Nursery, the oldest prison nursery in the United States, for up to 18 months. In addition, this is currently the only women's facility to offer its inmates a

Family Reunion Program, consisting of overnight, private visits with spouses, children, and other family members of the inmates. The Children's Center is an innovative program designed to make children feel comfortable while visiting their mothers. Both the Nursery and the Children's Center are staffed by inmate childcare workers. Other programs include education and advocacy in custody and foster care situations, and education workshops to improve parenting skills. Incarcerated parents lose their parental rights at a disproportionate rate due to the Adoption and Safe Families Act, which set strict timelines for initiating termination of parental rights (placement cannot exceed 15 of previous 22 months (Raimon, Lee, & Genty, 2009).

Bonta and Andrews (2017) provide numerous clinical intervention recommendations for women that are both consistent and inconsistent with the risk-need-responsivity (RNR) model, as well as recommendations for gender responsive interventions. Examples of women-specific needs that are consistent with the RNR model include focusing on unhealthy relationships and increasing decision-making abilities, controlling negative emotional responses, and providing substance abuse interventions. Examples of women-specific needs that are inconsistent with the RNR model include focusing on issues such as self-growth, interpersonal relationships, sexuality, and spirituality. Finally, examples of gender-responsive interventions that should be provided include offering women-only individual and group interventions, and utilizing female practitioners, service providers, and other staff who "model healthy relationships" (p. 347).

Trauma

Epidemiologic studies have found that trauma-related disorders are ubiquitous among women in treatment for addictions. Evidence based practices for trauma among those with addictions have brought the field to an important stage: examining mechanistic questions such as how, for whom and when evidence based practices work best and learning how to implement evidence-based practices in community treatment settings (Hien, Campbell, & Miele, 2014).

CASE EXAMPLE

The following case example illustrates the need to understand the experiences of special populations and accurately assess how public safety and public health risks can affect clinical and criminal justice interventions. As previously mentioned, offenders often experience multiple problems. They also experience a great deal of intersectionality between personal and individual characteristics, and social problems.

A 44-year-old Latino male and his 40-year-old Caucasian wife, Mr. and Mrs. Smith, are the custodians of three non-biological children. A child neglect petition was filed with the family court after an indicated investigation and subsequent report.

A simultaneous criminal case was ongoing, alleging possession of a controlled substance and public intoxication, for Mr. Smith. Mr. Smith's drugs of choice are alcohol and marijuana. After months of treatment program involvement and numerous significant positive drug tests for Tetrahydrocannabinol (THC), the Mr. Smith revealed to the Family Drug Court Program Administrator that he is HIV positive and taking a drug cocktail containing THC, the central ingredient in marijuana. These behaviors forced him to repeatedly test positive for marijuana in both drug court programs to adhere to medical treatment for his condition. Mr. Smith refuses to share his status with the other program personnel and court staff. Facing the possibility of incarceration and a termination of parental rights trial pending, Mr. Smith's medical condition can explain away what is perceived to be consistent relapses, drug-seeking behavior, and attempts to undermine clinical treatment.

SUMMARY

This chapter examined a number of special populations with criminal justice involvement. As this chapter has shown, these special populations are characterized by public safety and public health risks. More evidence-based practices are needed for special criminal justice populations.

REFERENCES

Aos, S., Mayfield, J., Miller, M., & Yen, W. (2006). *Evidence-based treatment of alcohol, drug, and mental health disorders: Potential benefits, costs, and fiscal impacts for Washington State*. Olympia, WA: Washington State Institute for Public Policy.

Aos, S., Miller, M., & Drake, E. (2006). *Evidence-based adult corrections programs: What works and what does not work*. Olympia: Washington State Institute for Public Policy.

Blandford, A., & Osher, F. (2012). *A checklist for implementing evidence-based practices and programs (EBPs) for justice-involved adults with behavioral health disorders*. Delmar, NY: SAMHSA's GAINS Center for Behavioral Health and Justice Transformation.

Bonta, J., & Andrews, D. A. (2017). *The psychology of criminal conduct* (6th ed.). New York: Routledge.

Bosworth, M. (2005a). *Encyclopedia of prisons and correctional facilities: Women's prisons* (Vol. 2. Thousand Oaks, CA: SAGE, 1050–1055.

Bosworth, M. (2005b). *Encyclopedia of prisons and correctional facilities: Bedford Hills correctional facility* (Vol. 1. Thousand Oaks, CA: SAGE, 66–69.

CDC Foundation. (2017). *What is public health?* Retrieved from https://www.cdcfoundation.org/content/what-public-health.

Centers for Disease Control and Prevention. (2011). *Hepatitis C: 2010 STD treatment guidelines*. Retrieved from https://www.cdc.gov/std/treatment/2010/hepc.htm.

Centers for Disease Control and Prevention. (2016). *TB treatment*. Retrieved from https://www.cdc.gov/tb/topic/treatment/default.htm.

Centers for Disease Control and Prevention. (2017). *Impaired driving: Get the facts motor vehicle safety*. Retrieved from https://www.cdc.gov/motorvehiclesafety/impaired_driving/impaired-drv_factsheet.html.

Center for Sex Offender Management. (1999). *Glossary of terms used in the management and treatment of sexual offenders*. Silver Springs, MD: Author.

Center for Substance Abuse Treatment. (1998). *Continuity of offender treatment for substance use disorders from institution to community*. Rockville, MD: Substance Abuse and Mental Services Administration. Treatment Improvement Protocol (TIP) Series, No. 30.

Center for Substance Abuse Treatment. (2004). Treating alcohol problems. *Substance Abuse in Brief*, *3*(1), 1–6.

Collins, S. P. K. (2014). *Alabama prisons are facing a record-breaking tuberculosis outbreak*. Retrieved from https://thinkprogress.org/alabama-prisons-are-facing-a-record-breaking-tuberculosis-outbreak-c8bb38f2f4c5.

CrimeSolutions.gov. (2011). *Program: Methadone maintenance treatment*. Retrieved from https://www.crimesolutions.gov/ProgramDetails.aspx?ID=158.

CrimeSolutions.gov. (2012). *Program: Assisted outpatient treatment (AOT)*. Retrieved from https://www.crimesolutions.gov/ProgramDetails.aspx?ID=228.

CrimeSolutions.gov. (n.d.a). Practice: Interventions for domestic violence offenders: Duluth model. Retrieved from https://www.crimesolutions.gov/PracticeDetails.aspx?ID=17.

CrimeSolutions.gov. (n.d.b). Practice: Interventions for domestic violence offenders: Cognitive behavioral therapy. Retrieved from https://www.crimesolutions.gov/PracticeDetails.aspx?ID=16.

CrimeSolutions.gov. (n.d.c). Topic: Gangs. Retrieved from https://www.crimesolutions.gov/TopicDetails.aspx?ID=13.

CrimeSolutions.gov. (n.d.d). Drunk driving. Retrieved from https://www.crimesolutions.gov/advsearch.aspx.

Epperson, M. W., Canada, K., Thompson, J., & Lurigio, A. (2014). Walking the line: Specialized and standard probation officer perspectives on supervising probationers with serious mental illnesses. *International Journal of Law and Psychiatry*, *37*(5), 473–483.

Epperson, M. W., Wolff, N., Morgan, R. D., Fisher, W. H., Frueh, B. C., & Huening, J. (2014). Envisioning the next generation of behavioral health and criminal justice interventions. *International Journal of Law and Psychiatry*, *37*(5), 427–438.

Fact Sheet, Women in Prison Project. (2017). Correctional Association of New York. http://www.correctionalassociation.org/pp/about-women-in-prison-projectCorrectional. Association of New York.

Fazel, S., Singh, J. P., Doll, H., & Grann, M. (2012). Use of risk assessment instruments to predict violence and antisocial behaviour in 73 samples involving 24 827 people: Systematic review and meta-analysis. *BMJ: British Medical Journal*, *345*, e4692.

Friedmann, P. D., Taxman, F. S., & Henderson, C. E. (2007). Evidence-based treatment practices for drug-involved adults in the criminal justice system. *Journal of Substance Abuse Treatment*, *32*(3), 267–277.

Glaze, L., & Maruschak, L. (2011). *Parents in prison and their minor children*. Washington, DC: Bureau of Justice Statistics.

Glover, A. J., Nicholson, D. E., Hemmati, T., Bernfeld, G. A., & Quinsey, V. L. (2002). A comparison of predictors of general and violent recidivism among high-risk federal offenders. *Criminal Justice and Behavior, 29*(3), 235–249.

Grady, M. D. (2009). Sex offenders part II: Policies that address sex offenders. *Social Work in Mental Health*, 7(4), 372–384.

Greenberg, G. A., & Rosenheck, R. A. (2008). Jail incarceration, homelessness, and mental health: A national study. *Psychiatric Services, 59*(2), 170–177.

Hammett, T. M., Gaiter, J. L., & Crawford, C. (1998). Reaching seriously at-risk populations: Health interventions in criminal justice settings. *Health Education & Behavior, 25*(1).

Hien, D. A., Campbell, A., & Miele, G. (2014). Synthesizing outcomes of evidence-based practices in a multi-site clinical trial for women with trauma and addictions. *Drug and Alcohol Dependence, 140*, e86–e168.

Kennedy-Hendricks, A., Huskamp, H. A., Rutkow, L., & Barry, C. L. (2016). Improving access to care and reducing involvement in the criminal justice system for people with mental illness. *Health Affairs, 35*(6), 1076–1083.

Lamb, H. R., & Weinberger, L. E. (2014). Decarceration of U.S. jails and prisons: Where will persons with serious mental illness go? *Journal of the American Academy of Psychiatry the Law, 42*(4), 489–494.

Leukefeld, C., Gullotta, T. P., & Gregrich, J. (2011). *Handbook of evidence-based substance abuse treatment in criminal justice settings*. New York: Springer.

Lurigio, A. J., Rollins, A., & Fallon, J. (2004). The effects of serious mental illness on offender reentry. *Federal Probation, 68*, 45.

Marsiglia, F. F., Miles, B. W., Dustman, P., & Sills, S. (2002). Ties that protect: An ecological perspective on Latino/a urban pre-adolescent drug use. *Journal of Ethnic and Cultural Diversity in Social Work, 11*(3–4), 191–220.

Maruschak, L. M. (1999). *DWI offenders under correctional supervision*. Washington, DC: U.S. Department Of Justice, Office of Justice Programs, Bureau of Justice Statistics.

McCarty, D., & Chandler, R. K. (2009). Understanding the importance of organizational and system variables on addiction treatment services within criminal justice settings. *Drug and Alcohol Dependence, 103*, 91–93.

Merrick, E. L., Horgan, C. M., Reif, S., Quinn, A., Stewart, M., Garnick, D. W., et al. (2015). Managing substance use treatment in private U.S. health plans. *Drug and Alcohol Dependence, 146*, e34–e117.

Meyer, J. P., Cepeda, J., & Altice, F. L. (2015). Longitudinal gender differences in HIV and criminal justice outcomes. *Drug and Alcohol Dependence, 146*, e39–e40.

Mills, K. L., Hodge, W., Johansson, K., & Conigrave, K. M. (2008). An outcome evaluation of the New South Wales Sober driver Programme: A remedial programme for recidivist drink drivers. *Drug and Alcohol Review, 27*(1), 65–74.

Navarro, M. (1992). *Panel proposes steps to control the spread of TB among inmates*. The New York Times.

Office for Victims of Crime. (2013). *Special Populations – 2013 OVC report to the nation: Fiscal years 2011-2012*. Retrieved from https://www.ovc.gov/pubs/reporttonation2013/sp_popl.html.

Olmstead, T., & Sindelar, J. L. (2004). To what extent are key services offered in treatment programs for special populations? *Journal of Substance Abuse Treatment, 27*, 9–15.

Oser, C., Knudsen, H., Staton-Tindall, M., & Leukefeld, C. (2009). The adoption of wraparound services among substance abuse treatment organizations serving criminal offenders: The role of a women-specific program. *Drug and Alcohol Dependence, 103*, 82–90.

Quinn, T. P., & Quinn, E. L. (2015). The effect of cognitive-behavioral therapy on driving while intoxicated recidivism. *Journal of Drug Issues, 45*(4), 431–446.

Quinsey, V. L., Harris, G. T., Rice, M. E., & Cormier, C. A. (1998). *Violent offenders: Appraising and managing risk*. Washington, DC: American Psychological Association.

Raimon, M., Lee, A., & Genty, P. (2009). *Sometimes good intentions yield bad results: ASFA's effect on incarcerated parents and their children*. New Jersey: National Resource Center on Children & Families of the Incarcerated.
Rice, M. E., Harris, G. T., & Lang, C. (2013). Validation of and revision to the VRAG and SORAG: The Violence Risk Appraisal Guide – Revised (VRAG-R). *Psychological Assessment, 25*(3), 951.
Robbins, M. S., Feaster, D. J., Horigian, V. E., Puccinelli, M. J., Henderson, C., & Szapocznik, J. (2011). Therapist adherence in brief strategic family therapy for adolescent drug abusers. *Journal of Consulting and Clinical Psychology, 79*(1), 43–53.
Sanders, B., Thomas, Y. F., & Griffin-Deeds, B. (2013). *Crime, HIV and health: Intersections of criminal justice and public health concerns*. New York: Springer.
Santisteban, D. A., Suarez-Morales, L., Robbins, M. S., & Szapocznik, J. (June 2006). Brief strategic family therapy: Lessons learned in efficacy research and challenges to blending research and practice. *Family Process, 45*(2), 259–271.
Skeem, J. L., & Louden, J. E. (2006). Toward evidence-based practice for probationers and parolees mandated to mental health treatment. *Psychiatric Services, 57*(3), 333–342.
Skeem, J. L., Emke-Francis, P., & Louden, J. E. (2006). Probation, mental health, and mandated treatment: A national survey. *Criminal Justice and Behavior, 33*(2), 158–184.
Spohr, S. A., Taxman, F. S., Rodriguez, M., & Walters, S.T. (2016). Motivational interviewing fidelity in a community corrections setting: Treatment initiation and subsequent drug use. *Journal of Substance Abuse Treatment, 65*, 20–25.
Springer, S. A., Azar, M. M., & Altice, F. L. (2011). HIV, alcohol dependence, and the criminal justice system: A review and call for evidence-based treatment for released prisoners. *The American Journal of Drug and Alcohol Abuse, 37*(1), 12–21.
Substance Abuse and Mental Health Services Administration. (2013). *Einstein expert panel: Medication-assisted treatment and the criminal justice system*. Retrieved from https://www.samhsa.gov/sites/default/files/mat-criminal-justice-panel-2011.pdf.
Substance Abuse and Mental Health Services Administration. (2015). *Screening and assessment of co-occurring disorders in the justice system*. Rockville, MD: HHS Publication No. (SMA) -15–4930 (Author).
Substance Abuse and Mental Health Services Administration. (2016a). *Co-occurring disorders*. Retrieved from https://www.samhsa.gov/disorders/co-occurring#criminal-justice.
Substance Abuse and Mental Health Services Administration. (2016b). *Medication-assisted treatment (MAT)*. Retrieved from https://www.samhsa.gov/medication-assisted-treatment.
Substance Abuse and Mental Health Services Administration. (2017). *Publications and resources on homelessness and housing*. Retrieved from https://www.samhsa.gov/homelessness-housing/publications-resources.
Szapocznik, J., Lopez, B., Prado, G., Schwartz, S. J., & Pantin, H. (2006). Outpatient drug abuse treatment for hispanic adolescents. *Drug and Alcohol Dependence, 84*, S54–S63.
Szapocznik, J., Prado, G., Burlew, A. K., Williams, R. A., & Santisteban, D. A. (2007). Drug abuse in African American and Hispanic adolescents: Culture, development, and behavior. *Annual Review of Clinical Psychology, 3*, 77–105.
Taxman, F. S., Young, D.W., & Fletcher, B.W. (2007). The National Criminal Justice Treatment Practices survey: An overview of the special issue. *Journal of Substance Abuse Treatment, 32*(3), 221.
Taxman, F. S., Young, D. W., Wiersema, B., Rhodes, A., & Mitchell, S. (2007). The national criminal justice treatment practices survey: Multilevel survey methods and procedures. *Journal of Substance Abuse Treatment, 32*(3), 225–238.
The Sentencing Project (2012). http://www.sentencingproject.org/doc/publications/cc_Incarcerated_Women_Factsheet_Dec2012final.pdf.

Todrys, K. W., & Amon, J. J. (2012). Criminal justice reform as HIV and TB prevention in African prisons. *PLoS Med, 9*(5), e1001215. https://doi.org/10.1371/journal.pmed.1001215.
Trimble, J. E., Scharrón-del-Río, M. R., & Hill, J. S. (2012). Ethical considerations in the application of cultural adaptation models with ethnocultural populations. In G. Bernal, & M. M. Domenech Rodriguez (Eds.), *Cultural adaptations: tools for evidence-based practice with diverse populations* (pp. 45–67). Washington, DC: American Psychological Association.
Truman, J. L., & Langton, L. (2015). *Criminal victimization, 2014.* Washington, DC: U.S. Department of Justice, Office of Justice Programs, Bureau of Justice Statistics.
U.S. Department of Justice, Office of Justice Programs. (2016). *Evidence integration: Gangs.* Retrieved from https://ojp.gov/programs/gangs.htm.
Underhill, K., Dumont, D., & Operario, D. (2014). HIV prevention for adults with criminal justice involvement: A systematic review of HIV risk-reduction interventions in incarceration and community settings. *American Journal of Public Health, 104*(11), e27–e53.
Valdez, A., Cepeda, A., Parrish, D., Horowitz, R., & Kaplan, C. (2013). An adapted brief strategic family therapy for gang-Affiliated Mexican American adolescents. *Research on Social Work Practice, 23*(4), 383–396.
Vanderplasschen, W., Colpaert, K., Autrique, M., Rapp, R. C., Pearce, S., Broekaert, E., et al. (2013). *Therapeutic communities for addictions: A review of their effectiveness from a recovery-oriented perspective.* The Scientific World Journal.
Wexler, H. K., & Fletcher, B. W. (2007). National criminal justice drug abuse treatment studies (CJ-DATS) overview. *The Prison Journal, 87*(1), 9–24.

FURTHER READING

Center for Sex Offender Management. (2007). *Managing the challenges of sex offender reentry.* Retrieved from http://www.csom.org/pubs/reentry_brief.pdf.
Substance Abuse and Mental Health Administration. (2016). *Criminal and juvenile justice.* Retrieved from https://www.samhsa.gov/criminal-juvenile-justice.

CHAPTER 10

Implementing Evidence-Based Practices and Principles With Criminal Justice Populations

George T. Patterson

GENERAL GUIDELINES FOR IMPLEMENTING EVIDENCE-BASED PRACTICES

Thomas Insel (2015), the former director of the National Institute of Mental Health, cited a recent Institute of Medicine report titled *Psychosocial Interventions for Mental and Substance Use Disorders: A Framework for Establishing Evidence-Based Standards*. The report describes significant differences that exist between the development and implementation of clinical interventions and medical interventions, notably medications. The Food and Drug Administration (FDA) regulations ensure the medication filled in a prescription is the same medication that was tested and determined effective in randomized controlled trials (RCTs). On the other hand, an FDA counterpart does not exist for clinical interventions. Consequently, no regulatory agency ensures that clinical interventions are implemented in the same way they were developed and tested in RCTs. Calls for a regulatory agency, or an FDA equivalent, for clinical interventions began in 1982, yet to date no regulatory agency has been established.

Despite the fact that no regulatory agency has been established to oversee the development and implementation of evidence-based practices, numerous recommendations have been proposed for implementing evidence-based practices. As outlined in Chapter 5, numerous organizations rate and classify clinical interventions as evidence-based practices. Interestingly, the rating systems and classification approaches are not uniform among organizations. Likewise, guidelines recommended to inform the implementation of evidence-based practices are not uniform.

Locating and retrieving information about evidence-based practices is among the earliest steps during the implementation process. Possessing

Clinical Interventions in Criminal Justice Settings
ISBN 978-0-12-811381-3
http://dx.doi.org/10.1016/B978-0-12-811381-3.00010-X

internet search skills has made this step relatively simple. Certainly, search strategies involve an understanding of best evidence, client needs, and relevant evidence-based interventions. Subsequent steps throughout the implementation process are not as easy to achieve.

Early guidelines in the medical field described four steps for implementing evidence-based medicine (EBM):

Step 1: Develop a question focused on the patient's presenting problem.

Step 2: Search and retrieve studies focused on the patient's presenting problem.

Step 3: Evaluate the evidence reported in the studies.

Step 4: Implement the findings gleaned from the studies (Rosenberg & Donald, 1995).

Straus, Richardson, Glasziou, and Haynes (2005) identified five steps for implementing EBM:

Step 1: Develop a clinical question.

Step 2: Locate and retrieve the "best research evidence" (p. 1) that answers the clinical question.

Step 3: Evaluate the research evidence in terms of applicability and validity.

Step 4: Supplement the evaluation of the research evidence with clinical expertise, and client values and situations.

Step 5: Conduct an evaluation of Steps 1–4 focused on improving each step for subsequent implementation efforts.

Social work scholars have proposed similar steps for implementing evidence-based practices. Mullen (2006) suggested eight components of successful implementation that highlight the significance of organizational support:

1. The internal organizational environment should develop and implement policies and procedures that support the evidence-based practice (funding, workload changes).
2. The external organizational environment should support the intervention (funder, accreditation organizations).
3. Assessment, intervention, and outcomes should be grounded in empirical evidence.
4. The intervention should be empirically supported in a systematic review.
5. Practice guidelines and manuals should be developed and utilized to support the intervention.
6. Implementation fidelity protocols should be developed and utilized.
7. Implementation fidelity and intervention outcomes should be evaluated and disseminated.
8. Social workers should be trained to provide the intervention.

Of course when implementing evidence-based practices in organizations, internal and external organizational support is essential. Without organizational support, full implementation is not likely to be successful and is more likely to fail. The need for organizational support is a common factor whether the organization is a criminal justice or noncriminal justice organization.

Proctor and Rosen (2006) proposed four steps for implementing evidence-based practices:

Step 1: Locate and retrieve an evidence-based intervention developed for a specific client population.

Step 2: Determine the most appropriate intervention for the client population.

Step 3: If necessary, modify the intervention using clinical expertise.

Step 4: Monitor and evaluate the intervention to assess effectiveness.

Each step for implementing evidence-based practice reviewed thus far is similar to the steps for implementing EBM proposed by Rosenberg and Donald (1995). Step 4 in the previous example is a crucial step, and is also articulated in the National Association of Social Workers (NASW) of Code of Ethics (2008). The NASW Code of Ethics states that social workers have an ethical obligation to monitor and evaluate interventions. It stands to reason that ethical practice demands that evaluation results be drawn upon to modify the intervention should results show that it is not achieving the intended outcomes. Clearly this requires expertise in implementation science. It also requires skills to conduct a program evaluation. Organizations most often lack expertise in these areas, and therefore will find the assistance of consultants invaluable.

Although initially articulated as EBM, over time as the principles of EBM were adopted in other fields the term evidence-based practice was used. Some sources even cite the EBM definition identifying it as the definition of evidence-based practice. Common characteristics among implementation steps for EBM and evidence-based practice suggests that such practices should be: (1) grounded in empirical evidence, and (2) evaluated following implementation to assess whether the intervention has been implemented properly and achieving the intended clinical and other outcomes.

The implementation of evidence-based practices range in complexity from manualized interventions such as anger and stress management techniques, and communication or listening skills which are considered relatively easy to implement without requiring in-depth supervision, technical assistance or training; to more complex interventions such as cognitive behavioral therapy. The latter require supervision, training, and/or technical assistance (Simpson, 2002).

GUIDELINES FOR IMPLEMENTING EVIDENCE-BASED PRACTICES IN CRIMINAL JUSTICE SETTINGS

The importance of following a systematic approach to implementing interventions in criminal justice settings has been well documented. Guidelines describing the implementation of evidence-based practices in criminal justice settings must consider the specific component of the criminal justice system in which the intervention will be located, as well as the social problems experienced by the criminal justice population. To facilitate the implementation process, checklists and guidelines have been developed. These materials are specific to a criminal justice setting and offender and former offenders' presenting problems.

Two checklists are briefly examined. Blandford and Osher (2012) suggest that behavioral evidence-based interventions should match the offender or former offender's behavioral health disorder, and needs and risk levels. The authors provide a checklist containing two sections. Section one emphasizes the importance of building partnerships across agencies. The checklist items include four steps for achieving these aims, rationale, and actions. These four steps receive a check mark indicating if a step is currently in progress, completed, or no progress has been made in achieving the step. The second section is used to conduct an assessment of agency readiness to implement a variety of evidence-based programs and practices, and promising programs and practices in the areas of adult mental health and substance abuse disorders. This section of the checklist contains a short summary describing the intervention, an area to identify the level of intervention (none, partial, or full implementation), and an area used to identify if agency capacity exists to implement the intervention.

Domurad and Carey (2010) describe a 19-item checklist that requires "yes", "no", or "unclear" responses. Checklist items include a range of implementation strategies such as whether or not actuarial risk assessment instruments are administered, and if so when, the types of community-based and/or institutional interventions provided, and whether or not needs and risks are reassessed. Based on the results of this assessment, an action plan is developed that assigns tasks to individuals together with specific completion dates. In addition to utilizing the checklist, involving leadership and front line staff, openness to change, and transparency and accountability are initial steps that should be performed.

Other approaches include guidelines or models for implementation. Bogue et al. (2004) describe the Integrated Model, useful for implementing eight evidence-based principles in community-based corrections settings. The goal of the model is to reduce recidivism. The model highlights the importance of three areas required for successful implementation; the use of effective evidence-based principles, organizational development, and partnership. Outcome and process measures are identified as well as definitions, sources of data, and data collection agencies and frequency. Similarly, Guevara and Solomon (2009) support use of the Integrated Model when implementing eight evidence-based principles in community-based corrections settings. They provide additional suggestions to aid with the implementation process which include:

- acquire knowledge about the components of correctional interventions.
- translate the research evidence demonstrating the effectiveness of the eight evidence-based principles into practice.
- apply the eight evidence-based principles with offenders and former offenders, the agency, and funders and policymakers.
- apply the following seven guidelines for implementing evidence-based practice:
  - implementation of new interventions must be congruent with the agency mission.
  - interventions implementation should be monitored using reliable and valid quantitative data.
  - utilize the expertise of an experienced professional.
  - provide staff development opportunities that emphasize research, training, and organizational change.
  - monitor staff attitudes, knowledge, skills and behaviors such as staff turnover. Use this information to improve the intervention or program.
  - measure staff, offender, and former offender's outcomes. Use this information to improve the intervention or program.
  - form partnerships between community-based agencies and corrections agencies.

Finally, SAMSHA (2017) provides guidelines describing successful strategies for implementing effective interventions during reentry among offenders who experience mental health and substance use disorders. The

10 guidelines are organized around the Assess, Plan, Identify, and Coordinate (APIC) model (Osher, Steadman, & Barr, 2002):

Assess clinical and other needs, and public safety risks

1. Use actuarial risk assessment instruments in applicable components of the criminal justice system to assess substance abuse, mental health, and co-occurring disorders, and criminogenic needs.
2. Among high-risk offenders and former offenders, complete thorough assessment that includes criminal history, social and community supports, and strengths and protective factors.

Plan treatment and other service needs

3. Develop a treatment plan based on actuarial risk assessment outcomes.
4. Establish partnerships between behavioral health and criminal justice agencies based on actuarial risk assessment outcomes and level of services assessment.

Identify correctional and reentry interventions

5. Identify and provide interventions early in the reentry process.
6. Develop and implement policies and practices that support seamless interventions and services during the reentry process.

Coordinate reentry plans, interventions, and services

7. Use effective strategies and programs such as problem-solving courts to enhance compliance with treatment plans and community supervision.
8. Develop and implement effective information-sharing strategies among relevant components of the criminal justice system.
9. Establish partnerships between agencies serving criminal justice populations with substance use, mental health, and co-occurring disorders, and establish joint training models.
10. Use data to evaluate and enhance program outcomes, and develop a plan for program sustainability.

These checklists and guidelines are practical for assisting agencies with identifying areas of strengths and areas that require improvement during the implementation process. In most instances technical assistance, training, or other support will be needed if agencies are not capable of implementing evidence-based practices and principles using these checklists and guidelines alone.

THE ROLE OF PRACTICE GUIDELINES IN IMPLEMENTING EVIDENCE-BASED PRACTICES

Clinical practice guidelines inform best practice approaches relevant for mental disorders and are intended to achieve specific outcomes. Practice guidelines are developed based on empirical evidence or expert consensus.

An example includes the clinical practice guidelines developed by the American Psychiatric Association (2017). The guidelines adhere to the PICO(TS) system, which emphasize: patient, intervention, comparison, and outcome. Some guidelines also include timing and setting.

Clinical practice guidelines can prove invaluable to assist clinicians with modifying an intervention when modifications are required. An informed decision can be made regarding which components of an intervention require modification. Indeed, practice guidelines and expert consensus guidelines can be valuable resources that support the implementation of evidence-based practices (Corcoran & Vandiver, 2006).

To illustrate further, the American Psychiatric Association developed practice guidelines for treating substance use disorders, which is a common problem among criminal justice populations. The guidelines identify numerous psychosocial interventions such as cognitive behavioral therapy, behavioral therapy, and 12-step programs, as well as issues to consider for intervention modification. These issues include client characteristics, cultural beliefs regarding health and recovery, and the difficulty conducting assessments and providing interventions when individuals use multiple substances (American Psychiatric Association, 2010). Clinical guidelines also provide information about community resources that are essential for referral and advocacy efforts such as the *Clinical guidelines for social work professionals discharge assistance* prepared by the Federal Bureau of Prisons (2002).

In spite of the usefulness of clinical practice guidelines, clinical practitioners are often unaware of these guidelines. Among 500 clinical agency staff employed in a large agency social service agency, 94.1% of psychiatrists were knowledgeable about clinical practice guidelines prior to participating in the study, 81.3% of psychologists, and only 42.3% of social workers were aware of clinical practice guidelines prior to participating in the study (Mullen & Bacon, 2006).

ACADEMIC TRAINING AND EMPLOYMENT

A national survey of accredited academic psychiatry, clinical psychology, and master's degree social work programs found that 4.3% of psychiatry programs did not offer rigorous academic training in evidence-based practices, 67.3% of clinical psychology PsyD programs, and 61.7% of social work programs did not offer such training (Weissman et al., 2006).

Among these three professional groups, clinical social workers are the largest group of mental health and substance abuse providers in the United States with 193,038 practitioners, followed by psychologists with 95,545 practitioners, and 33,727 psychiatrists (Substance Abuse and Mental Health Services Administration, 2013). The criminal justice system includes populations with high rates of mental illness, substance abuse disorders, and co-occurring disorders.

Although representing the largest group of mental health and substance abuse service providers, few social workers are employed in criminal justice settings. A survey of licensed clinical social workers who identified their employment setting as a criminal justice setting found that 0.30% identified a private for-profit agency, and 0.30% identified a private non-profit agency. Among governmental agencies, 5.3% identified a State agency, 4.4% a local governmental agency, and no social workers reported primary employment in a federal government criminal justice setting. Among all licensed clinical social workers, 1.7% reported a criminal justice agency as their primary employment (National Association of Social Workers, 2006).

It stands to reason that if rigorous academic training in evidence-based practice is not provided in accredited educational programs, other concepts such as implementation fidelity and implementation science are also not taught. Taken together, lack of educational training, knowledge about practice guidelines, and low rates of employment among licensed clinical professional in criminal justice settings influence evidence-based practice implementation.

IMPLEMENTATION SCIENCE

Implementation fidelity was discussed in Chapter 3. In this chapter, we examine implementation science. Przybylski and Orchowsky (2015) define implementation science as:

> *a field of research as well as a body of scientific knowledge that can be used to support high-quality implementation in complex, real-world settings. Although it is a relatively new and emerging discipline that only recently has become a part of programming conversations in the criminal justice and juvenile justice communities, implementation science has been embraced in the fields of public health and international development for years. (p. 5)*

As of 2013, Ducharme, Chandler, and Wiley (2013) reported that no published articles describing the implementation process in criminal justice settings were found in the journal *Implementation Science*. Implementation science can improve intervention outcomes in both criminal justice settings, and noncriminal justice community-based settings that provide clinical interventions to criminal justice populations.

Case Example

Background

Criminal justice populations often do not benefit from implementation science in real world settings. Moreover, the training agency staff receive to implement evidence-based practices is often less than ideal. The first author was contracted to conduct a program evaluation for a social service agency. The grant funded program provided services to a former offender female population. Grant funding was acquired prior to the involvement of the evaluator.

The goals of the gender-responsive approach to intervention were to increase access to HIV prevention and intervention, substance abuse treatment, HIV testing, treatment for co-occurring disorders, and reduce risk for HIV. The intervention was developed integrating components of an evidence-based intervention with modifications to address HIV.

The Problem

Although employing grant writers is not always possible among social service agencies, many social service agencies do employ grant writers. The agency employed a grant writer whose responsibilities included preparing and submitting the funding proposal. As a result, funding for the program, intervention, methodological approach, and outcomes were predetermined upon hiring the evaluator. Outcome measures were linked to the intervention and were created by the intervention developers. Little information was provided about the reliability and validity of the measures.

Some funding organizations provide suggestions to grant applicants for hiring an external program evaluator. As an illustration, The Office of Minority Health (OMH) at the U.S. Department of Health and Human Services (2011) prepared a report titled *How to hire an evaluator*. In the report, OMH suggests that evaluators should participate in the grant application writing process or agencies hire an evaluator soon after funding is awarded. Thus, either strategy is acceptable, although the latter offers less opportunities for an evaluator's contributions. OMH suggests early involvement of an evaluator in the funding application process for the following reasons:

1. It provides opportunities for the evaluator to become knowledgeable about the intervention, research design, and program.

2. It provides sufficient time for the evaluator to develop intervention outcomes and data collection procedures.
3. It provides sufficient time for the evaluator to develop the data collection instruments and pilot-test the instruments if necessary.
4. Early involvement provides the evaluator with sufficient time to obtain Institutional Review Board (IRB) approval prior to program participant enrollment and data collection.
5. Early involvement gives the evaluator sufficient time to engage staff in the evaluation process and increase their understanding of the intervention and outcome measures.
6. Early involvement allows the evaluator sufficient time to collect data and provide feedback to staff about program progress, outcomes, and areas that require improvement. Such early involvement also gives the evaluator sufficient time to develop and implement strategies intended to improve the program.

As these sample suggestions have shown, implementation science and fidelity are not specifically mentioned, although these concepts may be implied. Moreover, it may be less difficult for agencies to contract with evaluators skilled in research methodology, statistical analysis, and program evaluation methods than implementation science, implementation fidelity, and measurement and implementation research. The latter requires a unique skill set.

Several agency staff members were trained to administer the outcome measures and provide the intervention, which was described as an evidence-based practice. However, the intervention could not be found in any of the major registries identifying evidence-based practices. Empirical support for the evidence-based intervention and modified components consisted of a pre-experimental design with pretest and posttest data. Weissman et al. (2006) note that widespread agreement suggests that intervention efficacy should be demonstrated in two or more RCTs before an intervention can be classified as an evidence-based practice. While improved outcomes at posttest were statistically significant, no comparison group or random assignment to conditions were employed. Consequently, the intervention was not supported by RCTs.

During the course of the evaluation all of the staff members turned over. The quality of training new staff received to provide the intervention was unclear given that the intervention developers assumed responsibilities for staff training. The intervention developers were located off-site and a selected staff member was responsible for communications between the program and evaluator, and the developers.

Resolution

It would be ideal to have involved the evaluator in the grant application process from the onset. Although this was not the evaluation approach, the evaluator held regular meetings with agency staff and supervisors to identify ongoing issues that may have affected the intervention implementation.

These monitoring and evaluation activities also involved conducting focus groups with program participants. The IRB approved focus groups provided contextual information about the intervention from participants' perspectives. Implementation science and measuring implementation fidelity were not employed in this example. In real world settings, these activities are often not conducted. It requires an evaluator trained and experienced in implementation science or intervention research.

Positive intervention outcomes were found. Several factors could have contributed to the positive program results. The agency also provided housing and other community-based services as well as a gender-responsive approach to intervention. It is unknown whether these positive intervention results can be replicated in other settings among other former offender female populations. In fact, a review of implementation studies conducted in real world settings shows that positive intervention outcomes were reported among studies with approximately 60% implementation levels. Few studies reported implementation levels greater than 80%, and no study reported implementation levels approximating 100%. Overall, it is not practical to achieve full or close full intervention implementation (Durlak & DuPre, 2008).

Finally, agencies should employ strategies for building and sustaining capacity to support the intervention. This is particularly relevant when time-limited grant funding was used to initially implement the intervention and ongoing funding to sustain the intervention is nonexistent.

CRIME PREVENTION PROGRAMS IMPLEMENTED IN CRIMINAL JUSTICE AND NONCRIMINAL JUSTICE SETTINGS

Sherman et al. (1998) identified crime prevention programs that were implemented in criminal justice and noncriminal justice settings. These programs were categorized as what works, what doesn't, and what's promising, and were implemented in the following locations: (1) community-based settings, (2) family settings through home visits and family therapy, (3) school-based settings, (4) labor market settings, (5) business-settings, (6) law enforcement agencies, and (7) criminal justice agencies such as drug courts and prisons following an arrest.

EVIDENCE-BASED PRACTICES IMPLEMENTED IN CRIMINAL JUSTICE SETTINGS

Studies have examined the implementation of evidence-based practices in criminal justice settings. Analyzing data from the self-report National Crime Justice Treatment Practices survey, Henderson, Taxman, and Young (2008) listed the most frequent and least frequently implemented evidence-based practices in juvenile and adult corrections, and community-based substance abuse treatment organizations.

The five most frequently implemented interventions in juvenile justice settings were:

- comprehensive treatment.
- substance abuse assessment using a standardized instrument.
- family treatment.
- treatment for co-occurring disorders.
- use of methods to engage youth in treatment.

In order, beginning with the least frequently implemented evidence-based interventions listed first, these were:

- youth focused interventions.
- use of cognitive-behavioral, therapeutic community, or other manualized interventions.
- use of a standardized risk assessment instrument.
- use of sanctions.
- drug testing.

The most frequently implemented evidence-based interventions in adult settings were:

- comprehensive treatment.
- use of a standardized substance abuse assessment instrument.
- linkages among criminal justice system components.
- treatment for co-occurring disorders.
- methods to engage adults in treatment.

The least frequently implemented evidence-based practices, in ascending order, were:

- use of cognitive-behavioral, therapeutic community, or other manualized interventions.
- use of a standardized risk assessment instrument.
- use of sanctions.
- program outcomes are assessed.
- employing qualified staff.

Analyzing the same dataset, Friedmann, Taxman, and Henderson (2007) examined the implementation of evidence-based practices in correctional settings (jails, prisons, probation, and parole) and in community-based substance abuse organizations that treated adult criminal justice populations. Forty-one administrators employed in jails, 98 in prisons, and 151 employed in probation and parole settings reported a range of evidence-based practices that were implemented in these settings.

In jails, the five most frequently implemented evidence-based practices in order of most frequent listed first were:

- comprehensive services.
- linkages among criminal justice system components.
- use of incentives.
- use of a standardized substance abuse assessment instrument.
- treatment lasting more than 90 days.

The evidence-based interventions that were least used, in ascending order, include:

- family treatment.
- use of a standardized risk assessment instrument.
- use of cognitive-behavioral, therapeutic community, or other manualized interventions.
- use of methods to engage adults in treatment.
- use of sanctions.

In prisons, the five most implemented evidence-based practices were:

- comprehensive services.
- use of incentives.
- use of a standardized substance abuse assessment instrument.
- treatment lasting more than 90 days.
- linkages among criminal justice system components.

The five least implemented evidence-based practices, beginning with the least implemented listed first, were:

- family treatment.
- use of actuarial risk assessment instruments.
- use of cognitive-behavioral, therapeutic community, or other manualized interventions.
- drug testing.
- use of sanctions.

Finally, in probation and parole settings, the five most reported implemented evidence-based practices were:

- comprehensive services.
- linkages among criminal justice system components.
- drug testing.
- use of incentives.
- use of a standardized substance abuse assessment instruments.

The least implemented evidence-based practices, in ascending order, were:

- family treatment.
- use of cognitive-behavioral, therapeutic community, or other manualized interventions.
- use of methods to engage probationers and parolees.
- interventions for co-occurring disorders.
- use of actuarial risk assessment instruments.

Friedmann et al. (2007) concluded that prison settings used more evidence-based practices than jails, probation, or parole settings. Prisons also used standardized instruments to assess substance use more than other settings, used more methods to engage prisoners in treatment, were more likely to provide interventions for co-occurring disorders, and used incentives more than other criminal justice settings. Conversely, prisons were less likely than jails, probation, or parole settings to establish and maintain linkages between criminal justice and community-based settings. Probation and parole settings also used actuarial risk assessment instruments and conducted more drug testing than prisons and jails.

IMPLEMENTING EVIDENCE-BASED PRINCIPLES WITH CRIMINAL JUSTICE POPULATIONS

The opportunities for implementing evidence-based practices are different in a private practice setting, human service agency, or criminal justice setting. This occurs because each of these distinct settings presents unique organizational and practitioner and client characteristics.

Moreover, in some settings, it may be impossible to implement evidence-based practices that are long-term clinical interventions. In these instances, implementing evidence-based principles is more feasible.

Studies investigating the implementation of evidence-based practices in criminal justice settings have found support for the use of both evidence-based practices (which we view as manualized, replicable clinical interventions) as well as evidence-based principles (distinct components of evidence-based practices). For example, functional family therapy (FFT), a widely used empirically supported evidence-based intervention for at-risk adolescents and their families consists of three phases: (1) engagement and motivation, (2) behavior change, and (3) generalization. Each of the three phases is comprised of specific clinical techniques and goals relevant for that phase. In phase one, the focus is motivating at-risk adolescents and their families to change their behaviors including participating in FFT (Sexton & Alexander, 2003).

The engagement and motivation clinical techniques are components of FFT, and do not comprise the entire intervention. As we saw, increasing motivation and the use of engagement techniques are widely implemented evidence-based principles in criminal justice and community-based settings with criminal justice populations (Friedmann et al., 2007; Henderson et al., 2008). Increasing motivation among criminal justice populations, instead of using persuasion techniques, is an effective evidence-based principal for changing behavior (National Institute of Corrections, n.d.). Henderson et al. further suggested that in juvenile justice settings, the least frequently used interventions were cognitive behavioral therapy or other manualized, replicable evidence-based interventions. They concluded that evidence-based practices "requiring 'deep structure' modifications of service delivery" (p. 173) are less likely to be implemented in criminal justice settings.

Based on their literature review results, Golder et al. (2005) concluded that an inventory of effective interventions found to reduce recidivism are essentially "...intervention components or characteristics..." (p. 108). Among the list were previously identified principles for effective correctional intervention such as: provide a higher level of intervention to high-risk former offenders, provide interventions focused on criminogenic needs, provide interventions relevant for offender characteristics, provide cognitive behavioral interventions, recognize practitioner characteristics, and provide additional services such as housing assistance.

Further, because of the difficulties associated with implementing evidence-based practices in criminal justice settings, Belenko and Wexler (2007) asserted that evidence-based principles "may be easier to implement" (p. 27). Similar to evidence-based practices, empirical evidence demonstrates the effectiveness of evidence-based principles. The authors provide several examples of evidence-based principles that are appropriate for implementation with criminal justice populations. These include: (1) implementing cognitive and behavioral interventions, (2) targeting criminogenic risks and needs, (3) program monitoring, and (4) the provision of transitional services during reentry.

In sum, support exists for our perspective articulated in Chapter 1 in which we discussed that evidence-based practices are clinical interventions, whereas evidence-based principles are components of evidence-based practices. Our perspective is based on our clinical practice, teaching and program evaluation experiences. In our experiences, (1) frequent turnover among social service agency staff, (2) less than ideal training, supervision, and support for new staff, (3) the difficulty establishing buy-in from staff so that they do not view the implementation of evidence-based practices and assessing outcomes as extra work, and (4) the difficulty encountered with sustaining an intervention, particularly if the program was funded, after the funding period ends, has led us to perceive that evidence-based components may play a greater role in behavior change in some settings.

IMPLEMENTATION BENEFITS FOR CRIMINAL JUSTICE POPULATIONS

Clinical outcomes can be improved, and criminal justice populations can benefit when evidence-based practices and principles are used. These benefits have been discussed throughout the book and include improved public safety and public health, reduced recidivism and increased psychosocial wellbeing among offenders and former offenders. Additional benefits include benefits to taxpayers in terms of costs (Aos, Mayfield, Miller, & Yen, 2006).

IMPLEMENTATION CHALLENGES FOR CRIMINAL JUSTICE POPULATIONS

In a systematic review conducted to examine the effects of intervention implementation on programmatic outcomes, Durlak and DuPre (2008) assessed outcomes relevant for juvenile justice populations such as bullying, violence, drug use, and academic performance. Among more than 500 studies published between 1976 and 2006, five factors were found to affect the implementation of evidence-based practices in community-based settings: (1) community level factors (funding, policy, politics); (2) clinician characteristics (self-efficacy, skill level); (3) intervention characteristics (adaptability, compatibility); (4) prevention factors (organizational support, work environment), and (5) intervention factors (training, technical assistance).

Others have also noted the challenges that arise when implementing evidence-based practice and principles in criminal justice settings. Due the dissimilarities found among clinical practice and criminal justice settings, structural barriers, and funding issues implementing evidence-based practices in criminal justice settings can be a challenging undertaking (Ducharme et al., 2013).

In addition to the challenges that arise when implementing evidence-based practices in criminal justice settings due to the setting itself, the characteristics of criminal justice populations can present challenges to implementation. In other words, some implementation challenges are specific to the population's presenting problem. For instance, co-occurring disorders. Emphasis on public safety, different funding sources for mental health and substance use disorders, the lack of reentry transitional services for co-occurring disorders, and lack of resources and research for co-occurring disorders result in limited intervention options (Chandler, Peters, Field, & Juliano-Bult, 2004). Among prison-based programs providing substance use intervention, Farabee et al. (1999) identified six implementation challenges that emerged: (1) identifying, assessing, and providing referrals to the client population, (2) recruiting and training qualified staff, (3) maintaining corrections officer assignments in treatment programs, (4) use of institutional sanctions, (5) lack of reentry services, and (6) mandating offenders to substance abuse treatment. This diversity found among the population's presenting problems may also affect intervention participation levels.

Additional challenges that may affect intervention implementation include the population's need for other services as well as clinical interventions. These services include transportation, housing, employment, and health care, among others. In some instances lack of transportation may result in missed appointments.

Challenges associated with staffing include high rates of turnover, conflicts that arise with staff unions, lack of staff buy-in, a top-down organizational structure, large caseloads, inadequate education, training and resources, and varied views towards the criminal justice system and interventions (Belenko & Wexler, 2007). Consequently, a prerequisite to implementing evidence-based practices in criminal justice settings is to "identify staffs skill level, what skills require improvement, as well as the type of training needed to improve skills. Staff require training, coaching and feedback" (Ameen, Loeffler-Cobia, Clawson, & Guevara, 2010).

Case Example

Background

In 2007, a New York court received a four-year grant with supplemental funding to implement the Reclaiming Futures Initiative, and provide the foundation for a new juvenile drug court program to be housed in family court. In 2006, 855 juveniles entered the juvenile justice system in one community. In total, 2060 charges were filed against these youth, of which more than 43% were felony charges. Their average age was 15 years old. Among these youth, approximately 40% experienced a substance abuse issue (Graham, 2006).

To promote evidence-based care, Reclaiming Futures supports interventions such as cognitive behavioral therapy, motivational interviewing, the Adolescent Community Reinforcement Approach, The Seven Challenges, and the Global Appraisal of Individual Needs (GAIN) (Reclaiming Futures, 2017). A significant aspect of the initiative is a coordinated, individualized clinical approach to screening and assessment, which guides service coordination. A significant challenge in the juvenile justice system is identifying which adolescents meet the criteria for low-level offender status, and are therefore most appropriate for community-based interventions instead of custodial and other out-of-home placements. The GAIN instrument was an appropriate instrument for identifying risk and recidivism, yet considering protective factors, strengths, and person-in-environment.

The Problem

A major concern during the initial funding period was whether the current model of engagement allowed entry into the program from those program participants who were the most appropriate and eligible for these evidence-based models. Having spent considerable time and effort planning for programmatic success, a program survey found that a low-risk, African American male population was most eligible for services. The survey also found that African American males were not the juveniles who entered into the program, as white adolescents considered higher risk were being referred to the program at a higher rate by referral sources.

This was a significant event, as African American males are most often the recipients of social work services, experience embedded messages of micro-aggression and inequality, and disproportionate arrest rates (Otuyelo, Kennedy, & Graham, 2016). The increased referral of clients outside of the expected demographic resulted in a planning meeting with a referral source who articulated a race-based motivation for referrals to the program.

Differential treatment and disproportionate minority contact is a real concern in the juvenile justice system (Fix, Fix, Wienke-Totura, & Burkhart, 2017). In 2011, 14% of the total U.S. population consisted of African American adolescents, yet these youth comprised 41% of the juvenile incarcerated population (Sickmund, Sladky, Kang, & Puzzanchera, 2013). Recent data have shown how African Americans and other racial/ethnic minorities consistently experience more contact with criminal justice practitioners (e.g., law enforcement, judges) resulting in an overrepresentation of these groups within the judicial system (Leiber & Peck, 2015).

This case example highlights an additional layer of complexity resulting from the serviceable population receiving fewer referrals to the program. This phenomenon introduced conversations about whether racial bias was playing a role in the referral process, and whether that would eventually affect programmatic graduation rates, generalizable outcomes, and the self-efficacy of program participants.

Resolution

Following extensive meetings, it was determined that the narrative outlined in the grant proposal would be adhered to, and the program would regulate participation taking into account risk level regardless of other demographic characteristics such as race, ethnicity, or socio-economic status. At the risk of low program participant enrollment levels, the program would maintain fidelity to the program model originally described based on program population, referral, and screening.

One major problem affecting intervention implementation was disproportionality and its effects on referral to the program were initially ignored. Initially, program success was affected by race, micro-aggression, perceived negative programmatic outcomes, and future valuation of African American youth by criminal justice practitioners. It was assumed that the program benefits which included clinical outcomes, court case sealing, and expunging records was a futile effort as recidivism was "expected" for young African American males.

As this case example has illustrated, practitioner perceptions can affect the intervention implementation process. This case example demonstrates the need for ongoing evaluation and monitoring, and the need for an immediate corrective course of action.

SUMMARY

This chapter examined the implementation of evidence-based practices and principles in criminal justice and non-criminal justice settings. Implementation of evidence-based practices necessitates organizational capacity to sustain the intervention including ongoing training, fidelity, monitoring, and evaluation. While implementation science can promote successful implementation, it is rarely used in real world criminal justice settings.

REFERENCES

Ameen, C. A., Loeffler-Cobia, J., Clawson, E., & Meghan, G. (2010). *Evidence-based practice skills assessment for criminal justice organizations*. Washington, DC: National Institute of Corrections.

American Psychiatric Association. (2010). *Practice guideline for the treatment of patients with substance use disorders* (2nd ed.). Retrieved from. http://psychiatryonline.org/pb/assets/raw/sitewide/practice_guidelines/guidelines/substanceuse.pdf.

American Psychiatric Association. (2017). *Guideline development process*. Retrieved from http://www.psychiatry.org/psychiatrists/practice/clinical-practice-guidelines/guideline-development-process.

Aos, S., Mayfield, J., Miller, M., & Yen, W. (2006). *Evidence-based treatment of alcohol, drug, and mental health disorders: Potential benefits, costs, and fiscal impacts for Washington state*. Olympia: Washington State Institute for Public Policy.

Belenko, S., & Wexler, H. K. (2007). *Implementing evidence-based drug treatment in criminal justice settings: Final conference report*. Retrieved from www.tresearch.org/law_ethics/CEICAFinalReport2006.pdf.

Blandford, A. M., & Osher, F. C. (2012). *A checklist for implementing evidence-based practices and programs (EBPs) for justice-involved adults with behavioral health disorders*. Delmar, NY: SAMSHA's GAINS Center for Behavioral Health and Justice Transformation.

Bogue, B., Campbell, N., Carey, M., Clawson, E., Faust, D., Florio, K., et al. (2004). *Implementing evidence-based practice in community corrections: The principles of effective intervention*. Washington, DC: U.S. Department of Justice, National Institute of Corrections.

Chandler, R. K., Peters, R. H., Field, G., & Juliano-Bult, D. (2004). Challenges in implementing evidence-based treatment practices for co-occurring disorders in the criminal justice system. *Behavioral Sciences & the Law, 22*, 431–448.

Corcoran, K., & Vandiver, V. L. (2006). Implementing best practice and expert consensus procedures. In A. R. Roberts, & K. R. Yeager (Eds.), *Foundations of evidence-based social work practice* (pp. 59–66). New York: Oxford.

Domurad, F., & Carey, M. (2010). *Implementing evidence based practices: One in a series of coaching packets designed to assist jurisdictions in the implementation of effective practices that will support successful offender outcomes*. Washington, DC: Center for Effective Public Policy.

Ducharme, L. J., Chandler, R. K., & Wiley, T. R. A. (2013). Implementing drug-abuse treatment services in criminal justice settings: Introduction to the CJ-DATS study protocol series. *Health & Justice, 1*(1), 1–6.

Durlak, J. A., & DuPre, E. P. (2008). Implementation matters: A review of research on the influence of implementation on program outcomes and the factors affecting implementation. *American Journal of Community Psychology, 41*, 327–350.

Farabee, D., Prendergast, M., Cartier, J., Wexler, H., Knight, K., & Anglin, M. D. (1999). Barriers to implementing effective correctional drug treatment programs. *The Prison Journal, 79*(2), 150–162.

Federal Bureau of Prisons. (2002). *Clinical guidelines for social work professional discharge assistance*. Retrieved from https://www.bop.gov/resources/pdfs/discharge.pdf.

Fix, R. L., Fix, S. T., Wienke-Totura, C. M., & Burkhart, B. R. (2017). Disproportionate minority contact among juveniles adjudicated for sexual, violent, and general offending: The importance of home, school, and community contexts. *Crime & Delinquency, 63*(2), 189–209.

Friedmann, P. D., Taxman, F. S., & Henderson, C. E. (2007). Evidence-based treatment practices for drug-involved adults in the criminal justice system. *Journal of Substance Abuse Treatment, 32*, 267–277.

Golder, S., Ivanoff, A., Cloud, R. N., Besel, K. L., McKiernan, P., Bratt, E., et al. (2005). Evidence-based practice with adults in jails and prisons: Strategies, practices, and future directions. *Best Practices in Mental Health, 1*(2), 100–132.

Graham, W. (2006). *Reclaiming futures initiative/juvenile drug court grant application* (Unpublished manuscript).

Guevara, M., & Solomon, E. (2009). *Implementing evidence-based policy and practice in community corrections* (2nd ed.). Washington, DC: National Institute of Corrections.

Henderson, C. E., Taxman, F. S., & Young, D. W. (2008). A rash model analysis of evidence-based treatment practices used in the criminal justice system. *Drug and Alcohol Dependence, 93*, 163–175.

Insel, T. (2015). *Director's blog: Quality counts*. Retrieved from https://www.nimh.nih.gov/about/directors/thomas-insel/blog/2015/quality-counts.shtml.

Leiber, M., & Peck, J. H. (2015). Race, gender, crime severity, and decision making in the juvenile justice system. *Crime & Delinquency, 16*(6), 771–797.

Mullen, E. J. (2006). Facilitating practitioner use of evidence-based practice. In A. R. Roberts, & K. R. Yeager (Eds.), *Foundations of evidence-based social work practice* (pp. 152–159). New York: Oxford.

Mullen, E. J., & Bacon, W. (2006). Facilitating practitioner use of evidence-based practice. In A. R. Roberts, & K. R. Yeager (Eds.), *Foundations of evidence-based social work practice* (pp. 81–92). New York: Oxford.

National Association of Social Workers. (2006). *Assuring the sufficiency of a frontline workforce: A national study of licensed social workers*. Washington, DC: Author.

National Association of Social Workers. (2008). *Code of ethics of the national association of social workers*. Washington, DC: Author.

National Institute of Corrections. (n.d.). *The principles of effective interventions*. Retrieved from https://nicic.gov/theprinciplesofeffectiveinterventions.

Osher, F., Steadman, H. J., & Barr, H. (2002). *A best practice approach to community re-entry from jails for inmates with co-occurring disorders: The APIC model*. Delmar, NY: SAMSHA's GAINS Center.

Otuyelo, F., Kennedy, S., & Graham, W. K. (2016). The death of Black males: The unmasking of cultural competence and oppressive practices in a micro-aggressive environment. *Journal of Human Behavior in the Social Environment*, 26(3–4), 430–436.

Proctor, E. K., & Rosen, A. (2006). Concise standards for developing evidence-based practice guidelines. In A. R. Roberts, & K. R. Yeager (Eds.), *Foundations of evidence-based social work practice* (pp. 93–102). New York: Oxford.

Przybylski, R., & Orchowsky, S. (2015). *Implementing evidence-based practices*. Retrieved from http://www.jrsa.org/projects/ebp_briefing_paper2.pdf.

Reclaiming Futures National Program Office. (2017). *The model*. Retrieved from http://reclaimingfutures.org/model/model-solution/solution-better-treatment.

Rosenberg, W., & Donald, A. (1995). Evidence based medicine: An approach to clinical problem-solving. *Bmj: British Medical Journal, 310*(6987), 1122–1126.

Sexton, T. L., & Alexander, J. F. (2003). Functional family therapy: A mature clinical model for working with at-risk adolescents and their families. In T. L. Sexton, G. R. Weeks, & M. S. Robbins (Eds.), *Handbook of family therapy: The science and practice of working with families and couples* (pp. 323–348). New York: Brunner-Routledge.

Sherman, L. W., Gottfredson, D. C., MacKenzie, D. L., Eck, J., Reuter, P., & Bushway, S. D. (1998). *Preventing crime: What works, what doesn't, what's promising*. Washington, DC: U.S. Department of Justice, Office of Justice Programs, National Institute of Justice.

Sickmund, M., Sladky, T. J., Kang, W., & Puzzanchera, C. (2013). *Easy access to the census of juveniles in residential placement*. Retrieved from http://.ojjdp.gov.

Simpson, D. D. (2002). A conceptual framework for transferring research to practice. *Journal of Substance Abuse Treatment, 22*, 171–182.

Straus, S. E., Richardson, W. S., Glasziou, P., & Haynes, R. B. (2005). *Evidence-based medicine: How to practice and teach EBM* (3rd ed.). London: Elsevier Churchill Livingstone.

Substance Abuse and Mental Health Services Administration. (2013). *Behavioral health, United States, 2012*. Rockville, MD: Author.

Substance Abuse and Mental Health Services Administration. (2017). *Guidelines for successful transition of people with mental or substance use disorders from jail and prison: Implementation guide*. Rockville, MD: Author (SMA)-16–4998.

The Office of Minority Health, U.S Department of Health and Human Services. (2011). *How to hire an evaluator*. Retrieved from http://www.minorityhealth.hhs.gov.

Weissman, M. M., Verdeli, H., Gameroff, M. J., Bledsoe, S. E., Betts, K., Mufson, L., et al. (2006). National survey of psychotherapy training in psychiatry, psychology, and social work. *Archives of General Psychiatry, 63*, 925–934.

FURTHER READING

Aos, S., & Drake, E. (2013). *Prison, police, and programs: Evidence-based options that reduce crime and save money*. Olympia: Washington State Institute for Public Policy.

Bonta, J., & Andrews, D. A. (2007). *Risk-need-responsivity model for offender assessment and treatment* (No. 2007-06). User Report.

Casey, P. M., Elek, J. K., Warren, R. K., Cheesman, F., Kleiman, M., & Ostrom, B. (2014). *Offender risk & needs assessment instruments: A primer for courts*. Retrieved from http://www.ncsc.org/~/media/microsites/files/csi/bja%20rna%20final%20report_combined%20files%208-22-14.ashx.

Crime and Justice Institute at Community Resources for Justice. (2009). *Implementing evidence- based policy and practice in community corrections* (2nd ed.). Washington, DC: National Institute of Corrections.

Hughes, T., & Wilson, J. (2002). *Reentry trends in the United States*. Washington, DC: U.S. Department of Justice, Office of Justice Programs, Bureau of Justice Statistics.

MacKenzie, D. L. (2005). The importance of using scientific evidence to make decisions about correctional programming. *Criminology & Public Policy, 4*, 249–258.

Peters, R., & Wexler, H. K. (2005). Substance abuse treatment for adults in the criminal justice system. *TIP* (Vol. 44). Rockville, MD: SAMSHA. DHHS Publication No. (SMA) 05–4056.

Petersilia, J. (2003). *When prisoners come home: Parole and prisoner reentry*. New York: Oxford.

Prendergast, M. L. (2011). Issues defining and applying evidence-based practices criteria for treatment of criminal-justice involved clients. *Journal of Psychoactive Drugs, 7*, 10–18.

Seiter, R. P., & Kadela, K. R. (2003). Prisoner reentry: What works, what does not, and what is promising. *Crime & Delinquency, 49*, 360–388.

Serin, R. C. (2005). *Evidence-based practice: Principles for enhancing correctional results in prisons*. Washington, DC: Crime and Justice Institute, U.S. Department of Justice, National Institute of Corrections.

Solomon, A. L., Palmer, T., Atkinson, A., Davidson, J., & Harvey, L. (2006). *Prisoner reentry: Addressing the challenges in weed and seed communities*. Washington, DC: Urban Institute Press.

CHAPTER 11

Criminal Justice Initiatives Using Evidence-Based Practices and Principles

George T. Patterson

CRIMINAL JUSTICE INITIATIVES

The criminal justice system is a complex system comprised of four major components each with separate and distinct subcomponents. A diverse group of criminal justice practitioners are employed in these systems, including law enforcement officers, corrections officers, probation and parole officers, judges, attorneys, paralegals, mental health professionals, and paraprofessionals. Each of these professional groups, as well as individuals within these groups, hold different perspectives on offending behavior, punishment, and rehabilitation.

Coordinating these various systems and criminal justice practitioners, and establishing partnerships among them is also a complex task. To add to this complexity, there is much diversity among criminal justice populations and within communities. Consequently, including offenders and former offenders, and communities in criminal justice initiatives is also a huge undertaking. Further, communities are characterized by different laws, crime rates, and attitudes toward the criminal justice system, particularly towards police officers and police initiatives (Corsaro, Frank, & Ozer, 2015; Scaglion & Condon, 2006; Wehrman & De Angelis, 2011).

Latessa (2004) provided a summary of correctional programs and interventions that represent creative criminal justice initiatives implemented in three states: Oklahoma, Oregon, and Ohio.

In Oklahoma, the Department of Corrections implemented a statewide program evaluation of state and private corrections providers. These evaluations were conducted using the Correctional Program Assessment Inventory (Gendreau & Andrews, 1994). Initially, evaluation results showed that only 9% of correctional programs were rated as "satisfactory," whereas the remaining 91% of programs were "in need of improvement" or "unsatisfactory." After

Clinical Interventions in Criminal Justice Settings
ISBN 978-0-12-811381-3
http://dx.doi.org/10.1016/B978-0-12-811381-3.00011-1

implementing a statewide plan to improve services, and upon reassessing the correctional programs, 79% were rated "satisfactory" or higher, and no programs were rated "unsatisfactory." In Oregon, legislation was enacted that mandated the use of evidence-based interventions for adult and juveniles to reduce offending behavior, and utilization of emergency mental health services. This legislation also contained provisions mandating that state agencies spend a proportion of their funding on evidence-based interventions. Finally, the State of Ohio contracted with Dr. Latessa to conduct a program evaluation of all residential correctional programs in the state. The evaluation results suggested that high-risk offenders benefited most from participating in interventions, whereas low-risk offenders experienced higher recidivism. Based on these program evaluation results, residential correctional programs statewide were required to assess risk levels utilizing a standardizes risk assessment instrument within 5 days upon admission, base interventions on risks and needs assessment, integrate cognitive behavioral interventions with existing interventions, and address criminogenic needs, among other policy changes.

Some criminal justice initiatives use evidence in the form of biological evidence to improve criminal justice outcomes. Two notable examples are the Innocence Project and the DNA Field Experiment. The Innocence Project, founded in 1992 by Peter Neufeld and Barry Scheck (Innocence Project, 2017), uses deoxyribonucleic acid (DNA) evidence and testing to exonerate inmates wrongly convicted and incarcerated. In this way, the Innocence Project seeks to reform the criminal justice system and provide justice to innocent individuals who are wrongly convicted. Similarly, the DNA Field Experiment (National Institute of Justice, 2011) is based on DNA evidence, which is five times more likely to correctly identify a suspect when compared to fingerprints. Such evidence is used to identify suspects in residential and commercial burglaries, and car thefts.

Yet other initiatives are research initiatives aimed at improving criminal justice outcomes. One such research initiative is the Priority Criminal Justice Needs Initiative, which is a partnership between the National Institute of Justice, the RAND Corporation, the Police Executive Research Forum, RTI International, and the University of Denver (RAND Corporation, 2017). The initiative investigates the use of technology in the criminal justice, such as holding a trial using remote technology, to improve the functioning of the criminal justice system.

Another research initiative comprises the National Criminal Justice Drug Abuse Treatment Studies (CJ-DATS-1 and CJ-DATS-2) conducted by the National Institute on Drug Abuse (NIDA). The two research initiatives were conducted between 2002 and 2014 (National Institute on Drug Abuse, 2013). NIDA began the research initiative in 2002 to improve substance abuse treatment for criminal justice populations. This initiative was comprised of 13 research studies that investigated intervention needs such as improving reentry, screening, and referral (Wexler & Fletcher, 2007). Ducharme, Chandler, and Wiley (2013) describe the implementation studies that grew out of the CJ-DATS research initiative. The latter identified numerous challenges to implementing substance abuse interventions in criminal justice settings. Consequently, subsequent research initiatives concentrated on the application of implementation science.

Criminal justice initiatives to improve the criminal justice system have been implemented across the four components of the criminal justice system. These initiatives have been developed and implemented to enhance both policies and intervention practices. Therefore, we illustrate examples of both policies and practices, and organize these initiatives around the four components of the criminal justice system.

The Substance Abuse and Mental Health Service describes its criminal justice initiatives as the Sequential Intercept Model (SAMSHA, 2016). This model is organized around five intercepts in which individuals with mental illness, substance abuse, and co-occurring disorders can be diverted from the criminal justice system or experience reduced processing from one component of the criminal justice system to the next. These five areas are: (1) community and law enforcement, (2) arrest and initial detention including court hearings, (3) jails and specialty courts, (4) reentry, and (5) community corrections. A key feature of the initiative is its focus on enhancing collaboration between criminal justice settings and social service agencies, among other stakeholders.

EVIDENCE-BASED INITIATIVES IN THE FOUR COMPONENTS OF THE CRIMINAL JUSTICE SYSTEM

The implementation of creative evidence-based criminal justice initiatives have been encouraged, legislated, and/or implemented in each of the four components of the criminal justice system. It appears that more initiatives have been developed and implemented in corrections than any other criminal justice component. This stand to reason given the emphasis placed on reducing recidivism, the "what works" literature, the risk-needs-responsivity model, and the use of actuarial risk assessment instruments and evidence-based principles to guide correctional assessment and interventions.

Clearly, some criminal justice initiatives are appropriate for a specific criminal justice component or setting, and not others. This occurs as a result of the clear roles that each component performs in the criminal justice system.

Legislative Initiatives

Practitioners in the legislative component of the criminal justice system are comprised of policymakers at local, State, and Federal levels of government. These policymakers do not provide evidence-based practices, but do enact legislative policies that promote the use of implementation of evidence-based practices in criminal justice settings, oftentimes through the provision of funding.

Perhaps the most widely known work in the legislative component of the criminal justice system is the work of Aos and colleagues at the Washington State Institute for Public Policy (WSIPP). Beginning in the 1990s, the Washington State legislature requested that WSIPP classify evidence-based policies in the areas of education, child welfare, mental health, and criminal justice. In regards to criminal justice, the purpose of this initiative was to produce a list of evidence-based practices to aid the Washington State legislature with identifying effective interventions to reduce crime and reduce taxpayer spending. Thus, results are organized around taxpayer and non-taxpayer benefits, costs, and benefit to cost ratios, among others. Results are also organized around effective correctional interventions for juvenile and adult offenders, prison sentencing alternatives, police spending, and effective prevention programs (Aos & Drake, 2013). The 2007 Washington State legislature mandated that $48 million be provided to juvenile and adult justice system evidence-based programs (Drake, Aos, & Miller, 2009).

Policymakers also draft legislation and present it to Congress. For example, Senator Al Franken [D-MN] sponsored the bill S.993: Comprehensive Justice and Mental Health Act of 2015. The purpose of the bill was to amend the Omnibus Crime Control and Safe Streets Act of 1968 by providing coordination between mental health and criminal justice agencies, and providing interventions to reduce recidivism, among other provision. The last action taken on this bill shows that it was referred to the Subcommittee on Crime, Terrorism, Homeland Security and Investigations on January 1, 2016 (Library of Congress, n.d.).

In 1999, the New York State Legislature passed Kendra's Law. The law takes its name from Kendra Webdale. She was pushed into an oncoming subway train in New York City, and died in January 1999. The offender experienced a mental illness but was not receiving community-based treatment. This law is established in the New York State Mental Hygiene Law and legislates the provision of Assisted Outpatient Treatment (AOT) for criminal justice populations and others who experience mental illness, and require community-based treatment and supervision. In sum, court ordered or mandated treatment is provided (Office of Mental Health, 2006). Throughout New York State, regional implementation differences were found, suggesting that the New York State Legislature should reexamine how the law has been implemented (Robbins et al., 2010). AOT has been rated as an effective evidence-based intervention based on the results of several evaluation studies, and the majority of states have legislated some form of Kendra's Law (CrimeSolutions.gov, 2012).

"California's criminal justice realignment represents one of the most significant changes in criminal justice policy since statehood" (Criminal Justice Realignment Resource Center, 2017, p. 1). Criminal justice realignment legislation mandates the transfer of community supervision for low-level, non-violent felony offenders from the jurisdiction of the State of California to the jurisdiction of counties. Whereas the legislation does not change current laws or procedures prior to sentencing, it does shift the responsibility for community supervision. It also shifts the jurisdiction where these offenders are incarcerated. Offenders serve their sentences in county jails instead of state prisons.

Finally, as a result of State legislators turning their attention to the implementation of evidence-based practices and programs within their states, the Pew-MacArthur foundation has implemented the Pew-MacArthur Results First Initiative. This initiative is focused on evidence-based practices and programs, most of which are criminal and juvenile justice related. The initiative defines evidence-based policymaking, examined over 100 legislative policies enacted between 2004 and 2014; and identified states and bills that favor the implementation of evidence-based programs, require funded agencies to identify and categorize evidence-based programs, implement evidence and/or research-based programs, restrict the funding of those programs demonstrated to be ineffective, and legislate funding for agencies that implement evidence-based and research-based programs (The Pew Charitable Trusts, 2015). This summary of states and legislation associated with evidence-based practice and programs shows the wide range of innovative state activities in the legislative arena that support evidence-based practices and programs for adult criminal and juvenile justice populations.

Law Enforcement Initiatives

Similar to the legislative component, law enforcement officers do not provide clinical interventions. Some law enforcement agencies hire social workers to assist them with their service functions although their roles are focused on crisis intervention and referrals (Patterson, 2004, 2008; Zimmerman, 1988). Consequently, evidence-based policing efforts are practiced by law enforcement officers and driven by research, cost effectiveness, and crime reduction (Sherman, 2013).

Using the police response to domestic violence in which individuals are repeat victims of domestic violence, Sherman (1998) defined evidence-based policing as grounding policing activities in empirical evidence that demonstrates reductions in repeat victimization, thereby improving the police response. Sherman also suggested that evidence-based policing requires emphasis on research activities as well as implementation activities, a topic discussed throughout this book. Consistent with the importance of implementation activities and recognizing the need to translate research into practice among law enforcement agencies regarding evidence-based policing, Lum, Koper, and Telep (2011) proposed the Evidence-Based Policing Matrix to aid in these efforts.

The Byrne Criminal Justice Innovation Program (BCJI) exemplifies a law enforcement initiative that uses research and evidence-based practices to reduce crime, stimulate community development, and partner with community residents and community-based agencies. BCJI is associated with the Smart Suite of research-based programs housed at the U.S. Department of Justice Bureau of Justice Assistance. Since 2011, approximately $42.4 million in granting funding has been awarded to 65 sites to achieve the initiatives aims (Local Initiatives Support Corporation, 2017).

Several law enforcement initiatives have capitalized on law enforcement functions and using evidence to improve policing. SAMSHA (2015) describes three Law Enforcement and Behavioral Health Partnerships for Early Diversion grants that were awarded to achieve these aims. First, Project EDGE (Early Diversion, Get Engaged) was implemented in Colorado between 2013 and 2016. This evidence-based initiative diverts adults with mental health, substance abuse, and co-occurring disorders from further criminal justice system involvement through providing crisis intervention and referral skills training to police officers. Peer support specialists and evidence-based practices such as motivational interviewing are additional components of the initiative. Second, the Specialized Crisis Intervention

Teams for Young Adults (SCYA) Partnership was implemented in Connecticut also from 2013 to 2016. SCYA diverts young adults between the ages of 18 and 25 with mental health, substance abuse, and co-occurring disorders from further juvenile and criminal justice system involvement through partnerships formed between law enforcement and mental health agencies. Training, policy changes, and resources make up the primary initiative activities. Finally, the Knoxville Early Diversion Program was established in Knoxville, Tennessee during the same time period as the other two initiatives. The diversion program sought to decrease arrests and increase the use of community-based treatment among individuals having police contact. These aims were achieved through the development of a diversion team comprised of law enforcement, social service, mental health, and substance abuse agencies. Services are provided by a diversion team comprised of diversion liaisons, diversion case managers, and police officers.

Court Initiatives

Specialty courts are courts that hear cases about specific social problems. These courts adhere to principles of therapeutic jurisprudence. Judges and other court personnel are knowledgeable about the types of cases and social problems heard in their court. Examples of specialty courts include community courts, domestic violence courts, drug courts, mental health courts, and veterans courts, among others. Whereas specialty courts have been established throughout the country, New York City has established several specialty courts, some of which have also received evidence-based ratings from CrimeSolutions.gov.

The Midtown Community Court was founded in 1993, and is among the first specialty courts in the nation. Since 1993, community courts have emerged throughout the nation and in other countries as well. The court is based on partnerships formed with community residents, local businesses, social service and other community-based agencies to address community problems. Interventions include community service projects, the provision of social services, community restitution and workforce development, among others (Center for Court Innovation, n.d.-b). Although the Midtown Community Court is not among the evidence-based rated programs located in CrimeSolutions.gov, the Center for Court Innovation (2017) reports recent findings describing court operations. A total of 19,646 cases were heard in Midtown Community Court in 2015, the majority of which were summonses. The remaining cases were misdemeanor offenses such as trespassing, stolen property and marijuana possession. Evidence shows that the court issued fewer jail sentences than criminal court, and saves taxpayers approximately $1.2 million each year.

The Brooklyn Felony Domestic Violence Court was established in 1996, and hears all felony domestic violence cases in Brooklyn, NY. Sentences include both punitive sentences as well as sentences to mandated interventions such as batterer's interventions. Court personnel include judges, attorneys, and a victim advocate and resource coordinator. The court provides referrals, counseling, and domestic violence safety planning (Center for Court Innovation, n.d.-a). The Brooklyn Felony Domestic Violence Court has not been rated by CrimeSolutions.gov as an evidence-based program.

The Brooklyn Treatment Court (2005) hears cases involving nonviolent substance abuse offense. Alternative to incarceration activities include referrals to substance abuse treatment and community supports. Using a therapeutic jurisprudence perspective, case managers provide social services, and health care, educational and vocational services are provided as well. Cases are dismissed upon successful completion of treatment. The Brooklyn Treatment Court received an evidence rating of "effective" based on one study (CrimeSolutions.gov, 2011b). Likewise, the Bronx Treatment Court (CrimeSolutions.gov, 2011a) received an evidence rating of "effective" based on one study whereas the Bronx Mental Health Court was rated as having no effects on intervention outcomes based on the result of one study (CrimeSolutions.gov, 2016).

Correctional Initiatives

Perhaps more focus has been placed on evidence-based initiatives that have been implemented in corrections than any other criminal justice component. The correctional component is comprised of institutional and community-based residential facilities, and community supervision. While these settings serve as sanctions, they also emphasize public safety and decreased recidivism.

The development and implementation of innovative initiatives that employ evidence-based principles and practices in criminal justice settings must reflect the organizational characteristics found in a particular criminal justice component. Indeed, multiple factors that can adversely impact the implementation of evidence-based principles in prisons. These unique factors are unique to the prison setting and include: the prison organizational environment, (culture, priorities); staffing issues (recruitment and training, role of staff); gang activity; the availability of correctional programs; and reentry (Serin, 2005). It is plausible that these same factors should be considered in correctional initiatives. These factors are also relevant for jail setting initiatives.

A particularly relevant factor in jails and prisons is reentry. Reentry is a part of the corrections component and refers to "correctional programs (U.S. and Canada) that focus on the transition from prison to community (prerelease, work release, halfway houses, or specific reentry programs) and programs that have initiated treatment (substance abuse, life skills, education, cognitive/behavioral, sex/violent offender) in a prison setting and have linked with a community program to provide continuity of care" (Seiter & Kadela, 2003, p. 368). Petersilia (2003) defined reentry as "all activities and programming conduced to prepare exconvicts to return safely to the community and to live as law abiding citizens" (p. 3).

These definitions underscore the diverse types of correctional settings associated with reentry, and the types of social problems and service needs of the reentry population. Indeed, the reentry population requires housing, employment, education, community supports, health and mental health care, and substance abuse treatment, among other needs. For example, regarding reentry among sex offenders the Center for Effective Public Policy and the Council of State Governments created the Council of State Governments Sex Offender Reentry Project from 2013 to 2016. The initiative consists of resources helpful for assessing sex offenders risk levels, intervention needs, employing incentives and sanctions, and improving reentry.

Similarly, The Council of State Governments Justice Center (2017) identified 22 innovative reentry initiatives labeled as brand name programs and possessing an evidence base. A model initiative is Project Rio a statewide reentry program implemented in Texas. The goals of the program are to reduce recidivism and increase employment among the reentry population. Interventions are provided during incarceration and within the community.

In 2016, a $7.5 million Criminal Justice Investment Initiative (CJII) was initiated to provide more college-level educational programs in New York State prisons, make it easier to transfer college credits for courses taken inside prisons to colleges, improve reentry and public safety, and reduce recidivism. CJII will address problems associated with the private funding of New York State prison college programs such as waitlist and lack of standardization across curricula. It is anticipated that CJII will increase the number of state prisoners taking college level credit course from 1000 to 1500 over a five-year period (The New York County District Attorney's Office, 2016).

An evaluation report of the Bureau of Justice Assistance FY 2011 Second Chance Act Adult Offender Reentry Demonstration Projects highlights seven of 22 sites that implemented resourceful reentry initiatives. Common components among these seven sites, implemented in seven different states, were a focus on evidence-based practices such as targeting high-risk former offenders, employing actuarial risk assessment instruments, and providing case management interventions to individuals while incarcerated and during reentry (Rossman, Willison, Lindquist, Walters, & Lattimore, 2016). The Substance Abuse and Mental Health Services Administration (2017) highlighted statewide reentry initiatives implemented in Hawaii, North Carolina, and New York that focused on the reentry process and interventions for former offenders with mental health and substance use disorders. SAMSHA suggests that whereas these initiatives are specific to three geographic locations, they can be implemented in other communities with modifications.

Some reentry initiatives provide reentry services to youth. In 2011, a U.S. Department of Labor grant, as part of its former offender initiative, developed a reentry initiative for 16–24year old youth and young adults that has been implemented in nine communities characterized by high crime rates and poverty. Interventions begin during incarceration and continue during reentry (YouthBuild USA, 2017).

SUMMARY

This chapter reviewed various criminal justice initiatives that use empirical evidence to improve criminal justice outcomes. Although not exhaustive, the reviewed initiatives illustrate examples of both research and intervention initiatives. The Appendix provides resources for locating additional initiatives.

REFERENCES

Aos, S., & Drake, E. (2013). *Prison, police and programs: Evidence-based options that reduce crime and save money*. Olympia, WA: Washington State Institute for Public Policy.

Brooklyn Treatment Court. (2005). *About the court*. Retrieved from http://www.courts.state.ny.us/courts/2jd/brooklyntreatment/about.shtml.

Center for Court Innovation. (n.d.-a). Brooklyn domestic violence court. Retrieved from http://www.courtinnovation.org/project/brooklyn-domestic-violence-court.

Center for Court Innovation. (n.d.-b). Midtown community court. Retrieved from http://www.courtinnovation.org/project/midtown-community-court.

Center for Court Innovation. (2017). *Midtown community court: Documented results*. Retrieved from http://www.courtinnovation.org/sites/default/files/documents/MCC_Results_1.pdf.

Corsaro, N., Frank, J., & Ozer, M. (2015). Perceptions of police practice, cynicism of police performance, and persistent neighborhood violence: An intersecting relationship. *Journal of Justice, Criminal Justice, 43*, 1–11.

CrimeSolutions.gov. (2011a). *Program: Bronx (NY) treatment court*. Retrieved from https://www.crimesolutions.gov/ProgramDetails.aspx?ID=70.

CrimeSolutions.gov. (2011b). *Program: Brooklyn (NY) treatment court*. Retrieved from https://www.crimesolutions.gov/ProgramDetails.aspx?ID=44.

CrimeSolutions.gov. (2012). *Program: Assisted outpatient treatment (AOT)*. Retrieved from https://www.crimesolutions.gov/ProgramDetails.aspx?ID=228.

CrimeSolutions.gov. (2016). *Program: Bronx (NY) mental health court*. Retrieved from https://www.crimesolutions.gov/ProgramDetails.aspx?ID=475.

Criminal Justice Realignment Resource Center. (2017). *Criminal justice realignment*. Retrieved from http://www.courts.ca.gov/partners/realignment.htm.

Drake, E. K., Aos, S., & Miller, M. G. (2009). Evidence-based public policy options to reduce crime and criminal justice costs: Implications in Washington State. *Victims and Offenders, 4*, 170–196.

Ducharme, L. J., Chandler, R. K., & Wiley, T. R. A. (2013). Implementing drug-abuse treatment services in criminal justice settings: Introduction to the CJ-DATS study protocol series. *Health & Justice, 1*(1), 1–6.

Gendreau, P., & Andrews, D. A. (1994). *The correctional program assessment inventory*. Saint John, New Brunswick, Canada: University of New Brunswick. OpenURL.

Innocence Project. (2017). *About – innocence project*. Retrieved from https://www.innocenceproject.org/about/.

Latessa, E. J. (2004). The challenge of change: Correctional programs and evidence-based practices. *Criminology and Public Policy, 3*(4), 547–560.

Library of Congress. (n.d.). S.993–99114th Congress (2015–2016): Comprehensive justice and mental health act of 2015. Retrieved from https://www.congress.gov/bill/114th-congress/senate-bill/993.

Local Initiatives Support Corporation. (2017). *Byrne criminal justice innovation program overview*. Retrieved from http://www.lisc.org/media/filer_public/a2/68/a2684311-a554-4b76-b0f5-b5967d543689/bcji_program_overview_feb2017.pdf.

Lum, C., Koper, C. S., & Telep, C. W. (2011). The evidence-based policing matrix. *Journal of Experimental Criminology, 7*, 3–26.

National Institute of Justice. (2011). *Program: DNA field experiment*. Retrieved from https://www.crimesolutions.gov/ProgramDetails.aspx?ID=155.

National Institute on Drug Abuse. (2013). *Justice system research initiatives*. Retrieved from https://www.drugabuse.gov/researchers/justice-system-research-initiatives.

Office of Mental Health. (2006). *AOT summary*. Retrieved from https://www.omh.ny.gov/omhweb/Kendra_web/Ksummary.htm.

Patterson, G. T. (2004). Police social work crisis teams: Practice and research implications. *Stress, Trauma and Crisis, 7*, 93–104.

Patterson, G. T. (2008). Police social work. In T. Mizrahi, & L. Davis (Eds.), *Encyclopedia of social work* (20th ed.) *Vol. 20*. (pp. 357–362). New York: Oxford.

Petersilia, J. (2003). *When prisoners come home: Parole and prisoner reentry*. New York: Oxford University Press.

RAND Corporation. (2017). *Priority criminal justice needs initiative*. Retrieved from https://www.rand.org/jie/justice-policy/projects/priority-criminal-justice-needs.html.

Robbins, P. C., Keater, K. J., Steadman, H. J., Swanson, J. W., Wilder, C. M., & Swartz, M. S. (2010). Regional differences in New York's assisted outpatient treatment program. *Psychiatric Services, 61*(10), 1–6.

Rossman, S. B., Willison, J. B., Lindquist, C., Walters, J. H., & Lattimore, P. (2016). *Second chance act adult offender reentry demonstration projects*. Washington, DC: Urban Institute.

Substance Abuse and Mental Health Services Administration. (2015). *Law enforcement and behavioral health partnerships for early diversion*. Retrieved from https://www.samhsa.gov/gains-center/grants-grantees/early-diversion.

Substance Abuse and Mental Health Service. (2016). *SAMHSA's efforts on criminal and juvenile justice issues*. Retrieved from https://www.samhsa.gov/criminal-juvenile-justice/samhsas-efforts.

Scaglion, R., & Condon, R. G. (2006). Determinants of attitudes toward city police. *Criminology*, *17*, 485–494.

Seiter, R. P., & Kadela, K. R. (2003). Prisoner reentry: What works, what does not, and what is promising. *Crime and Delinquency*, *49*, 360–388.

Serin, R. C. (2005). *Evidence-based practice: Principles for enhancing correctional results in prisons*. Washington, DC: Crime and Justice Institute, U.S. Department of Justice, National Institute of Corrections.

Sherman, L.W. (1998). *Evidence-based policing*. Washington, DC: Police Foundation.

Sherman, L.W. (2013). The rise of evidence-based policing: Targeting, testing, and tracking. *Crime and Justice*, *42*(1), 377–451.

Substance Abuse and Mental Health Services Administration. (2017). *Guidelines for successful transition of people with mental or substance use disorders from jail to prison: Implementation guide. (SMA)-16–4998*. Rockville, MD: Author.

The Council of State Governments Justice Center. (2017). *Brand name programs: What works in reentry clearinghouse*. Retrieved from https://whatworks.csgjusticecenter.org/focus-area/topics.

The New York County District Attorney's Office. (2016). *Governor CUOMO and DA Vance announce statewide initiative to provide college classes in prison*. Retrieved from http://manhattanda.org/press-release/governor-cuomo-and-da-vance-announce-statewide-initiative-provide-college-classes-pris.

The Pew Charitable Trusts. (2015). *Legislating evidence-based policymaking*. Retrieved from http://www.pewtrusts.org/~/media/assets/2015/03/legislationresultsfirstbrief-march2015.pdf?la=en.

Wehrman, M. M., & De Angelis, H. (2011). Citizen willingness to participate in police-community partnerships: Exploring the influence of race and neighborhood context. *Police Quarterly*, *14*(1), 48–69.

Wexler, H. K., & Fletcher, B.W. (2007). National criminal justice drug abuse treatment studies (CJ-DATS) overview. *The Prison Journal*, *87*(1), 9–24.

YouthBuild USA. (2017). *Criminal justice initiatives*. Retrieved from https://www.youthbuild.org/criminal-justice-initiatives.

Zimmerman, S. I. (1988). *Police social work in twenty-three programs: Program description and analysis of interdisciplinary relations* (Unpublished doctoral dissertation). Chicago, IL: The Graduate College of the University of Illinois at Chicago.

FURTHER READING

Department of Criminal Justice Services. (2007). *Blueprints for change: Criminal justice policy issues in Virginia, evidence-based practice in community corrections*. Retrieved from https://www.dcjs.virginia.gov/sites/dcjs.virginia.gov/files/publications/dcjs/evidence-based-practices-community-corrections.pdf.

Lansing, S. (2012). *New York State COMPAS – probation risk and need assessment study: Examining the recidivism scale's effectives and predictive accuracy*. Retrieved from http://www.northpointeinc.com/downloads/research/DCJS_OPCA_COMPAS_Probation_Validity.pdf.

The Center for Effective Public Policy. (2016). *Reentry projects*. Retrieved from http://cepp.com/expertise/reentry/projects.

APPENDIX: RESOURCES FOR EVIDENCE-BASED CRIMINAL JUSTICE PRACTICE

George T. Patterson

RESOURCES FOR EVIDENCE-BASED PRACTICES

American Psychiatric Association Practice Guidelines

http://psychiatryonline.org/guidelines

The American Psychiatric Association practice guidelines describe treatment for adults. Examples relevant for criminal justice populations include substance use disorders and HIV/AIDS. Guidelines are dated and the website mentions these guidelines have not been updated in more than 5 years. Links are provided for learning about mental health, using evidence in practice, and publications.

American Psychological Association, Society for Clinical Psychology Empirically Supported Treatments

https://www.div12.org/psychological-treatments

This website is relevant for the general public, clinicians, researchers, and students. It includes links to membership and student/early career sections, an alphabetized listing of treatments, clinical resources, and training opportunities.

Campbell Collaboration

https://www.campbellcollaboration.org

The Campbell Collaboration is an international, nonprofit organization consisting of six coordinating groups: crime and justice, education, international development, methods, social welfare, and knowledge translation and implementation. The website contains useful links to receive Campbell training, a listing of Campbell systematic reviews, as well as the Campbell library, funding opportunities, and news and events.

Center for Evidence-Based Crime Policy

http://cebcp.org

The Center for Evidence-Based Crime Policy (CEBCP) is located at George Mason University, Department of Criminology, Law and Society. The CEBCP conducts evaluations of criminal justice programs and focuses on knowledge translation.

Links are provided to free tools such as David Wilson's Systematic Review Toolbox, a Crime and Place Bibliography, and the CEBCP Video Library that contain informational and training videos.

Center for the Study and Prevention of Violence, Blueprints for Healthy Youth Development

http://www.blueprintsprograms.com

Blueprints for Healthy Youth Development is located at the University of Colorado Boulder, Center for the Study and Prevention of Violence. Blueprints identifies evidence-based prevention and intervention practices relevant for youth, and categorize these as "model" or "promising" programs. Interventions can be found using the user-friendly program search link that identifies three methods for finding an intervention.

Coalition for Evidence-Based Policy

http://coalition4evidence.org

The Coalition for Evidence-Based Policy is a nonprofit, nonpartisan organization focused on using empirical evidence to promote social policies in the areas of education, poverty, and crime prevention. All are relevant areas for criminal justice populations. The website contains links to publications, social programs that work, and what works in social policy, for example. Interventions are rated as "top-tier" or "near top tier" evidence and can be found by content area such as crime/violence prevention.

Cochrane Collaboration

http://www.cochrane.org

The Cochrane collaboration is an international, nonprofit organization that produces systematic reviews and meta-analysis on health and healthcare. The website is appropriate for doctors, nurses, patients, and researchers. The website has links to the Cochrane library which contains systematic reviews, publications, and resources helpful for understanding evidence-based practice.

Council of State Governments Justice Center

https://csgjusticecenter.org

The Council of State Governments (CSG) Justice Center is focused on enhancing public safety and the criminal justice system by disseminating nonpartisan research, which includes public policy. The website contains links to timely updates from Capitol Hill, publications, and a Press Room which contains recent releases of newsworthy issues.

CrimeSolutions.gov

https://www.crimesolutions.gov

CrimeSolutions.gov is housed within the National Institute of Justice, Office of Justice Programs. The website is useful for criminal justice practitioners, policymakers, trainers, and researchers, and contains listings of effective programs and practices in criminal justice, juvenile justice, and crime victim service settings. These programs and practices are rated as "effective," "promising" or "no effects," and can be found using a user-friendly search site. The website also contains links to A to Z topics, FAQs, and other evidence-based resource materials.

International Community Corrections Association

http://iccalive.org/icca

The International Community Corrections Association (ICCA) is a community corrections membership organization. The website contains information about conferences, the Journal of Community Corrections, links for members, resources and events. An e-mail Listserv for up-to-date information is also available.

Office of Juvenile Justice and Delinquency Prevention: Model Programs Guide

https://www.ojjdp.gov/mpg

The Model Programs Guide (MPG) provides information about evidence-based prevention, intervention, and reentry programs relevant for the juvenile justice system. The MPG utilizes the same rating and review process as crimesolutions.gov. The website provides links to implementation guides, literature reviews, and other resources useful for policymakers and juvenile justice practitioners.

Substance Abuse and Mental Health Services Administration: National Registry of Evidence-Based Programs and Practices

http://nrepp.samhsa.gov

The National Registry of Evidence-Based Programs and Practices (NREPP) describes the website as "an evidence-based repository and review system designed to provide the public with reliable information on mental health and substance use interventions". The website contains information about the submission and review process, FAQs, a link to find an intervention, and a learning center to assist researchers, practitioners, and the public obtain additional information about the NREPP and how to use the website.

University of Washington, Human Services Library, Evidence-Based Practice

http://guides.lib.uw.edu/hsl/ebp

This Libguide provides links to reviews of clinical research, clinical practice guidelines, classic papers describing evidence-based practices, evidence-based practice research centers, an evidence-based calculator, and organizations that produce systematic reviews and meta-analyses.

Washington State Institute for Public Policy

http://www.wsipp.wa.gov

The Washington State Institute for Public Policy (WSIPP) conducts nonpartisan research to inform policymakers. The website contains reports describing the benefit–cost estimates calculated when evidence-based practices are implemented. For example, a benefit–cost estimate is provided for Functional Family Therapy (FFT) provided to youth in state institutions. The website describes the date the last systematic review was conducted, taxpayer and non-taxpayer benefits, and intervention costs.

RESOURCES FOR PROGRAM IMPLEMENTATION AND EVALUATION

Bureau of Justice Assistance

https://www.bja.gov

The Bureau of Justice Assistance (BJA) website contains practical links to funding opportunities, publications, training, technical assistance, and programs and events. Importantly, a link to request training and technical assistance from the BJA focused implementing evidence-based programs, and conducting data analysis can be requested online for state local and tribal organizations, and an A to Z index of criminal justice related topics are also provided.

Bureau of Justice Assistance: Center for Program Evaluation & Performance Measurement

http://www.ncjp.org/BJA%20Center%20for%20Program%20Evaluation%20and%20Performance%20Measurement

This BJA website contains program evaluation and performance measures resources. Links to very useful resources such as the Guide to Program Evaluation, suggestions for selecting a program evaluation team, and in-house versus outside evaluation teams, among other program evaluation topics are provided.

Gather, Assess, Integrate, Network, and Stimulate Center

https://www.samhsa.gov/gains-center

The purpose of the Gather, Assess, Integrate, Network, and Stimulate (GAINS) Center is to increase the availability of services for criminal justice populations with mental and/or substance use disorders. The GAINS Center provides information and training to local, state, regional, and national organizations focused on implementing effective interventions. The website contains links to contact the GAINS Center, locate mental health treatment courts, a listing of grants and grantees, and trauma training for criminal justice practitioners.

National Implementation Research Network

http://nirn.fpg.unc.edu

The National Implementation Research Network's (NIRN) mission is to advance the use of implementation science in human service settings and to disseminate information about implementation science and best practice approaches. The website contains user-friendly links to articles, books, and reports; cases and examples; an instrument for screening new practices for adoption; and other useful implementation, evaluation, and planning resources.

National Institute of Corrections

https://nicic.gov

The National Institute of Corrections (NIC) is a government agency housed in the U.S. Department of Justice, Federal Bureau of Prisons. The NIC provides training, technical assistance, and program and/or policy development directly to local, state, and federal corrections agencies. Technical assistance services include on-site consultation and training. Organizations can request technical assistance for a variety of needs including implementing effective practices, program evaluation, and evaluation of staff training programs. The website provides useful links to training resources, technical assistance for agencies, a library including program evaluation resources, blogs, and a listing of current projects.

RESOURCES FOR CRIMINAL JUSTICE RELATED INFORMATION

American Society of Criminology

https://www.asc41.com

The American Society of Criminology (ASC) is an international membership organization focused on preventing and treating crime and delinquency. The website provides resources for members, publications, and criminal justice and research archives.

Bureau of Justice Statistics

https://www.bjs.gov

The mission of the Bureau of Justice Statistics (BJS) is to collect, analyze, publish, and disseminate information about crime, criminal offenders, victims of crime, and the operation of the criminal justice system at all governmental levels. The website contains useful links to publications, and recent reports summarizing statistics on crime and victimization, among other topics.

Center for Advancing Correctional Excellence

https://www.gmuace.org

The Center for Advancing Correctional Excellence (ACE!) is a research center located at George Mason University, Department of Criminology, Law and Society. ACE!'s mission is to improve correctional outcomes, disseminate information about effective interventions, improve research methods used in criminal justice settings, and support students and faculty at George Mason University.

Center for Court Innovation

http://www.courtinnovation.org

The Center for Court Innovation was founded as a public, private partnership to focus on community-based violence prevention initiatives, alternatives to incarceration, reentry initiatives, and court-based programs, Useful links are provided to access criminal justice related topics such as bail reform, violence prevention, problem-solving justice, risk assessment, and families and children, among other relevant topics.

Center for Effective Public Policy

http://cepp.com

The Center for Effective Public Policy (CEPP) is a nonprofit organization. The CEPP's list of clients is a resource unto itself, identifying numerous local, state, federal, and private or nonprofit agencies with criminal justice-related interests. The website has links to the Center for Sex Offender Management, National Parole Resource Center, National Resource Center on Justice Involved Women, and the Collaborative Justice Resource Center; all associated with the CEPP.

Council for Court Excellence

http://www.courtexcellence.org

The Council for Court Excellence (CCE) is a nonprofit, nonpartisan civic organization whose mission is to improve the justice process in local and federal courts and other agencies in the Washington, DC area. Several areas of interest include speeding cases through civil and appellate courts, victims' rights issues, and child abuse and neglect cases.

Federal Bureau of Investigation

https://www.fbi.gov

The Federal Bbureau of Investigation (FBI) is both a law enforcement and intelligence agency that employees approximately 35,000 individuals. The website contains links to resources that include victim assistance, and reports and publications. The FBI also produces the Annual Uniform Crime Report, which summarizes crime data obtained from thousands of law enforcement agencies throughout the United States.

National Center for Juvenile Justice

http://www.ncjj.org

The National Center for Juvenile Justice (NCJJ) is the research division of the National Council of Juvenile and Family Court Judges. As such, the NCJJ is a private, nonprofit organization that conducts research on crime and delinquency. The website describes the NCJJ as the oldest research group focused on the juvenile justice system in the United States. The website also provides links to publications, and current national projects such as the Juvenile Justice Model Data Project and National Juvenile Court Data Archive.

National Criminal Justice Reference Service

https://www.ncjrs.gov

The National Criminal Justice Reference Service (NCJRS) is a useful resource for the public, policymakers, criminal justice practitioners, researchers, educators, and community leaders. The NCJRS provides copies of

Bureau of Justice statistics reports, criminal justice statistics, assistance with data analysis, and referrals to other sources of crime data. The website contains links to register for JUSTINFO, a biweekly electronic newsletter, e-mail notifications describing new publications and resources, and a Listserv invitation. Links are also provided to search questions and answers containing hundreds of criminal justice-related questions and answers, publications, and funding opportunities. The NCJRS has established one of the largest and most comprehensive criminal justice and juvenile justice libraries and databases in the world.

National Institute of Justice

https://www.nij.gov

The National Institue of Justice (NIJ) is a research, program development, and evaluation agency housed within the U.S. Department of Justice. The NIJ focuses on crime reduction in local and state governments and provides free on-line and in-class courses for criminal justice practitioners. The website lists priority areas, funding opportunities, events, publications, and multimedia, and listings of A to Z topics.

National Reentry Resource Center

https://csgjusticecenter.org

The National Reentry Resource Center (NRRC) is a project of the BJA. The website contains links to publications, webinars and videos, technical assistance, funding opportunities, reentry facts and trends, up-to-date projects, a directory consisting of reentry services, information about emerging issues in reentry such as tribal affairs, mentoring, and juvenile reentry, among others.

Office of Sex Offender Sentencing, Monitoring, Apprehending, Registering and Tracking

https://www.smart.gov

The Office of Sex Offender Sentencing, Monitoring, Apprehending, Registering and Tracking (SMART) is a governmental office established in the Adam Walsh Child Protection and Safety Act of 2006. The SMART's mission is to enhance public safety through national implementation of the sex offender registration notification system. This is achieved through the provision of technical assistance, tracking legislation, and funding opportunities.

Office of Juvenile Justice and Delinquency Prevention

https://www.ojjdp.gov

The Office of Juvenile Justice and Delinquency Prevention (OJJDP) was established in the Juvenile Justice and Delinquency Prevention (JJDP) Act as a government office focused on improving the juvenile justice system and preventing delinquency. OJJDP promotes research, programs, funding, and training opportunities. The website provides links to publications, statistics, and annual reports.

Office of Victims of Crime

https://www.ovc.gov

The Office of Victims of Crime (OVC) website provides links to information about crime victims' rights; a library containing publications, videos, and mobile apps; A to Z topics focused on victimization, information for providers and community leaders; assistance and resources for victims of crime; and grant and funding opportunities.

The Vera Institute of Justice

https://www.vera.org

The Vera Institute of Justice focuses its efforts on major issues facing the criminal justice system such as mass incarceration, crime and violence, racial disparities, and public safety. Vera establishes partnerships with government organizations and uses empirical evidence to address these issues. The website identifies up-to-date information about priorities and current issues of interest to Vera.

U.S. Department of Justice

https://www.justice.gov

One feature of the Department of Justice's (DOJ) mission, among many, is to operate as a source of federal leadership in the prevention and control of crime. The website includes links to DOJ resources such as publications, other federal government agencies such as Federal Bureau of Prisons (BOP), U.S. Parole Commission, Community Oriented Policing Services (COPS), and a summary of historical legislative case.

INDEX

'*Note*: Page numbers followed by "f" indicate figures and "t" indicate tables.'

F

G

H

I

J

L

S

T

V

W

Y

84035782R00124

Made in the USA
Middletown, DE
16 August 2018